Introduction to Logic
Predicate Logic

SECOND EDITION

Introduction to Logic
Predicate Logic

Howard Pospesel
University of Miami

With an Appendix on Metatheory by

William G. Lycan
University of North Carolina at Chapel Hill

Prentice
Hall

Upper Saddle River, New Jersey 07458

Library of Congress Cataloging-in-Publication Data
Pospesel, Howard
    Introduction to logic: predicate logic / Howard Pospesel; with an appendix on
metatheory by William G. Lycan.–2nd ed.
        p. cm.
    Includes bibliographical references and index.
    ISBN 0-13-164989-2
    1. Predicate (Logic) I. Title

    BC181 P62 2003
    160–dc21   2001059600

VP, Editorial Director: Charlyce Jones-Owen
Acquisition Editor: Ross Miller
Editorial Assistant: Carla Worner
Sr. Managing Editor: Jan Stephan
Production Liaison: Fran Russello
Project Manager: Jennifer Murtoff/Lithokraft II
Prepress and Manufacturing Buyer: Brian Mackey
Art Director: Jayne Conte
Cover Art: FOXTROT © Bill Amend. Reprinted with permission of UNIVERSAL
        PRESS SYNDICATE. All rights reserved.
Permissions Specialist: Marlene Gassler
Marketing Manager: Chris Ruel
Marketing Assistant: Scott Rich

This book was set in 10/12 Baskerville by Lithokraft II
and was printed and bound by R. R. Donnelley & Sons Company.
The cover was printed by Phoenix Color Corp.

 © 2003 by Pearson Education, Inc.
Upper Saddle River, New Jersey 07458

Printed in the United States of America

10   9   8   7   6   5   4   3

ISBN: 0-13-164989-2

Pearson Education LTD, *London*
Pearson Education Australia PTY, Limited, *Sydney*
Pearson Education Singapore, Pte. Ltd
Pearson Education North Asia Ltd, *Hong Kong*
Pearson Education Canada, Ltd, Toronto
Pearson Educación de Mexico, S.A. de C.V.
Pearson Education–Japan, *Tokyo*
Pearson Education Malaysia, Pte. Ltd
Pearson Education, *Upper Saddle River, New Jersey*

For Clara

Contents

Student's Preface

I have three aims for this book. The *first* goal is to teach you the vocabulary and grammar of predicate logic so that you will be able to translate the sentences of English (or other natural languages) into the notation of this important branch of symbolic logic. The *second* goal concerns three techniques for evaluating predicate arguments: formal proofs, counterexamples, and truth trees. I aim to help you become proficient in employing these logical methods. The *third* goal of the book is to develop your ability to identify and assess those predicate arguments you encounter daily as you read books and newspapers, carry on conversations, and watch television. Most of the examples and exercises in the text involve arguments of this everyday variety.

I enjoyed writing the book. If you enjoy studying it (as I hope you will), I think my goals will be achieved.

Howard Pospesel
University of Miami

Teacher's Preface

This text presupposes familiarity with propositional logic and, in particular, acquaintance with the natural-deduction approach to formal proofs and the technique of two-sided truth trees. Appendix One contains a review of this material, but it is too compact to be fully intelligible to the complete novice. A discussion of these techniques is provided in the companion volume, *Introduction to Logic: Propositional Logic*, revised third edition.

Predicate logic is developed gradually in this book, starting with the simplest monadic symbolizations and proceeding through multiple quantification to the logic of relations. Students learn to symbolize *and* evaluate arguments of a given degree of complexity before addressing the symbolization of more complex problems.

The formal-proof system presented here does not include a universal-quantifier introduction rule. The advantages of this approach are that the quantifier rules can be stated more simply and that proofs (although often longer) are often easier to devise. A universal-quantifier introduction rule is provided in a footnote at the start of section 4.2 to accommodate students of teachers who prefer to include this rule.

Most of the examples and exercises center around arguments similar to those encountered by students. The majority of these arguments are *natural*, rather than contrived; many are presented by direct quotation from newspapers and other sources. My purposes in employing natural everyday arguments are (1) to evoke the reader's interest, (2) to counter the common but mistaken view that formal logic is just an impractical academic diversion, and (3) to improve students' capacity to notice and assess the arguments they encounter. The final chapter explicitly addresses the problems that arise when predicate logic is applied to natural arguments.

The second edition has been extensively revised. It differs from the first edition mainly in these ways:

- The book has been reorganized to allow students to develop symbolization and proof-construction skills even more gradually.
- There is a chapter on two-sided truth trees. Some instructors prefer to teach one-sided trees; a chapter explaining that technique is included on the CD-ROM disk packaged with the book.
- New sections treat possible-world counterexamples, intensional contexts, quantifier scope, and quantifier order.
- There are more exercises, and most of the original exercises and examples have been replaced by better and more current ones.
- The book is accompanied by a tutorial program, "PredLogic," written by Mark Pospesel and me. This Windows-based software provides an environment in which students symbolize sentences, construct proofs of validity, devise counterexamples, and create truth trees. The program enables students to catch errors as they are made, and it offers hints for solving problems.
- William G. Lycan has provided an appendix on the metatheory of predicate logic.
- This edition uses parenthesis-free quantifier symbols. These symbols have become standard since the first edition was published, and they are more suitable for doing logic on a computer.
- Gender-neutral language is used throughout.
- The chapter on logic diagrams (that appeared in the first edition) has been moved to the CD-ROM disk that accompanies the book.

Acknowledgments

First edition: William Hanson and David Marans read and criticized the manuscript; their comments led to numerous improvements. David contributed thirty examples and helped with proofreading chores.

These friends contributed exercises: Harold Zellner, Jo Anne Zarowny, Bruce Whitcomb, Fred Westphal, Charles Werner, Bill Webber, Steven Wasserman, Randy Swanson, Linda Stubbs, Marilyn Sher, Linda Schreiber, Miguel Sanabria, James Rachels, Paul Qubeck, Clara Pospesel, Denise Oehmig, Jorge Morales, Virginia Miller, Robert McCleskey, Tommie Kushner, Peter Koujoumis, Stephanie Kazarian, Owen Herring, Elizabeth Hermelee, Jean Henderson, Robert Grier, Caroline Echarte, Robert Dietz, Osvaldo del Rey, Jerry Crangi, Nancy Cain, Edward Braverman, Mark Borgelt, Ray Bielec, Richard Beikirch, and George Bailey.

Second edition: William Lycan, Tony Hill, and the publisher's reviewers (Richard Arthur, Cynthia Bolton, Nicholas Dixon, and Glenn Lesses) provided very helpful comments on the first edition. Carmen Pospesel and Tony read the revision and made good suggestions for improvement; Carmen also read proofs. Leonard Carrier, Alan Goldman, Robert Hanna, Len Olsen, Robert E. Rodes, Jr., Charles Sola, and Mary Sutton helped with the project in various ways. The project manager, Jennifer Murtoff of Lithokraft II, exhibited uncommon care and attention to detail as she oversaw the production of the book.

Tony Hill contributed more than a dozen excellent logic examples, and Jessica Lewis, David Marans, and Carmen Pospesel each supplied several as well. These friends contributed exercises: Stuart Adriance, Robert Bruderman, Christopher Chung, Jane Connolly, Michelle Eustache, Beatriz F. Fernandez, Shameka Gainey, Robin Gomez, Elliott Hinkes, Eric Khoury, Javier Lopez, Karen Marcus, Aman Mehan, Régine Mondé, David Mount, Rebecca Nako, Leo de la Peña, Daniel Rhoads, Ahmed Riesgo, Jonathan Sanders, Michael Strande, and Geff Zamor.

These friends helped with the development of the computer program *PredLogic:* Jessica Blair, Jens Bratz, Linda Fulop, Owen Herring, William Lievens, Chris Paniewski, Fernando Patterson, Waleed Sneij, and Mary Sutton. Owen Herring class-tested beta versions of the program twice. The program exists only because of the hard work of its lead author, Mark Pospesel. His skills in program design and code writing will be evident to anyone who examines the program.

Howard Pospesel
University of Miami

1

Introduction

1.1 Predicate Logic and Propositional Logic

As the second inning of a baseball game (in a coed youth league) was starting, the umpire asked the Boca Raton Dodger catcher, "Are you wearing a [protective] cup?" The catcher, 12-year-old Melissa Raglin, took off her helmet (to reveal her hair) and replied, "I'm a girl." The umpire responded, "So, I'm the umpire and any catchers under my supervision have to wear cups." As Melissa wasn't wearing a cup she was banished to the outfield. Later she explained to a reporter why she was unhappy about the move, "[When you play in the outfield] you're not in the game. Catchers are always in the game. It's just more competitive." She also thought it silly to apply to girls a rule whose language was appropriate only for boys. Melissa played the next two games in the outfield because she refused to wear a cup, but at the beginning of the third game she appeared behind home plate wearing a cup *on her ankle!* Once again she was exiled to the outfield. Melissa, recognizing that the time had come to yield to authority, obtained female protective gear (which was not readily available and had to be rush-ordered from an athletic company in another state). The league officials were placated, and Melissa resumed her accustomed assignment behind the plate.[1]

The umpire, citing the league's (outdated) rule book, advanced an argument that we may formulate as follows:

> All catchers are required to wear cups.
> Melissa is a catcher.
> So, Melissa is required to wear a cup.

[1]See John Pacenti (AP), "This jock won't put on a cup; Girl: Eject rule for boys," *Miami Herald* (May 22, 1997), p. 6B.

Gary L. Rothstein

Let's call this argument "Cup I." Melissa also employed an argument that we can set out like this:

"Cup II"

> If I wear a protective cup tied to my ankle, then I satisfy the rule.
> I am wearing a cup tied to my ankle.
> So, I satisfy the rule.

League officials were not persuaded by Melissa's argument, presumably because they rejected its first premise.

Let's symbolize these two arguments in propositional logic.[2]

"Cup I": A, M ⊢ R
"Cup II": W → S, W ⊢ S

The first of these sequents[3] is invalid, the second one is valid.[4] It is hardly surprising that the first sequent is invalid; note that no two of the three formulas composing the sequent have anything in common. By contrast, the statements composing the English argument "Cup I" do have elements in common: *catcher* is common to the premises, *required to wear a cup* occurs in both the first premise and the conclusion, and *Melissa* is found in the second premise and the conclusion. Propositional logic cannot represent these elements because they are not propositions (or propositional connectives); rather they are parts of simple propositions.[5] (We know they are not propositions because they are not true or false.) In order to treat the "Cup I" argument adequately we need to use a logic that can represent elements like *Melissa* and *is a catcher*. That is where predicate logic, the subject of this book, comes in. Predicate logic is able to represent these expressions. I will return to "Cup I" in Chapter Three and show that it is a valid argument (in the sense that it has a valid form). Why is this branch of logic called *predicate logic?* Because it has mechanisms for representing general terms (like *catchers*) and logicians call such terms *predicates*. Predicate logic provides a deeper analysis of "Cup I" than does propositional logic. For some arguments ("Cup II," for example) propositional logic is an adequate tool of analysis, but for other arguments it is insufficient. Many arguments falling beyond the scope of propositional logic can be treated successfully in predicate logic. A rough description of predicate logic is that it is the logic of the expressions *all, no,* and *some.*[6] Your grasp of the nature of this discipline will increase as you work through the book.

---

[2] *Propositional logic* is, roughly, the logic of the five expressions *not, and, or, if . . . then,* and *if and only if.* This volume presupposes a knowledge of propositional logic. The first appendix provides a review of this branch of logic and describes the specific techniques of propositional logic that are used in the book. If your knowledge of this part of logic is sketchy, it will be to your advantage to study Appendix One before addressing Chapter Two.

[3] A *sequent* is a sequence of one or more formulas where the last formula follows a turnstile. We commonly employ sequents to represent arguments expressed in English (or other natural languages).

[4] A *valid* argument is one having a form such that if all its premises are true, then its conclusion must also be true. A sequent is *valid* if and only if every argument it can represent is valid.

[5] I use the terms *proposition* and *statement* interchangeably to refer to sentences that are either true or false. (Many logicians give these terms other meanings.)

[6] Predicate logic was developed around 1880 by the American philosopher-logician Charles Peirce and the German mathematician-logician Gottlob Frege working independently. For more about the history of this branch of logic see William and Martha Kneale's *The Development of Logic* (Oxford: The Clarendon Press, 1985).

The sample predicate argument discussed above ("Cup I") is quite simple. Some predicate arguments, of course, are more complex. Here is an example contained in dialogue from the movie, *Jurassic Park*.[7]

PARK SCIENTIST: *Actually, they can't breed in the wild. Population control is one of our security precautions. There's no unauthorized breeding [among dinosaurs] in Jurassic Park.*

IAN MALCOLM: *How do you know they can't breed?*

PARK SCIENTIST: *Oh, because all of the animals [i.e., dinosaurs] in Jurassic Park are female. We've engineered them that way.*

The park scientist's argument:

Two dinosaurs can breed only if one is female and one is not.
All of the dinosaurs in Jurassic Park are female.
So, the dinosaurs in Jurassic Park can't breed.

If you saw the movie you know that the conclusion of this argument is false (according to the story line), even though the argument is valid. That can happen because the second premise is false. As the theme of the movie puts the matter, *nature will find a way*. One feature of the argument that adds to its complexity is that it involves the relational predicate *breeds*. We will examine the structure of the Jurassic Park argument in Chapters Ten and Eleven.

The good news for students embarking on the study of predicate logic is that predicate logic and propositional logic are intimately connected. Having mastered propositional logic you are already well on your way toward learning predicate logic. For example, all of the symbols of propositional logic appear in the formulas of predicate logic, and all of the propositional inference rules and truth tree rules are also employed in predicate logic. (Obviously it is essential that a person studying this book know the logic of propositions.) In the chapters that follow, I will develop a formal system of predicate logic by grafting new "branches" onto the "trunk" of propositional logic. The symbols of predicate logic will be added to your vocabulary in Chapter Two. Four predicate inference rules are introduced in Chapters Three and Four to accompany the eighteen propositional rules listed on page 278. In Chapter Eight, four predicate truth-tree rules are added to the ten propositional rules listed on page 280. In the last third of the book I extend predicate logic to encompass relational predicates.

[7]Universal Pictures, 1993. Directed by Steven Spielberg. Screenplay by Michael Crichton and David Koepp, based on the book by Michael Crichton.

2

Basic Symbolization

This chapter treats sentences of the following five types:

> All watermelons are vegetables.
> No Lutherans are Methodists.
> Some computers are antiques.
> Some numbers are not odd.
> Kelly is ambitious.

The point of the chapter is to teach you how to symbolize such sentences. Many sentences that you encounter (in this book and in your life) exhibit one of these five forms. So, it is well worth knowing how to analyze them. Many other sentences are a lot like these five types of sentences, so learning how to symbolize the basic five will help you grasp the structure of these sentences.

Nearly twenty-four hundred years ago the first systematic logician, Aristotle, studied sentences of the first four types,[1] and today they are still recognized by logicians as being of fundamental importance. Logicians call them *standard categorical propositions*.

---

[1]Aristotle subsumed sentences of the fifth type under the first kind.

2.1   Singular Statements

Many English sentences can be viewed as consisting of two parts: an expression that is used to refer to an individual and another expression that is used to ascribe a property to the individual. We will call expressions of the former sort *singular terms* and expressions of the latter kind *predicates*. Sentences composed of singular terms and predicates are known as *singular statements*. Some examples:

Singular Statement	Singular Term	Predicate
George W. Bush is a Republican.	George W. Bush	is a Republican
Stephanie's dog is a rottweiler.	Stephanie's dog	is a rottweiler
He sings poorly.	he	sings poorly
The richest person lives in Seattle.	the richest person	lives in Seattle

The key characteristic of a singular term is that it is customarily used to refer to an individual. I use *individual* broadly, counting not only people but pets, rivers, rocks, roads, bridges, cars, cities, planets, numbers, and so on, as individuals. Singular terms are expressions that function like proper nouns, but the concept is a logical, not a grammatical one. Singular terms may be proper nouns (*Shakespeare*), pronouns (*she*), or noun phrases (*David's right ear, the janitor*). In predicate logic we abbreviate singular terms with lower-case letters of the alphabet from *a* through *v*. (The letters *w, x, y,* and *z* are reserved for another use, which is explained in the next section.) Normally the letter chosen as an abbreviation will be the first letter of a prominent word occurring in the singular term; for example, *the janitor* will typically be abbreviated with a *j*. Let's call the letters that abbreviate singular terms *individual constants*.

A predicate or general term is an expression that may be used to ascribe a property (such as *being a cartoonist*) to an individual or to assert that several individuals stand in some relationship (like *hating*). At present we will concentrate on property predicates, postponing our treatment of relational predicates until Chapter Ten. Predicates may be composed of various parts of speech. Some examples:

Predicate	Part of Speech
sleeps	verb
sleeps poorly	verb + adverb
speaks German	verb + noun
is greedy	copula[2] + adjective
is a Texan	copula + noun phrase

---

[2]A copula is a word or expression (such as a form of the verb *to be*) that links the subject of a sentence with its grammatical predicate without asserting action.

It will become clear as we proceed that our concept of *predicate* does not correspond exactly to the grammarian's notion. Predicates are abbreviated in our logic by capital letters. The letter selected will usually be the first letter of one of the words comprising the predicate; for example, *is a Texan* will typically be abbreviated by *T.* We call the letters that abbreviate English predicates *predicate letters* (or just *predicates*). A predicate letter in a wff (well-formed formula) will always be followed by one or more lower-case letters. (A capital letter standing alone in a wff is not a predicate letter but the abbreviation of a statement.)

To symbolize an (affirmative) singular statement in the notation of predicate logic, we write the capital that abbreviates the predicate followed by the lower-case letter that serves as the abbreviation of the singular term. S1 is symbolized by F1.

(S1) Stephanie's [d]og is a (r)ottweiler.
(F1) Rd

I use two conventions for designating abbreviations: (1) placing square brackets around a letter in the singular term indicates that it will serve as the individual constant that abbreviates the term, and (2) enclosing in parentheses a letter in the predicate shows that it will serve as the predicate letter. Notice that the predicate-first order displayed by F1 is not the standard pattern of English sentences.

Some singular statements are negative; S2 is an example.

(S2) Thomas [E]dison did not attend (c)ollege.

A negative singular statement is symbolized as the negation of an affirmative one. S2 is symbolized by F2.

(F2) −Ce

This is our first example of the use of a symbol of propositional logic in a predicate-logic wff.

2.2 Existential Statements (*I* and *O*)

Let's define a *singular statement* as a statement containing one or more singular terms. We shall call a statement that has no singular terms a *general statement.* (Does it follow from these definitions that every statement is either singular or general? Do the definitions imply that no statement is both?)[3] A singular

---

[3]Yes and yes. You will establish the correctness of these answers in an exercise in Chapter Six.

statement mentions a specified individual; a general statement concerns individuals of certain kinds or types but does not name any specific individual. S1 is a sample general statement:

(S1) Some rabbis are Japanese.

S1 concerns rabbis but it refers to no specific rabbi. In this regard S1 contrasts sharply with the singular statement S2.

(S2) Hiroshi Okamoto is a rabbi.

As I mentioned at the beginning of the chapter, logicians have long been interested in general statements (or *categorical propositions*) that exhibit any of four simple forms. These forms are given in the following table.

Standard Categorical Proposition Forms

Form	Example	Code Letter
All F are G	All pines are conifers.	*A*
No F are G	No snakes are warm-blooded.	*E*
Some F are G	Some senators are principled.	*I*
Some F are not G	Some psychologists are not atheists.	*O*

Obviously the script F and G in each statement-form mark gaps that are to be filled by predicates (like *pines* and *conifers*). Code letters have been used for many centuries to identify these four statement-forms. We will call A and E statements *universal* and I and O statements *existential*. (The traditional label for I and O statements is *particular*, but that term would seem to fit singular statements better than I and O statements.) In the remainder of this section we concentrate on statements of the I and O types. Section 2.3 treats statements of types A and E.

"I" Statements.   In predicate logic a statement exhibiting one of the four basic general forms is regarded as containing two predicates. Consider again S1.

(S1) Some rabbis are Japanese.

Without altering the content of S1 we can rephrase it as S1′.

(S1′) There exists at least one individual who *is a rabbi* and *is Japanese*.

The two predicates are brought to the surface in S1'; they can be abbreviated with *R* and *J*. Two other symbols of predicate logic are required if we are to symbolize S1': the *individual variable* (or *variable* for short) and the *existential quantifier*. We employ the lower-case letters *w, x, y,* and *z* as individual variables. If a wff requires more than four variables, we can form additional ones with the prime mark (thus *x'* or *y"*). Until we reach Chapter Ten, however, we will manage with just one variable: *x*. The variable is a symbolic device for achieving cross-reference. The closest analogue in English to the variable is the pronoun. The existential quantifier consists of an inverted *E* followed by a variable; $\exists x$ is read *there exists an x such that.*

We now have the machinery required to symbolize S1' (and thus S1).

There exists at least one individual who	is a rabbi	and	is Japanese
$\exists x$	(Rx	&	Jx)

So, we reach F1 as our symbolization of S1.

(F1) $\exists x(Rx \& Jx)$

F1 may be read *There exists an x such that x is a rabbi and x is Japanese.* Every *I* statement is symbolized in similar fashion. The pair of parentheses in F1 indicate that the scope of the quantifier includes all of "Rx & Jx" (and not just "Rx"). This matter will be explained further in Chapters Five and Thirteen. It is sufficient at present to note that each wff symbolizing an *I* statement (or an *O, A,* or *E*) has a left-hand parenthesis after the quantifier and a right-hand one as concluding symbol.

I statements exhibit both *vagueness* and *ambiguity.* As an example of the former, consider again S1:

(S1) Some rabbis are Japanese.

How many Japanese rabbis must there be if S1 is to express a truth? There is no definite answer to this question, if it is a question about English usage. However, in deciding to paraphrase S1 as S1', we have stipulated (for the purposes of logic) that *one* Japanese rabbi is sufficient for the truth of S1.

(S1') There exists at least one individual who is a rabbi and is Japanese.

As an example of the *ambiguity* of sentences of the *I*-type consider S3:

(S3) Some dogs are mammals.

Is S3 true? One who utters S3 may be intending to claim S4, or may be making the stronger claim expressed by S5.

(S4) At *least* some dogs are mammals.

(S5) Some dogs (and at *most* some dogs) are mammals.

Of course, S4 is true and S5 false. In logic, we will regard S3 as equivalent to S4; so, we count S3 a truth.

I statements can be disguised in different English garments. All of the statements in this list are regarded as *I* statements by logicians and are symbolized by F1.

> At least one rabbi is Japanese.
>
> Rabbis are sometimes Japanese.
>
> There are rabbis who are Japanese.
>
> Rabbis who are Japanese do exist.

The list is not exhaustive.

"O" Statements.   Having learned how to symbolize *I* statements, it is an easy step to the symbolization of *O* statements. S6 serves as an example.

(S6) Some psychologists are not atheists.

S6 may be rephrased as S6′, which in turn is symbolized by F6.

(S6′) There exists an *x* such that *x* is a (p)sychologist and *x* is not an (a)theist.

(F6) $\exists x(Px \text{ \& } -Ax)$

Every *O* statement may be symbolized in this way. Notice that the dash is properly located after the ampersand. Neither of the following wffs symbolizes S6.

(F7) $\exists x-(Px \text{ \& } Ax)$

(F8) $-\exists x(Px \text{ \& } Ax)$

F7 and F8 symbolize S7 and S8, respectively, and neither S7 nor S8 is equivalent to S6.

(S7) Someone is not both a psychologist and an atheist.

(S8) It is false that there is a psychologist who is an atheist.

O statements can be expressed in English in various ways, for example:

> At least one psychologist is not an atheist.
>
> There are psychologists who aren't atheists.

Each of these sentences is correctly symbolized by F6.

EXERCISES

Note: You can check your symbolizations of exercises with the computer tutorial "PredLogic."

1. (1) Symbolize each statement using the suggested abbreviations. (Each statement is either singular (affirmative or negative), an *I*, or an *O*.) (2) Provide a *dictionary* for the abbreviating symbols. For example, the symbolization and dictionary for (a) are:

    Pt (t = three, Px = x is prime)

    Of course, there is no need to provide a dictionary entry where I have already done so, as I have for *J* in exercise (c).

    (a) [T]hree is (p)rime.

    *(b) (*this text*) "Some (s)ingular statements are (n)egative."

    (c) Some statements that we are (j)ustified in believing are not (t)rue. (Jx = x is a statement that we are justified in believing)

    (d) (*The Koran*) "There are some who (d)ispute about Allah and (s)erve rebellious devils."

    (e) The [h]ighest point in the eastern United States is not in (T)ennessee. (Tx = x is in Tennessee) *Note that the use of "x" in this dictionary entry does not imply that "x" will appear in the symbolization of the sentence.*

    *(f) At least one (h)orse-drawn bus (o)perated in London after 1911. (Ox = x operated in London after 1911)

    (g) Some 1-800 (n)umbers are not (t)oll-free. (Tx = x is toll-free)

    (h) (G)olden (f)aucets exist.

    (i) (*children's book*) "There are . . . (p)eople who cannot (t)ell the difference between an alligator who is smiling and an alligator who is not smiling." (Px = x is a person, Tx = x can tell the difference between an alligator who is smiling and an alligator who is not smiling)

    *(j) (*Pliny the Elder*) "Individuals are occasionally born who belong to both sexes." (Mx = x is male, Fx = x is female)

2. Translate each wff into an English sentence using this dictionary: r = Janet Reno, Px = x is a politician, Ox = x lives in Ohio.

    (a) Pr

    *(b) −Or

    (c) ∃x(Px & Ox)

    (d) ∃x(Ox & Px)

    (e) ∃x(Px & −Ox)

    *(f) ∃x(Ox & −Px)

---

*Solutions (or partial solutions) to starred problems are provided in Appendix Four.

2.3   Universal Statements (*A* and *E*)

"A" Statements.   *A* and *E* statements are called *universal* statements because they allow us to make claims about *all* individuals of a certain kind (that is, individuals possessing a certain property), either the claim that each possesses some further specified property or the claim that each lacks some specified property. The introduction of one more symbol of predicate logic–the *universal quantifier*–will enable us to symbolize *A* and *E* statements. (No additional symbols will be needed until we reach Chapter Ten.) The universal quantifier consists of an inverted *A* followed by a variable; $\forall x$ is read *for any x*. How shall we symbolize S1?

(S1)   All pines are conifers.

As a first step we paraphrase S1 as S1′.

(S1′)   For any individual, if it is a (p)ine, then it is a (c)onifer.

S1′ is composed exclusively of predicates and expressions that correspond to symbols in our logical vocabulary. We symbolize S1′ (and hence S1) with F1.

(F1) $\forall x(Px \rightarrow Cx)$

F1 is read *For any x, if x is a pine, then x is a conifer.* Any *A* statement may be symbolized in this fashion.

Why employ an arrow rather than an ampersand; why not symbolize S1 with F2?

(F2) $\forall x(Px \& Cx)$

F2 is read *For any x, x is a pine and x is a conifer.* It symbolizes S2, which, of course, does not have the same content as S1.

(S2)   Everything is a pine and a conifer.

A statements (or sentences equivalent to such statements) occur very often in natural languages. It is not surprising then that English offers many ways of expressing *A* statements. Some are included in this list.

Every pine is a conifer.	A pine is a conifer.
Each pine is a conifer.	Pines are all conifers.
Each and every pine is a conifer.	Pines are always conifers.
Any pine is a conifer.	Pines are conifers.

Each of these sentences is properly symbolized by F1. Notice that the order of the predicates in an *A* wff is crucial. Switching the predicates of F1 yields F3.

(F3) $\forall x(Cx \rightarrow Px)$

But F3 does not represent S1 or any of the *A* variants listed above. F3 symbolizes (the false) S3.

(S3) All conifers are pines.

How should we symbolize S4?

(S4) Not all (F)orest Service trucks are (g)reen.

We can view S4 as an abbreviation of S5, and accordingly symbolize it with F5:

(S5) It is not the case that all Forest Service trucks are green.
(F5) $-\forall x(Fx \rightarrow Gx)$

Note that S4 has the same content as S6:

(S6) Some Forest Service trucks are not green.
(F6) $\exists x(Fx \,\&\, -Gx)$

A statements and *O* statements (having the same grammatical subjects and predicates) are exact opposites. Logicians term them *contradictories*. That *A*'s and *O*'s are contradictories explains the equivalence of S5 (or S4) and S6. Because S4 and S6 are equivalent we can use F6 to symbolize S4. So, we can symbolize S4 with either F5 or F6. Is one of these two symbolizations preferable? I favor F5 because it *tracks* S4 better than F6 does. (A wff *tracks* a sentence when the two have the same or comparable logical structures. The structure of a predicate logic wff is shown by the pattern of quantifiers, variables, connectives, and grouping symbols it contains.) For example, the universal quantifier (coupled with an arrow) in F5 corresponds to the word *all* in S4; the existential quantifier in F6 does not track *all*.

Two *A* variants involving the expressions *only* and *none but* are troublesome and deserve special treatment. S7 and S8 serve as representatives.

(S7) Only males are [Roman Catholic] priests.
(S8) None but males are priests.

Let's begin with S7. S7 has the same content as S9 and S10:

(S9) All (p)riests are (m)ales.

(F9) $\forall x(Px \rightarrow Mx)$

(S10) All non-males are non-priests.

(F10) $\forall x(-Mx \rightarrow -Px)$

Either F9 or F10 will serve as a symbolization of S7. It is hard to say which wff tracks S7 better; I prefer F9 because it is more concise. We can formulate this principle for transforming *only* statements into standard *A* statements:

Only F are G = All G are F

People are often confused by *only* statements. For example, some may believe that S7 has the same content as S11.

(S7) Only males are priests.

(S11) All males are priests.

We can prove conclusively that S7 and S11 are not equivalent. S7 is true while S11 is false. If they were logically equivalent,[4] they would have the same truth value. So, they are not logically equivalent. We can also prove that S7 and S9 are equivalent. Consider these four statements:

(S9) All priests are males.
      No priests are non-males.
      No non-males are priests.

(S7) Only males are priests.

Each of the first three statements in this list is logically equivalent to the statement directly beneath it. Therefore, S7 is logically equivalent to S9. (This argument is assessed in Chapter Thirteen.)

Having mastered the treatment of *only* statements, we can handle *none but* statements easily. This principle suffices:

None but F are G = only F are G

S8 is equivalent to S7, and therefore to S9.

(S8) None but males are priests.

(S7) Only males are priests.

(S9) All priests are males.

"E" Statements.   Of the four standard categorical statement-forms, only the *E* form remains to be treated. S12 is a representative *E* statement:

[4]Two statements are logically equivalent if and only if it is logically impossible in virtue of their forms for one to be true and the other false.

(S12) No catchers are left-handed.[5]

We can paraphrase S12 in a way that employs two predicates and certain other readily symbolized expressions.

(S12′) For any *x*, if *x* is a (c)atcher, then *x* is not (l)eft-handed.

S12′ (and also S12) is symbolized by F12.

(F12) $\forall x(Cx \rightarrow -Lx)$

The dash is properly located after the arrow (as in F12). None of the following wffs symbolizes S12:

$$-\forall x(Cx \rightarrow Lx)$$
$$\forall x-(Cx \rightarrow Lx)$$
$$\forall x(-Cx \rightarrow Lx)$$

There are many ways of expressing *E* statements in English; here are some:

Catchers who are left-handed don't exist.

Catchers aren't left-handed.

There are no catchers who are left-handed.

Catchers are never left-handed.

No one is both a catcher and left-handed.

Catchers are not left-handed.

F12 symbolizes each of these sentences.

An introduction-to-philosophy exam I graded contained this sentence:

(S13) All events are not caused.

Had S13 not been imbedded in an essay, I would not have known whether the student was asserting S14 or S15.

(S14) No events are caused.
(S15) Some events are not caused.

---

[5]S12 is an overstatement, but *nearly* all catchers are right-handed. The explanation: right-handed catchers have a better lane to throw out runners who are trying to steal second base if the batter is standing to the left of home plate, and most hitters stand on that side of the plate.

Sentences of the form "All F are not G" are amphibolous.[6] (Distinguish this form from the unambiguous form "Not all F are G," that was discussed above.) In deciding whether to view a sentence such as S13 as an E or an O statement, we must pay attention to intonation (for speech) and to the context in which the sentence occurs. A person who dislikes unnecessary ambiguity will avoid formulating sentences of S13's type.

A question on a national high school mathematics examination concerned these statements:

I.   All shirts in this store are not on sale.
II.   There is some shirt in this store not on sale.
III.   No shirt in this store is on sale.
IV.   Not all shirts in this store are on sale.

Sentence II is an O statement, sentence III is an E statement, and sentence IV amounts to the negation of an A statement, making it equivalent to an O statement. Each of these statements is quite clear. Sentence I, on the other hand, is an amphibolous statement of the type just discussed. It can be read as an E or as an O statement. (If that is not evident, read the sentence several times stressing different components.) I think the test item is poor because of the ambiguity involved.

In this chapter we have learned how to symbolize singular statements and standard categorical propositions. In the next two chapters we will examine arguments composed of statements of these kinds (and their negations).

EXERCISES

Instructions for exercises 3 and 4: (1) Symbolize each statement using the suggested abbreviations. (Each statement belongs to one of the five types discussed in the chapter.) (2) Provide a dictionary for the abbreviating symbols. There is no need to provide a dictionary entry where I have already done so.

3. (a) (*lyric*) "All who (l)ove are (b)lind."
    *(b) (*Alan Dershowitz*) ". . . No (w)ealthy people are ever (e)xecuted."
    (c) (*bumper sticker*) "ANY DAY SPENT (A)BOVE GROUND IS A (G)OOD DAY." (Ax = x is a day spent above ground)
    (d) Ted [T]urner (f)ounded CNN.
    (e) (*ABC News*) "(N)eutrinos have (m)ass."
    *(f) (*bumper sticker*) "(W)OMEN WHO SEEK TO BE EQUAL TO MEN LACK (A)MBITION." (Ax = x has ambition)

---

[6]*Amphiboly* is ambiguity rooted in poor sentence structure.

(g) Every (t)reaty ever made between the U.S. government and native Americans has been (b)roken by the U.S. government.

(h) (*jar lid*) "[S]alsa is (f)at-free." (Fx = x contains fat)

(i) (S)alsa is (f)at-free." (Fx = x contains fat)

*(j) Some royal (p)oincianas have (y)ellow blossoms.

(k) (*Catch-22*) "What's good for M & M (E)nterprises is good for the (c)ountry." (Ex = x is good for M & M Enterprises, Cx = x is good for the country)

(l) (*newspaper*) "There's no (w)all in Washington to (r)emember the thousands of Cherokees who died during the removal [of 1838]." (Rx = x commemorates the Cherokees who died during the removal of 1838)

(m) (*bumper sticker*) "HE WHO D(I)ES WITH THE MOST TOYS IS D(E)AD." (Ix = x dies with the most toys)

*(n) (*Andrew Carnegie*[7]) "The man who dies (r)ich dies (d)isgraced."

(o) Some (w)ater birds lack (o)il glands. (Ox = x has oil glands)

4. (a) (*newspaper*) "All loitering (l)aws are unconstitutional." (Cx = x is constitutional)

*(b) (*conversation*) "(I)nsects all have (a)ntennae."

(c) (*bumper sticker*) "[H]ATRED IS NOT A FAMILY (V)ALUE."

(d) (*anti-smoking crusader*) "Only s(u)ckers s(m)oke."

(e) Whenever it rains our telephone has no dial tone. (Rx = it is raining at time x, Tx = our telephone has a dial tone at time x)

*(f) (*Charlie Brown*) "To (k)now me is to (l)ove me." (Kx = x knows Charlie, Lx = x loves Charlie)

(g) (*Ellen Goodman*) "Not all (p)oliticians today are (r)otten."

(h) (*USFS sign at trailhead*) "If you pack it (i)n, pack it (o)ut." (Ox = you should pack x out)

(i) (*dialogue from* It's a Wonderful Life) "No man is a f(a)ilure who has f(r)iends." (Ax = x is a failure, Rx = x is a person who has friends)

*(j) (*movie title*) (L)onely are the (B)rave.

(k) (*Lincoln*) "Those who deny freedom to (o)thers deserve it not for (t)hemselves." (Ox = x denies freedom to others, Tx = x deserves to be free)

(l) (*Samuel Johnson*) "No man but a (l)unatic would be a (s)ailor."

(m) (*Erskine Caldwell*) "You cannot be both a good (s)ocializer and a good (w)riter."

*(n) (*W. C. Fields*) "A thing worth (h)aving is a thing worth (c)heating for." (Hx = x is worth having, Cx = x is worth cheating for)

---

[7]Steel magnate Andrew Carnegie (1835–1919) gave away $4.6 billion (in dollars adjusted for the year 2000) during his lifetime. Among his many gifts were more than 2,800 public libraries.

5. Translate each wff into a colloquial English sentence using the dictionary provided.

> Nx = x is a newt
> Sx = x is a salamander
> Rx = x is a reptile

(a) $\forall x(Nx \rightarrow Sx)$ (c) $\forall x(Rx \rightarrow -Sx)$

*(b) $\forall x(Sx \rightarrow -Rx)$ (d) $-\forall x(Sx \rightarrow -Nx)$

6. For each of the following sentences decide whether it is best viewed as a singular statement, an *A* statement, or an *I*.

(a) A whale is a mammal.

*(b) A whale has just surfaced off the port side of the ship.

(c) Manatees are mammals.

(d) Manatees live in Blue Spring Run in the winter.

(e) The oldest daughter of Bill and Ruth is a veterinarian.

*(f) The parent of a parent is a grandparent.

Note: The next two exercises are more difficult than any of the preceding ones; they require ingenuity. If you enjoy a challenge, you will want to tackle them. There are challenging problems in most of the exercise sets in this volume. To distinguish them from the other exercises, I have marked them with the word CHALLENGE.

7. (CHALLENGE) Symbolize these statements using the suggested abbreviations. Each statement is an instance of one of the five types discussed in the chapter, or the negation of such a statement.

(a) (*Oliver Goldsmith*) "Honour (s)inks where commerce long (p)revails." (Sx = x is a place where honor recedes, Px = x is a place where commerce has long prevailed)

(b) (*radio commercial*) "(S)moke and (m)ake your doctor rich." (Sx = x smokes, Mx = x makes x's doctor rich)

(c) (*proverb*) "All that g(l)itters is not g(o)ld."

(d) (*banker Charles Rice*) "The Harvard Business School never graduated an (M)BA that can't be hornswoggled by the businessmen of the Florida (p)anhandle." (Mx = x is a Harvard MBA, Px = x can be hornswoggled by Florida panhandle businessmen)

(e) (*newspaper*) "The only senators ever (e)xpelled were those found guilty of (t)reason." (Ex = x is an expelled senator, Tx = x is found guilty of treason) (Note: Distinguish "The only *f* are *ℊ*" from "Only *f* are *ℊ*." Can you formulate a translation principle for statements such as (e)?)

(f) (*Walt Kelley's Pogo*) "There's nothing but (l)osers in a (w)ar." (Wx = x is involved in a war)

(g) (*Milton*) "Nothing of all these evils hath (b)efallen me but justly." (Bx = x is an evil that has befallen me, Dx = x is an evil I deserve)

(h) (*newspaper letter*) "(H)umans are not the only creatures that (m)atter."

(i) (*J. M. Hilary*) "The perfect (c)ake is the sine qua non of the carefully planned modern (w)edding." (Cx = x includes a perfect cake, Wx = x is a carefully planned modern wedding)

(j) (*Nigerian general Abubakar*) "There is no (n)ation in the world that hasn't made (m)istakes." (Mx = x has made mistakes)

(k) (*newspaper*) "The only way to survive an accident on water at that speed [300 mph] is not to have one." (Sx = accident x has survivors, Wx = x is an accident on water at 300 mph)

8. (CHALLENGE) Symbolize these statements, employing the suggested abbreviations. (Neither (e) nor (f) is an instance of one of the five types discussed in the chapter.)

(a) All (p)arents are (e)ligible.

(b) Any parent is eligible.

(c) Not all parents are eligible.

(d) Not any parent is eligible.

(e) If all parents are eligible, [R]ita is.

(f) If any parent is eligible, Rita is.

(F4) Ca → Da
(F5) Cb → Db

F6 and F7 are not instances of F1. Why not?[4]

(F6) Ca → Db
(F7) Cy → Dy

The first predicate inference rule is simplicity itself.

The Universal Quantifier Out Rule (∀O): From a universal quantification derive any instance of it.

(How should "∀O" be pronounced? I suggest "AO.") The ∀O Rule (as well as the other predicate inference rules introduced later) is to be applied to *whole* lines only. To illustrate the use of the rule I will construct a proof for "Kodiak I," which was symbolized:

$$\forall x(Lx \rightarrow Fx), Lt \vdash Ft$$

The proof is short and sweet:

(1) ∀x(Lx → Fx)   A
(2) Lt   A
(3) Lt → Ft   1 ∀O
(4) Ft   3,2 →O

Line 3 is an instance of the universal quantification on line 1; hence the ∀O Rule was correctly applied in deriving line 3. The individual constant I chose to *instantiate* to on line 3 was *t*. I selected *t* because it occurred in the second premise and the conclusion of the sequent. Had I instantiated to any other constant on line 3 I would have been unable to complete the proof. The Arrow Out step on line 4 can be made only if the antecedent of line 3 is identical with line 2; thus line 3 must contain *t*.

Either of two questions may have occurred to you: *Why is the ∀O Rule sound?* and *Why is it needed?* Let's consider these questions in turn. The rule is based on the elementary logical principle that what is true of *every* individual is true of *any named* individual. Thus if it is true of every number that it has a successor, then it is true of 17 that it has a successor. A universal quantification represents a claim about every individual; an instance of that universal quantification represents the same claim applied to a specific (named) individual. The universal quantification on line 1 of the above proof says of every individual that if it is a legal request [made by a dying child], then it will be funded. The instance on line 3 says of the Minnesota teenager's request that if it is legal, then it will be funded.

---

[4]F6: *a* and *b* are not the same constant. F7: *y* is not a constant but a variable.

Why is the ∀O Rule needed? The rule allows us to derive from a universal quantification a wff that essentially belongs to propositional logic; it allows us to derive a wff to which we can apply the propositional inference rules. Contrast lines 1 and 3 of the above proof. The main symbol in line 1 (that is, the symbol with the greatest scope) is the universal quantifier, not the arrow; line 1 is a quantification, not a conditional. Thus a propositional rule such as Arrow Out cannot be applied correctly to line 1. By contrast, the main symbol in line 3 is the arrow; line 3 is a conditional. Arrow Out can be applied to that line. So, the main purpose of the ∀O Rule is to allow us to derive from universal quantifications wffs that lend themselves to manipulation by the inference rules of propositional logic.

For a second illustration of the use of the ∀O Rule I will construct a proof for "Kodiak II." This inference was symbolized:

$$Lp, -Fp \vdash -\forall x(Lx \rightarrow Fx)$$

A proof for this sequent:

1	(1) Lp	A
2	(2) −Fp	A
3	(3) ∀x(Lx → Fx)	PA
3	(4) Lp → Fp	3 ∀O
1,3	(5) Fp	4,1 →O
1,2,3	(6) Fp & −Fp	5,2 &I
1,2	(7) −∀x(Lx → Fx)	3-6 −I

The fact that the conclusion is a negation suggests that we employ the Dash In strategy; so a provisional assumption of the conclusion less its dash was made on line 3. When a standard contradiction[5] was reached on line 6, an application of Dash In finished the proof. The employment of a provisional assumption in the proof above required the inclusion (on the left) of an assumption-dependence column. This column makes it evident that line 7, the sequent's conclusion, depends only on the original assumptions and not on the provisional assumption. Note that the standard assumption-dependence principle applies to the ∀O Rule (and all the other predicate inference rules to be introduced). That is, the statement derived by ∀O depends on all of the assumptions on which the premise of the step depends.

The proof above is not the only correct proof that can be devised for "Kodiak II." For example, instead of employing Arrow Out, I might have used Modus Tollens. For any valid predicate sequent there are multiple correct proofs. A practical corollary: if a proof you construct for a starred exercise differs from the proof given in Appendix Four, your proof may yet be correct.

---

[5]A *standard contradiction* is a conjunction whose right conjunct is the negation of the left conjunct.

When Dr. Calvin Shirley, an African-American physician, applied to join the staff at Broward General Hospital in Ft. Lauderdale in the 1950's, he found that he was prevented from doing so by the combination of two rules; one was a hospital rule and the other a rule of the Broward County Medical Society.[6] The situation he faced is summarized by this argument:

> Only members of the (m)edical society are (p)ermitted to join the hospital staff. No (b)lacks are in the medical society. Dr. [S]hirley is black. Therefore, Dr. Shirley is not permitted to join the hospital staff.
>
> $\forall x(Px \rightarrow Mx), \forall x(Bx \rightarrow -Mx), Bs \vdash -Ps$

(Note how the first premise is symbolized.) A proof of the validity of this sequent:

(1) $\forall x(Px \rightarrow Mx)$ A
(2) $\forall x(Bx \rightarrow -Mx)$ A
(3) Bs   A
(4) $Ps \rightarrow Ms$ 1 $\forall$O
(5) $Bs \rightarrow -Ms$ 2 $\forall$O
(6) $-Ms$ 5,3 $\rightarrow$O
(7) $-Ps$ 4,6 MT

Dr. Shirley won his rightful place on the hospital staff by obtaining a court order forcing the medical society to admit him.

EXERCISES

1. Complete the following proofs. Every assumption has been identified. An assumption-dependence column is required for proof (b).

   (a) (1) $\forall x(Ax \rightarrow -Bx)$ A
        (2) Bc   A
        (3)   1 $\forall$O
        (4) $Bc \rightarrow -Ac$
        (5) $-Ac$

   *(b) 1   (1) De   A
             (2) $\forall x(Dx \rightarrow Fx)$ A
             (3) $-Ge$ A
             (4) $\forall x(Fx \rightarrow Gx)$ PA
             (5) $De \rightarrow Fe$
             (6)

[6]"Dedicated doctor is still in," *Miami Herald* (February 7, 1998), pp. 1G & 5G.

(7) Fe

(8)

(9) Ge & −Ge

1,2,3 (10) −∀x(Fx → Gx)

Note: To practice proof construction without the need for prior symbolization, see the Chapter Three practice problems in the Proofs section of the computer tutorial "PredLogic."

Instructions for exercises 2 through 7: Symbolize each argument on one horizontal line, using the suggested abbreviations. Construct a proof for each sequent. (These exercises are arranged so that the simplest problems occur first. This practice is followed throughout the book.)

2. Air Force Major Robert Lawrence, Jr., was killed in a plane crash during a training exercise in 1967, six months after he was named to the Air Force's manned orbiting laboratory program.[7] By NASA standards, he was an astronaut because he had been selected for astronaut training. NASA's reasoning:

    (a) Anyone (s)elected for astronaut training is an (a)stronaut. Major [L]awrence was selected for astronaut training. Hence, he was an astronaut.

By the standards employed by the Air Force in the 1960's, Major Lawrence was *not* an astronaut because he never flew 50 miles above the surface of the earth. The Air Force's argument:

*(b) Only those who have (f)lown 50 miles above the earth are (a)stronauts. Major [L]awrence never flew 50 miles above the earth. Therefore, he was not an astronaut.

Because of the Air Force's stand, Major Lawrence's name was not etched on the Space Mirror, the granite monument at Cape Canaveral that honors astronauts killed in the line of duty, when that monument was erected. Major Lawrence's family worked for years to persuade the directors of the monument foundation to include his name. One of the arguments they employed:

    (c) Christa [M]cAuliffe's name is on the (S)pace Mirror.[8] Ms. McAuliffe never (f)lew 50 miles above the earth. So, it is false that only those who have flown 50 miles above the earth have their names inscribed on the mirror.

(m = Christa McAuliffe, Sx = x's name is on the Space Mirror)

Major Lawrence's name was added to the Space Mirror 30 years after his death.

[7]"First black astronaut belatedly recognized," *Miami Herald* (December 8, 1997), p. 4A.

[8]Teacher Christa McAuliffe died in the *Challenger* explosion.

3. C(r)uel and unusual punishment is unconstitutional. So, c[a]pital punishment is unconstitutional because it is cruel and unusual.

   $(Ox = $ x is constitutional$)$

4. A topless club in New York City discovered that it could evade a law designed to put strip clubs out of business by admitting children as patrons.[9] The lawyer for the club devised this argument (which was accepted by the state supreme court):

   > The anti-smut (l)aw applies only to (a)dult establishments. No adult establishment admits (m)inors. [T]en's World Class Cabaret admits minors. It follows that the anti-smut law does not apply to Ten's.

   $(Lx = $ the anti-smut law applies to x$)$

*5. When Serena Williams announced that she wanted to play on the men's tennis tour, a spokesperson for the men's tour responded,

   > *To be able to play an ATP tournament, you have to be a member of the Association of Tennis Professionals. Serena Williams cannot become a member of the ATP because she is a woman. That answers the question.*[10]

   The argument reformulated:

   > Only members of the (A)TP (p)lay in ATP tournaments. Only (m)en are members of the ATP. Therefore, [S]erena Williams will not play in ATP tournaments because she is not a man.

6. Some years ago, when the Rev. Bailey Smith, president of the Southern Baptist Convention at the time, made public his opinion that God does not hear the prayers of Jews, protests came from all quarters. One man wrote *Time* magazine:

   > *If God cannot hear a Jew's prayers, how could he hear those of Jesus, a Jew?*[11]

   The man's reasoning seems to be:

   > Jesu[s] is a Je(w). God (h)ears Jesus' prayers. Hence, it is false that God hears the prayers of no Jews.

   $(s = $ Jesus, $Wx = $ x is a Jew, $Hx = $ God hears x's prayers$)$

   (Rev. Smith's bigoted view deserves to be challenged, but this argument may not do the job. The argument appears to trade on an ambiguity in the term *Jew*: that word can identify ethnicity or religious

---

[9]"'Adult' club admits kids to remain open (AP)," *(Fort Lauderdale) Sun-Sentinel* (November 7, 1998), p. 3A.

[10]"Sorry, Serena, you can't enter," *Miami Herald* (October 8, 1999), p. 3D.

[11]October 20, 1980, p. 5.

adherence. If our symbolization of the argument is to be acceptable, then the word must be used in the same sense throughout the argument. If it is used to identify ethnicity, the conclusion does not contradict Rev. Smith's position; and if it is used in the other sense, one can argue that the first premise is false. Note that this criticism of the reasoning in the letter is itself an argument.)

7. Officials in Deltona, Florida, informed Deborah Housend that she could no longer keep her pet Vietnamese potbellied pig, Harley, in her backyard.[12] The bureaucrats argued as follows:

> [H]arley is a pot(b)ellied pig. Potbellied pigs are pi(g)s. Pigs are (l)ivestock. Livestock are not permitted in (r)esidential areas. It follows that Harley is not permitted in residential areas.

$(Rx = x$ is permitted in residential areas$)$

3.2 ∃O

A newspaper columnist writes:

The predominant idea that only whites owned slaves is not correct. There were also Indian slave holders, particularly among the so-called "Five Civilized Tribes." [13]

The columnist reasons:

> Some (I)ndians (o)wned slaves.
> No Indians are (w)hites.
> So, it is false that only whites owned slaves.

$$\exists x(Ix \ \& \ Ox), \forall x(Ix \rightarrow -Wx) \vdash -\forall x(Ox \rightarrow Wx)$$

The second premise was assumed, and not stated. This is an obviously valid argument, but we cannot construct a proof for its sequent until we adopt a rule of inference that allows us to make inferences from wffs that begin with existential quantifiers.

> *The Existential Quantifier Out Rule* (∃O): **From an existential quantification derive any instance of it,** *provided that* **the individual constant being introduced is a dummy name that is new to the proof.**

(I suggest that "∃O" be pronounced "EO.") I need to define several terms appearing in the ∃O Rule. An *existential quantification* is a wff beginning with an

---

[12]"Deltona is no hog heaven for Harley the potbellied pig," *Orlando Sentinel* (April 30, 1997), pp. C-1 & C-4.

[13]MariJo Moore, "'Five Civilized Tribes' were owners of African American slaves," *Asheville Citizen-Times* (June 14, 1998), p. A11.

existential quantifier whose scope is the entire wff. An *instance* of an existential quantification is a wff that results from deleting the quantifier (and groupers showing the scope of the quantifier) and replacing each of the remaining occurrences of the variable by the same individual constant. A *dummy name* is an individual constant in a proof that does not appear in the sequent being tested. (We call a constant that *does* appear in the sequent a *genuine name*.) Note that the ∃O Rule incorporates two restrictions (in the clause following *provided that*): (1) the constant must be a dummy name, and (2) it must be new to the proof. The need for these restrictions will be explained below.

We can now construct a proof for (the symbolization of) the argument about slave ownership:

1	(1)	∃x(Ix & Ox)	A
2	(2)	∀x(Ix → −Wx)	A
3	(3)	∀x(Ox → Wx)	PA
1	(4)	Ia & Oa	1 ∃O
2	(5)	Ia → −Wa	2 ∀O
3	(6)	Oa → Wa	3 ∀O
1	(7)	Ia	4 &O
1,2	(8)	−Wa	5,7 →O
1	(9)	Oa	4 &O
1,3	(10)	Wa	6, 9 →O
1,2,3	(11)	Wa & −Wa	10,8 &I
1,2	(12)	−∀x(Ox → Wx)	3-11 −I

Line 4 is an instance of the existential quantification on line 1. Furthermore, the individual constant introduced on line 4 is a dummy name and it is new to the proof (it does not occur on any line above line 4), so the restrictions on the ∃O Rule are satisfied. The individual constant employed on the fourth line was selected at random; any other constant letter would have served as well. However, having chosen *a* for line 4, I had to instantiate to it again on lines 5 and 6 in order to complete the proof. The purpose of the ∃O Rule is to permit us to derive from existential quantifications wffs to which the propositional inference rules apply. Consider the above proof. The Ampersand Out Rule cannot be applied to line 1, because that wff is not a conjunction (its main symbol is not an ampersand), but the rule *can* be applied to line 4 (which was derived from line 1 by the ∃O Rule).

I will construct a second proof employing the ∃O Rule. It was long thought that an email message (as opposed to an *attachment* to an email message) could not harbor a computer virus.[14] The reasoning behind that view:

---

[14] In 1999 a virus (*Bubbleboy*) was created that could be activated (assisted by a glitch in Microsoft Outlook Express) simply by highlighting its subject line.

Anything that harbors a computer (v)irus is an executable (p)rogram. No (e)mail message is an executable program. Therefore, it is false that some email messages harbor viruses.

∀x(Vx → Px), ∀x(Ex → −Px) ⊢ −∃x(Ex & Vx)

(Vx = x harbors a virus) A proof of validity for this sequent:

1	(1)	∀x(Vx → Px)	A
2	(2)	∀x(Ex → −Px)	A
3	(3)	∃x(Ex & Vx)	PA
3	(4)	Eb & Vb	3 ∃O
1	(5)	Vb → Pb	1 ∀O
2	(6)	Eb → −Pb	2 ∀O
3	(7)	Vb	4 &O
1,3	(8)	Pb	5,7 →O
3	(9)	Eb	4 &O
2,3	(10)	−Pb	6,9 →O
1,2,3	(11)	Pb & −Pb	8,10 &I
1,2	(12)	−∃x(Ex & Vx)	3-11 −I

Notice that the existential quantification on line 3 was instantiated *before* the universal quantifications on lines 1 and 2. This was done to ensure satisfaction of the second restriction on the ∃O Rule–the requirement that the individual constant introduced not appear on any higher line. This procedural principle should be followed:

Wherever possible, employ the ∃O Rule before using the ∀O Rule.

Note that the ∀O rule is not encumbered with either of the restrictions that are imposed on the ∃O Rule. The constant introduced by a step of ∀O may be either a genuine name or a dummy name, and it need not be new to the proof.

I will conclude the section by considering two questions: *Why is the ∃O Rule sound?* and *Why are the two restrictions needed?*

Consider the statement "Some (r)abbis are (J)apanese" and the existential quantification, F1, that symbolizes it.

(F1)   ∃x(Rx & Jx)

You certainly couldn't validly infer F2 (where *b* functions as a genuine name, denoting George W. Bush, let's say) from F1.

(F2)   Rb & Jb

It is unsound to reason that what is true of some individual (namely, that he or she is a rabbi and also Japanese) must be true of a particular named individual (George W. Bush). F2 may be correctly inferred from F1 when and only when *b* is a dummy name (and also new to the proof containing these wffs). F1 is true iff (if and only if) there is at least one individual to whom the predicates R and J can be correctly ascribed. Now we probably don't know who that individual is, but we can agree to let *b* function (in the context of the proof) as the name of that individual (or one of those individuals if there are several).[15] If F1 is true, then F2 will also be true. And that is all we need to ask of a rule of inference, that it be *truth-preserving*. It is important that we not attach any additional significance to *b,* and that is why we require that it be a dummy name new to the proof.

We can re-emphasize the necessity of the two restrictions by showing that without them it would be possible to construct "proofs" for invalid sequents. Here is an obviously invalid argument:

> Some (D)emocrats are (p)oliticians. Thus, [E]lizabeth Dole is a Democrat.
>
> $\exists x(Dx \ \& \ Px) \vdash De$

A "proof" for its sequent:

(1) $\exists x(Dx \ \& \ Px)$ A
(2) $De \ \& \ Pe$ 1 $\exists$O (*ERROR!*)
(3) De 2 &O

The move to line 2 violates the first restriction on the $\exists$O Rule, since the individual constant introduced is a genuine name (it appears in the conclusion), not a dummy name. In symbolizing the argument I chose *e* to refer to Elizabeth Dole. Thus, when I instantiated on line 2, *e* was not functioning as a dummy name.

A second obviously fallacious argument:

> Some Democrats are not politicians. So, it is false that some Democrats are politicians.
>
> $\exists x(Dx \ \& \ -Px) \vdash -\exists x(Dx \ \& \ Px)$

We know that this argument is invalid because it has a true premise and a false conclusion. (The conclusion denies a true assertion.) A "proof" for its sequent:

1   (1) $\exists x(Dx \ \& \ -Px)$ A
2   (2) $\exists x(Dx \ \& \ Px)$ PA

---

[15]But what if there is no such individual? In that case F1 is false, and it really doesn't matter what individual the dummy name denotes; we can let the name designate any arbitrarily chosen individual.

1	(3)	De & −Pe	1 ∃O
2	(4)	De & Pe	2 ∃O (*ERROR!*)
2	(5)	Pe	4 &O
1	(6)	−Pe	3 &O
1,2	(7)	Pe & −Pe	5,6 &I
1	(8)	−∃x(Dx & Px)	2-7 −I

The derivation of line 4 violates the second restriction on the ∃O Rule, since the individual constant used on line 4 occurs on a preceding line (3) and so is not new to the proof. As *e* was already assigned a use on line 3 (to name some individual that makes line 1 a truth), it was not free on line 4 to function simply as a dummy name in relation to line 2.

Now we should wrap up some loose ends relating to the assignment of meanings to dummy names. (1) When a dummy name is initially introduced into a proof by a step of ∀O (or in a provisional assumption or via vI), what significance do we attach to the name? Answer: the name represents an individual selected at random. (2) When a dummy name is brought into a proof for a second (or third, etc.) time by a step of ∀O (or in a provisional assumption or via vI), what significance do we attach to the name? Answer: it has the same significance given when the name was first introduced to the proof. (3) In a propositional-logic proof, each line in a proof is correlated with a sequent whose validity is established when that line is reached. The conclusion of the sequent is the wff on the line in question, and the premises are the assumptions on which that wff depends. In a predicate-logic proof this result holds only for lines that do not contain dummy names. Because a dummy name has a reference only in the context of the proof in which it occurs, it cannot be a part of a sequent considered independently of the proof.

EXERCISES

8. Complete the following proof.

	(1)	∀x(Ax → Bx)	A
	(2)	∃x(Ax & Cx)	A
	(3)	∀x(Cx → −Bx)	PA
	(4)	Ad & Cd	2 ∃O
	(5)		1 ∀O
	(6)		3 ∀O
	(7)		4 &O
	(8)		5,7 →O
	(9)		4 &O
	(10)		6,9 →O
	(11)		8,10 &I
1,2	(12)		3-11 −I

Instructions for exercises 9 through 14: Symbolize each argument on one horizontal line, using the suggested abbreviations. Construct a proof for each sequent.

9. *A* and *O* statements with the same grammatical subjects and predicates are *contradictories*; *E*'s and *I*'s are also. Two statements are contradictories when and only when, by virtue of their forms, they must have opposite truth values. We can begin to establish these results by showing that the arguments below are valid.

   (a) All (o)rthodontists are (d)entists. So, it is false that some orthodontists are not dentists.

   *(b) No (B)uddhists are (A)mish. So, it is false that some Buddhists are Amish.

10. A newspaper story describes Wabash College, one of three remaining all-male colleges in the United States (as of 1999), and its effective honor code.[16] The article advances this argument (paraphrased):

    A (W)abash man is a (g)entleman. No gentleman (c)heats. Thus, it is not the case that there are Wabash men who cheat.

11. Sociologist Amati Etzione, in a newspaper interview:

    Community is . . . not a sufficient condition for a noble social life. There can be a Nazi community. There can be a community that decides to burn books.[17]

    Etzione's reasoning reformulated:

    There are (N)azi (c)ommunities. No Nazi institutions (f)oster a noble social life. Therefore, it is false that all communities foster a noble social life.

    The second premise was taken for granted, and so not made explicit.

12. An appellate court decision includes the following reasoning:

    The plaintiff Pestana contends . . . that the contract herein is a destination contract. . . . He relies for this position on the notation at the bottom of the contract between the parties which provides that the goods were to be sent to Chetumal, Mexico. We cannot agree. A "send to" or "ship to" term is a part of every contract involving the sale of goods where carriage is contemplated and has no significance in determining whether the contract is a shipment or destination contract for risk of loss purposes.[18]

---

[16]Jon Jeter, "School of Manners, Not Miss Manners," *Washington Post* (March 12, 1999), p. 2-A.

[17]Bob von Sternberg and Martha Sawyer Allen, "Hey, can't we all just get along?" *Minneapolis Star Tribune* (October 14, 1994), p. 22A.

[18]*Pestana* v. *Karinol Corp.* District Court of Appeal of Florida, Third District (1979), 367 So. 2d 1096.

The court's thinking may be expressed:

All sales contracts involving (c)arriage contain the (t)erm "send to." So, since at least some sales contracts involving carriage are not (d)estination contracts, it is false that every contract containing the term "send to" is a destination contract.

The second premise was unstated in the decision.

*13. On an exam in Introduction to Philosophy I asked:

How would the hard determinist answer the question, "Could a machine have free will?"

One student answered (in part):

The hard determinist says that all events are caused. Therefore all machine actions (which are also events) are caused. Therefore a machine could not have free will.

Formalizing this a bit more we reach:

All (e)vents are (c)aused. All (m)achine actions are events. Nothing caused is (f)ree. Therefore, it is false that there are free machine actions.

14. A traveling museum show called *Big Bugs* included this sign beside a giant wooden replica of a scorpion:

Can you tell . . .

Is a scorpion an insect? Count its legs. Insects have six, while arachnids (spiders and their relatives) have eight.

The scorpion model had eight legs. Perhaps the naturalist who wrote the sign text was encouraging children to reason like this:

(I)nsects have si(x) legs. (A)rachnids have (e)ight legs. Nothing with six legs has eight legs. S(c)orpions are arachnids. Thus, it is false that some insects are scorpions.

(We hope that the naturalist was not also encouraging this reasoning: Arachnids have eight legs. Scorpions have eight legs. Hence, scorpions are arachnids.)

15. (CHALLENGE) Construct a seven-line proof for exercise 9(a).

4

Proofs: ∃I and 2E

The inference rules presented in Chapter Three are both "out" rules; they allow us to move *from* quantified wffs, but of course not *to* such wffs. For this reason, the conclusions of the sequents we have proven so far have been either the negations of quantifications (which can be reached by the Dash In Rule) or wffs without quantifiers. In this chapter we extend the proof system so that we can handle sequents whose conclusions are quantifications.

4.1   ∃I

The Existential Quantifier In Rule allows us to infer existential quantifications.

> *The Existential Quantifier In Rule* (∃I): **Derive an existential quantification from any instance of it.**

F2 is an existential quantification and F1 is an instance of it; therefore, we may derive F2 from F1 by ∃I.

(F1) Fa & Ga
(F2) ∃x(Fx & Gx)

Why is this rule sound? Because if some *named* individual bears a property, then surely some individual bears it. (Note that predicate logic assumes that each individual constant names some individual.) This rule works whether the constant in the instance is a genuine or dummy name.

We can illustrate the use of the rule by constructing a proof for the argument "Dead Voters." A newspaper story under the headline, *Dead Men* do *Vote— Miami Probe Widens,* begins:

> *Manuel Yip died in 1993 at age 75. Last week, he voted in the Miami city election.[1]*

The reporters' tongue-in-cheek argument:

> [M]anuel Yip is a (d)ead man. Yip (v)oted in the Miami election. So, some dead man voted in the Miami election.
>
> Dm, Vm ⊢ ∃x(Dx & Vx)

We have here a valid argument with a false conclusion. How can that be? Answer: The second premise is false. Mr. Yip didn't vote; rather, someone voted using his identity. However, our present concern is not with determining the truth or falsity of the statements making up the argument, but with establishing the validity of the argument. The proof couldn't hardly be simpler:

(1) Dm	A	
(2) Vm	A	
(3) Dm & Vm	1,2 &I	
(4) ∃x(Dx & Vx)	3 ∃I	

The deduction of line 4 from line 3 is correct because line 3 is an instance of line 4.

For a second sample proof we turn to an argument (call it "False Beliefs") advanced by Plato in the dialogue *Gorgias[2]*:

> All (k)nowledge is (t)rue. Some (b)eliefs are not true. Hence, at least some beliefs are not knowledge.
>
> ∀x(Kx → Tx), ∃x(Bx & −Tx) ⊢ ∃x(Bx & −Kx)

(1) ∀x(Kx → Tx)	A	
(2) ∃x(Bx & −Tx)	A	
(3) Ba & −Ta	2 ∃O	
(4) Ka → Ta	1 ∀O	
(5) Ba	3 &O	
(6) −Ta	3 &O	

[1]Manny Garcia, Frances Robles, and Joseph Tanfani, *Miami Herald* (November 9, 1997), p. 1A.

[2]454d. *The Collected Dialogues of Plato,* ed. by Edith Hamilton and Huntington Cairns (Princeton, N.J.: Princeton University Press, 1961), p. 238.

(7) −Ka   4,6 MT
(8) Ba & −Ka   5,7 &I
(9) ∃x(Bx & −Kx)   8 ∃I

Note that line 8 is an instance of line 9. Also note that the ∃O move was made before the ∀O move in order to avoid violating one of the restrictions on the ∃O Rule.

EXERCISES

1. The *converse* of a categorical proposition is the statement that results when you switch the (logical) predicates. An *I* statement and its converse (S1 and S2, for example) are logically equivalent.

   (S1) Some (M)ethodists are (O)hioans.
   (S2) Some Ohioans are Methodists.

   Complete the proof below to show that S1 entails[3] S2. An isomorphic proof would show that S2 entails S1. Since logical equivalence is mutual entailment, we see that the two statements are equivalent. We can generalize the result and state that *I* statements are (validly) convertible. (There is only one assumption line in this proof.)

   (1) ∃x(Mx & Ox)   A
   (2)
   (3) Mb
   (4)
   (5)
   (6) ∃x(Ox & Mx)

Note: To practice proof construction without the need for prior symbolization, see the Chapter Four practice problems in the Proofs section of "PredLogic."

Instructions: Symbolize each argument on one horizontal line, using the suggested abbreviations. Construct a proof for each sequent.

2. Liz Heaston, a place kicker for Willamette University, broke the gender barrier in American college football in 1997,[4] giving us the following argument:

   [H]easton is a (w)oman. She is a college (f)ootball player. Hence, some college football players are women.

---

[3]One statement *entails* a second iff the argument that has the first statement as sole premise and the second statement as conclusion is valid.

[4]"Kicking down barriers; It's a 1st: Woman plays in college football game," *Miami Herald* (October 21, 1997), pp. 1D & 4D.

*3. Bertrand Russell writes in *A History of Western Philosophy*:

> *The syllogism is only one kind of deductive argument. In mathematics, which is wholly deductive, syllogisms hardly ever occur.*[5]

As Russell notes, syllogisms (this term is defined in the next section) are uncommon in mathematics, but they are more common in philosophy—this passage being a case in point. Russell's syllogism:

> Some (d)eductive arguments are not (s)yllogisms. Proof: (M)athematical arguments are all deductive. Some mathematical arguments are not syllogisms.

4. [T]wo is not (o)dd. Two is (p)rime. Therefore, some primes are not odd.

5. Some arguments with (f)alse premises are (v)alid. This proves that some valid arguments do not (e)stablish their conclusions, because no argument that establishes its conclusion has false premises.

(Fx = x is an argument with false premises, Ex = x is an argument that establishes its conclusion)

6. Since 1992 it has been illegal in Australia to sterilize retarded women without court approval.[6] In the five years following this decision, court permission was granted only 17 times, but at least 1,045 retarded women were sterilized. The reasoning (applied to sterilizations of retarded Australian women) is obvious:

> Sterilizations are (l)egal only if they are done with court (a)pproval. Some (s)terilizations were done without court approval. Hence, some of the sterilizations were illegal.

(Lx = x is a legal case of sterilization, Ax = x is done with court approval, Sx = x is a case of sterilization)

*7. Philosopher James Rachels advances this argument:

> *1. If an action promotes the (b)est interests of everyone concerned and violates no one's rights, then that action is (m)orally acceptable.*
>
> *2. In at least some cases, active (e)uthanasia promotes the best interests of everyone concerned and violates no one's rights.*
>
> *3. Therefore, in at least some cases active euthanasia is morally acceptable.*[7]

(Bx = x is an action that promotes the best interests of everyone concerned and violates no one's rights, Mx = x is morally acceptable, Ex = x is an act of active euthanasia)

---

[5](New York: Simon and Schuster, 1945), p. 198.

[6]"Panel: Illegal sterilizations in Australia," (AP), *Miami Herald* (December 16, 1997), p. 30A.

[7]"Euthanasia," in *Matters of Life and Death: New Introductory Essays in Moral Philosophy*, 2nd ed., ed. by Tom Regan (New York: Random House, Inc., 1986), p. 52.

8. A naive boy (growing up in a less-sophisticated era) reasoned as follows:

    > Whoever engages in (i)ntercourse is (e)vil. (M)inisters are not evil. Some ministers have (c)hildren. Therefore, some who have children have never had intercourse.

    (The reasoning is valid but, of course, most of the statements are false.) An unusual logical feature of this argument is that it contains all of the basic statement forms (A, E, I, and O).

9. The political cartoon below skewering Canadian politician Jean Charest advances this argument:

    > (M)oney is being put in my [Charest's] pocket. [I] am a (T)ory. Tories are (C)anadians. So, money is being put in the pocket of some Canadians.

    (Mx = money is being put in the pocket of x)

Reprinted with permission from the *Halifax Herald Limited*.

4.2   QE

Our proof system is still incomplete. We are not yet equipped to deal with sequents whose conclusions are universal quantifications or with sequents having a premise that is the negation of a quantification. We could solve the first problem by adding a Universal Quantifier In Rule ($\forall$I) to our stockpile of rules, and logicians commonly do this.[8] Adding this rule would provide two advantages: it would enable elegant proofs for sequents whose conclusions are universal quantifications, and it would provide a symmetrical set of rules, with an *In* rule and an *Out* rule for each quantifier. But there are considerations on the other side. The main one is that the set of conditions that must be imposed on an ∀I Rule in order to make it valid are so cumbersome that the benefit of having the rule available for use in proofs is more than neutralized by the difficulty of remembering, and determining the satisfaction of, its conditions. Why must an ∀I Rule be laden with conditions? You can see that, in general, universal quantifications make much more sweeping claims than do existential quantifications. To hold that *every*thing bears some property is to assert a lot more than merely that *some*thing bears that property. So, a move to a universal quantification is an inherently risky move. In order to insure that it is properly done a number of restrictions must be observed. A second consideration is that even if we added an ∀I Rule to our set we would still not be equipped to deal with certain valid sequents, those containing premise wffs that are the negations of quantifications.

My plan is to introduce a fourth inference rule that will solve both problems mentioned above. The addition of this rule will make it unnecessary to include an ∀I Rule. The rule allows us to interchange dashes and quantifiers:

The Quantifier Exchange Rule (QE): (1) From the negation of a universal quantification derive the wff that results from replacing the quantifier by an existential quantifier and interchanging the dash and the quantifier, and vice versa.

(2) From the negation of an existential quantification derive the wff that results from replacing the quantifier by a universal quantifier and interchanging the dash and the quantifier, and vice versa.

The rule can be expressed more simply as follows:[9]

From −∀x⁄x derive ∃x−⁄x, and vice versa.

From −∃x⁄x derive ∀x−⁄x, and vice versa.

---

[8]An ∀I Rule may be formulated as follows:
Derive a universal quantification from any instance of it, *provided that* the individual constant is a dummy name that does not occur in:

(1) any line derived by ∃O,
(2) any provisional assumption on which the instance depends, or
(3) the universal quantification itself.

[9]"−∀x⁄x" represents the negation of any universal quantification and "∃x−⁄x" represents the wff that results from replacing the quantifier by an existential quantifier and interchanging the dash and the quantifier. Analogous comments apply to the second version of the rule.

We can illustrate the use of this rule with a proof that shows that E statements are validly convertible. We will show that S3 entails S4. (An isomorphic proof would establish the reverse entailment.)

(S3) No (T)exans are (I)owans.
(S4) No Iowans are Texans.

1	(1)	$\forall x(Tx \rightarrow -Ix)$	A
2	(2)	$-\forall x(Ix \rightarrow -Tx)$	PA
2	(3)	$\exists x-(Ix \rightarrow -Tx)$	2 QE
2	(4)	$-(Ic \rightarrow -Tc)$	3 $\exists$O
1	(5)	$Tc \rightarrow -Ic$	1 $\forall$O
1	(6)	$Ic \rightarrow -Tc$	5 CN
1,2	(7)	$(Ic \rightarrow -Tc)$ & $-(Ic \rightarrow -Tc)$	6,4 &I
1	(8)	$\forall x(Ix \rightarrow -Tx)$	2-7 $-$O

The last line in the proof is a universal quantification. Because we do not have at our disposal an $\forall$I Rule, we adopt a Dash Out strategy for reaching line 8. Accordingly we provisionally assume on line 2 the negation of the wff on line 8. Notice that the $\forall$O Rule cannot be applied to the wff on line 2 because it is not a quantification. (It is not a quantification because it begins with a dash rather than a quantifier.) With the help of the QE Rule we can deduce from line 2 a quantification on line 3; then we can apply the $\exists$O Rule to that wff. What is true in this proof is true generally: the main purpose of the QE Rule is to transform *the negation of a quantification* into *a quantification,* so that the $\forall$O or $\exists$O Rule may then be used.

We can justify the QE Rule by noting the intuitive soundness of English versions of the rule. An English counterpart of the first form of the rule:

> From "It is false that everything is A" derive "Something is not A," and vice versa.

By substituting a specific predicate for the A and employing more colloquial English, we reach an instance of the rule that is even more obviously correct:

> From "Not all things are physical" derive "Some things aren't physical," and vice versa.

Two English counterparts of the second form of the rule—one abstract and the other concrete:

> From "It is false that there is an A" derive "Each thing is not A," and vice versa.
> From "It's false that ghosts exist" derive "Nothing is a ghost," and vice versa.

I will provide a second example of a proof that uses the QE Rule, a proof for this argument (call it "Smoking Collegians"):

> Those who knowingly and needlessly (e)ndanger their health act (i)rrationally. College students who (s)moke knowingly and needlessly endanger their health. It follows that college students who smoke act irrationally.

$$\forall x(Ex \to Ix), \forall x(Sx \to Ex) \vdash \forall x(Sx \to Ix)$$

(Ex = x knowingly and needlessly endangers x's health, Sx = x is a college student who smokes) A proof of validity:

proof stages

1	(1)	$\forall x(Ex \to Ix)$	A	1
2	(2)	$\forall x(Sx \to Ex)$	A	
3	(3)	$-\forall x(Sx \to Ix)$	PA	2
3	(4)	$\exists x-(Sx \to Ix)$	3 QE	3
3	(5)	$-(Sa \to Ia)$	4 ∃O	4
1	(6)	$Ea \to Ia$	1 ∀O	5
2	(7)	$Sa \to Ea$	2 ∀O	
1,2	(8)	$Sa \to Ia$	7,6 CH	6
1,2,3	(9)	$(Sa \to Ia) \ \& \ -(Sa \to Ia)$	8,5 &I	
1,2	(10)	$\forall x(Sx \to Ix)$	3-9 $-$O	7

(The column on the right is not part of the proof.) Many proofs for sequents whose conclusions are universal quantifications follow the same general pattern, which I call *the seven stages of a Dash Out predicate proof*:

1. The premises of the sequent are assumed.
2. A provisional assumption is made of the negation of the conclusion (in anticipation of stage seven).
3. The QE Rule is applied to assumptions that are negations of quantifications.
4. The ∃O Rule is applied to existential quantifications.
5. The ∀O Rule is applied to universal quantifications.
6. A standard contradiction is derived (by propositional inference rules) from the wffs reached in stages four and five.
7. The conclusion is obtained by Dash Out.

This strategy will work not only for sequents whose conclusions are universal quantifications, but also for sequents with existential quantifications as conclusions. Here is such a proof for "False Beliefs" from the previous section.

1	(1)	$\forall x(Kx \to Tx)$	A
2	(2)	$\exists x(Bx \ \& \ -Tx)$	A

3	(3)	$-\exists x(Bx \ \& \ -Kx)$	PA
3	(4)	$\forall x-(Bx \ \& \ -Kx)$	3 QE
2	(5)	$Bd \ \& \ -Td$	2 $\exists$O
1	(6)	$Kd \rightarrow Td$	1 $\forall$O
3	(7)	$-(Bd \ \& \ -Kd)$	4 $\forall$O
2	(8)	$-Td$	5 &O
1,2	(9)	$-Kd$	6,8 MT
1,2,3	(10)	$-Bd$	7,9 CA
2	(11)	Bd	5 &O
1,2,3	(12)	$Bd \ \& \ -Bd$	11,10 &I
1,2	(13)	$\exists x(Bx \ \& \ -Kx)$	3-12 $-$O

This proof is four lines longer than the proof displayed in the last section, and this is typical of the difference in length between $\exists$I and $-$O proofs for sequents whose conclusions are existential quantifications. Note also that the shorter proof had no provisional assumption and so no assumption-dependence column was needed. For both of these reasons we prefer the $\exists$I proof. But there is an important theoretical point to make in this connection. The $\exists$I Rule is superfluous. The other three predicate rules ($\forall$O, $\exists$O, and QE), when added to the group of eighteen propositional inference rules listed on page 278, form a set that is sufficient for constructing a formal proof for *any* valid sequent that uses the vocabulary presented in Chapter Two. (Of course, it does not follow that a given individual will be able to devise a proof for a particular sequent.) In logicians' terminology, the set of rules is *complete* for this portion of predicate logic. (But it is not complete for relational predicate logic, the subject of Chapters Ten through Thirteen.) The set of inference rules (with or without the addition of $\exists$I) is also *consistent;* that is, no proof for an invalid sequent can be constructed using just these rules.[10]

Buckle up your seat belts; it's time for a quick lesson in the history of logic. "False Beliefs" and "Smoking Collegians," as well as most of the arguments featured in the exercises of this chapter, are *categorical syllogisms*.

A categorical syllogism is an argument with these features:
  (1) It consists of three statements.
  (2) Each statement is an *A, E, I,* or *O* statement.
  (3) Each (logical) predicate occurs in two statements.

There are 256 forms of categorical syllogisms. Contemporary logicians assess 15 of these forms as valid, and the remaining 241 as invalid.[11] For practical

---

[10]For more information on these matters see Appendix Two.

[11]Medieval logicians regarded 24 forms as valid and 232 invalid. The difference between the two positions relates to the issue of *existential import* explored in Chapter Nine.

purposes, the 15 valid syllogism forms may be reduced to the six forms listed in this table:[12]

Six Valid Syllogism Forms

All D are E All F are D So, all F are E	No D are E All F are D So, no F are E
All D are E Some F are D So, some F are E	No D are E Some F are D So, some F are not E
Some D are not E All D are F So, some F are not E	All E are D Some F are not D So, some F are not E

"False Beliefs" has the form shown in the bottom row, right column, and the form of "Smoking Collegians" is displayed in the top row, left column. Most of the arguments treated in the exercises in this chapter exhibit one or another of these six forms (or variations on them).

The study of categorical syllogisms, called *syllogistic logic* or *Aristotelian logic,* dominated formal logic from the fourth century B.C. through the nineteenth century. Medieval logicians assigned (or in some cases invented) women's names to identify the valid syllogism forms. The vowels in the names indicate the kinds of statements making up the form. The form of "Smoking Collegians," for example, was dubbed *Barbara* because it is composed of three *A* statements. Medieval logicians did not use the same kinds of techniques for determining argument validity that are employed today. They typically devised sets of rules (rules like "No valid syllogism has two negative premises") to be applied to syllogisms. A syllogism is valid iff it adheres to all of the rules in the set.[13] The shortcoming of this approach is that it is restricted to syllogisms. Predicate logic, developed largely in the twentieth century, includes within its scope all syllogisms plus a great many arguments that syllogistic logic is unable to treat.

A *sorites* is a syllogism on steroids. If you don't care for that definition, try this one.

A sorites is an argument with these features:

(1) It consists of four or more statements.

[12]The reduction is accomplished by changing the order of predicates in convertible statements (*E* and *I*).

[13]For a fuller account of syllogistic logic see Chapter Two of Stephen F. Barker, *The Elements of Logic* (5th ed.; New York: McGraw-Hill Book Company, 1989).

(2) **Each statement is an *A, E, I,* or *O* statement.**
(3) **Each predicate occurs in two statements.**

In the 1960s NASA trained 13 women (known as *the Mercury 13*) to be astronauts, but then NASA officials had second thoughts because they feared the public reaction to the death of women in a space accident. So, NASA prevented the women from entering space with the help of a sorites and some convenient regulations:[14]

> Being a jet test (p)ilot is a necessary condition for being an (a)stronaut. Attending jet test-pilot (s)chool is a necessary condition for being a jet test pilot. No (w)omen [are permitted to] attend jet test-pilot school. Thus, no women are astronauts.

$$\forall x(Ax \rightarrow Px), \forall x(Px \rightarrow Sx), \forall x(Wx \rightarrow -Sx) \vdash \forall x(Wx \rightarrow -Ax)$$

Note the symbolization of the first two premises. The proof for this sequent is very similar to the proof for a syllogism, just a few lines longer.

1	(1)	$\forall x(Ax \rightarrow Px)$	A
2	(2)	$\forall x(Px \rightarrow Sx)$	A
3	(3)	$\forall x(Wx \rightarrow -Sx)$	A
4	(4)	$-\forall x(Wx \rightarrow -Ax)$	PA
4	(5)	$\exists x-(Wx \rightarrow -Ax)$	4 QE
4	(6)	$-(We \rightarrow -Ae)$	5 ∃O
1	(7)	$Ae \rightarrow Pe$	1 ∀O
2	(8)	$Pe \rightarrow Se$	2 ∀O
3	(9)	$We \rightarrow -Se$	3 ∀O
1,2	(10)	$Ae \rightarrow Se$	7,8 CH
1,2	(11)	$-Se \rightarrow -Ae$	10 CN
1,2,3	(12)	$We \rightarrow -Ae$	9,11 CH
1,2,3,4	(13)	$(We \rightarrow -Ae) \& -(We \rightarrow -Ae)$	12,6 &I
1,2,3	(14)	$\forall x(Wx \rightarrow -Ax)$	4-13 -O

EXERCISES

10. In exercise 9 of Chapter Three you began the task of showing that *A* and *O* statements with the same grammatical subjects and predicates are *contradictories,* and that the same holds true for *E*'s and *I*'s. Finish the job by completing the proofs for the following arguments. Every assumption has been identified.

[14]"These astronaut trainees never left the earth," *Miami Herald* (October 17, 1998), pp. 1E & 2E.

(a) It is false that some (o)rthodontists are not (d)entists. So, all (o)rthodontists are (d)entists.

```
1  (1)  −∃x(Ox & −Dx)        A
   (2)                        PA
   (3)                        1 QE
   (4)                        2 QE
   (5)                        4 ∃O
   (6)                        3 ∀O
   (7)  Oe → De               6 AR
1,2 (8)                       7,5 &I
1  (9)  ∀x(Ox → Dx)          2-8 −O
```

*(b) It is false that some (B)uddhists are (A)mish. So, no Buddhists are Amish.

```
1  (1)   −∃x(Bx & Ax)              A
   (2)   −∀x(Bx → −Ax)             PA
   (3)   ∀x−(Bx & Ax)
   (4)   ∃x−(Bx → −Ax)
   (5)   −(Bf → −Af)
   (6)   −(Bf & Af)
   (7)   −Bf v −Af
   (8)   Bf → −Af
1,2 (9)  (Bf → −Af) & −(Bf → −Af)
1  (10)  ∀x(Bx → −Ax)
```

Instructions for exercises 11, 12, and 14 through 16: Symbolize each argument on one horizontal line, using the suggested abbreviations. Construct a proof for each sequent.

11. In the Sixth *Meditation,* Descartes writes:

> *I first take notice here that there is a great difference between the mind and the body, in that the body, from its nature, is always divisible and the mind is completely indivisible.*[15]

He is reasoning syllogistically:

(B)odies are always (d)ivisible. (M)inds are indivisible. Thus, no minds are bodies.

12. A contestant on the television game show *Who Wants to Be a Millionaire?* faced this question:

Which of these is not a reptile?	
A. Gila Monster	B. Komodo Dragon
C. Salamander	D. Python

[15]Rene Descartes, *Meditations on First Philosophy,* tr. by Laurence J. Lafleur (Indianapolis, Ind.: The Bobbs-Merrill Company, Inc., 1951, 1960), p. 81.

5

Intermediate Symbolization

In Chapter Two we discussed the symbolization of singular statements and statements of the *A, E, I,* and *O* types. However, there are many other forms of statements that can be analyzed in predicate logic. This chapter is devoted to the symbolization of such statements. Along the way we will introduce the concept of *domain,* and further discuss the concept of *quantifier scope.*

5.1 Other Statement Forms

One-Predicate Statements. We will begin with statements containing only one predicate, then consider more complex statements. The Roman poet-philosopher Ovid (43 B.C.–17 A.D.) wrote *All things change, nothing is extinguished.* We can symbolize the first of these claims as follows:

All things (c)hange.
∀xCx

You can read the symbolization as "for any individual x, x changes" (or, more briefly, "for any x, x changes"). Note that we don't need a predicate letter to represent *things;* that concept is captured by the quantifier itself. Note also that we do not need parentheses to show the scope of the quantifier because the scope is obvious. When it comes to symbolizing Ovid's second claim we have a choice between two wffs.

Nothing is (e)xtinguished.
∀x−Ex
−∃xEx

These wffs may be read, respectively:

For any x, x is not extinguished.
It is not the case that there exists an x such that x is extinguished.

We know from the QE Rule that these two wffs are equivalent.
Three more simple statements and their symbolizations:

Something is (m)aterial.
∃xMx

Something is not material.
∃x−Mx

Not everything is material.
−∀xMx

"∃x−Mx" is a possible symbolization for the third statement, but it does not track well.

Two-Predicate Statements.   Every *A, E, I,* or *O* statement contains two predicates, but some statements having two predicates do not exhibit any of these four forms. Here are some examples:

Some things are either (t)asty or (f)attening.	∃x(Tx ∨ Fx)
Some things are neither tasty nor fattening.	∃x−(Tx ∨ Fx)
Each thing is either tasty or fattening.	∀x(Tx ∨ Fx)
Everything is both tasty and fattening.	∀x(Tx & Fx)
A thing is tasty iff it is fattening.	∀x(Tx ↔ Fx)

Definitions may be symbolized as universally quantified biconditionals. Definition S1, for example, is symbolized by F1.

(S1)   "Heavy (s)par: (b)arite." (Webster)
(F1)   ∀x(Sx ↔ Bx)
(F1X) ∀x(Sx → Bx)

F1X is inadequate as a symbolization of S1. S1 and F1 claim that each piece of heavy spar is barite *and vice versa,* while F1X makes only the first of these claims. Here are some additional examples of the symbolization of statements containing two predicates:

(*refrigerator magnet*) "If you can't wash dishes, don't eat."
∀x(−Wx → −Ex)
(Ex = x is welcome to eat)

(*Hester Mundis*) "There is no such thing as a non-(w)orking (m)other."
−∃x(−Wx & Mx)
(Wx = x works)

Statements with Three (or More) Predicates.   Some statements differ from *A, E, I,* and *O* statements principally in containing three (rather than two) predicates. Consider these statements:

Sentence	Symbolization	Source
"All (b)irds have two (l)egs and two (w)ings."	∀x[Bx → (Lx & Wx)]	*Scientific American*
"Each (p)assenger was either a (d)warf or a (m)idget."	∀x[Px → (Dx v Mx)]	(pre-PC) children's book
"[No matter how you look at it,] a (g)oal without a (p)lan is still a (d)ream."	∀x[(Gx & −Px) → Dx] Px = x involves a plan	sign in Hixton, Wisconsin, post office
Years ending in (h)undreds are (l)eap years only if (d)ivisible by 400.	∀x[Hx → (Lx → Dx)]	policy implemented by Pope Gregory XIII

All of these wffs resemble *A*-wffs in that they employ a universal quantifier and the main connective within the scope of the quantifier is an arrow. Recognizing that the sentence is *A*-like gives you a head start on devising the correct symbolization, for you know that the overall structure will be:

∀x[... → ...]

All that remains is to determine where to place the predicate letters in this matrix. Letters representing the grammatical subject will precede the arrow and those representing the grammatical predicate will follow it. Consider the sentence above about birds as an example. "Bx," representing the grammatical subject, will precede the arrow, while "(Lx & Wx)," representing the grammatical predicate, will follow it. The grammatical subject of the third sentence in the table is "a (g)oal without a (p)lan;" so "(Gx & −Px)" will precede the arrow.

These sentences resemble *E* statements:

No (L)utheran (r)ock climbers play (b)ridge.
∀x[(Lx & Rx) → −Bx]

No Lutherans are rock climbers who play bridge.
∀x[Lx → −(Rx & Bx)]

Are these sentences (wffs) logically equivalent?
These sentences are similar to *I* statements:

(*newspaper*) "Some newborn (b)abies are (i)rritable and (j)umpy."
∃x[Bx & (Ix & Jx)]

Some newborn babies who are irritable are also jumpy.
∃x[(Bx & Ix) & Jx]

Are these sentences (wffs) logically equivalent?
Some sentences contain more than three predicates. I symbolize four such sentences in the following table. Many complicated general sentences can be viewed as approximating the pattern of *A, E, I,* or *O* statements. Recognizing this resemblance is an important first step in devising the symbolization. Consider the first sentence; the claim it makes is both universal and affirmative, that is, the sentence is *A*-like. Once you realize that the third sentence makes an existential negative claim (like an *O* statement), you see that its symbolization will have this structure:

∃x[. . . & − . . .]

Sentence and Symbolization	Source and Dictionary
"When (w)omen are (d)epressed they either (e)at or go (s)hopping. [Men invade another country. It's a whole different way of thinking.]" ∀x{Wx → [Dx → (Ex v Sx)]} *or* ∀x[(Wx & Dx) → (Ex v Sx)]	(Elayne Boosler)
Coast (G)uard personnel may not (p)atronize Hooters while on (d)uty or in (u)niform. ∀x{Gx → [(Dx v Ux) → −Px]} *or* ∀x{[Gx & (Dx v Ux)] → −Px}	(Coast Guard policy in effect in Clearwater, Florida) Px = x may patronize Hooters
There are (c)hildren in (A)merica who have neither an adequate (d)iet nor a (r)oof over their heads. ∃x[(Cx & Ax) & −(Dx v Rx)]	Ax = x lives in America
No (l)ifer will be (p)aroled unless the person is (e)lderly or terminally (i)ll. ∀x{Lx → [−(Ex v Ix) → −Px]}	(pledge of Maryland governor Glendening) Lx = x is serving a life sentence in Maryland

The main connective in a universal quantification is usually the arrow, and the main connective in an existential quantification is generally the ampersand. These correlations obtain so often that you should double check any symbolization that deviates.

Exceptives.   Consider this statement containing *except:*

(S2) All (f)aculty except (i)nstructors are provided health (b)enefits.

At least one of the following wffs correctly symbolizes S2, but which one?

(F2) $\forall x[(Fx \ \& \ -Ix) \rightarrow Bx]$
(F2$'$) $\forall x[(Fx \ \& \ Ix) \rightarrow -Bx]$
(F2$''$) $\forall x[Fx \rightarrow (Bx \leftrightarrow -Ix)]$

Consider two cases: (**Case 1**) Beth is on the faculty and she is not an instructor (but a professor), yet she lacks health benefits. Her case shows S2 to be false, but it is consistent with F2$'$. It is consistent with F2$'$ because that wff makes a claim only about faculty who are instructors, and Beth is not an instructor. Since Beth's case is consistent with F2$'$ but inconsistent with S2, F2$'$ is not a correct symbolization of S2. (**Case 2**) Carl is an instructor on the faculty, and he has health benefits. Does his case show S2 to be false? It is reasonable to hold that it does not. On this view S2 functions as a guarantee to faculty who aren't instructors that they have health benefits, but it does not also function as a prohibition against the provision of benefits for the instructor in special circumstances. Those who take this view give a *weak* interpretation to S2, and accept F2 as the correct symbolization. Those who think that Carl's case falsifies S2 give that statement a *strong* interpretation, and accept F2$''$ (which is equivalent to the conjunction of the other two wffs) as the proper symbolization. I believe the weak interpretation is preferable. For some statements the weak interpretation is the only plausible one. For instance, no one would regard the following statement from the U.S. Constitution in the strong way:

> *No Person except a natural born (C)itizen . . . shall be eligible to the Office of (P)resident. . . .*

If you took it in the strong way you would have to agree that all six-year-olds who are natural born citizens are eligible to be president (at their current age).

Rainy Mondays.   One type of sentence typically containing three predicates is particularly tricky. A line from a 70's pop song (popularized by the Carpenters) provides an example:

(S3) "(R)ainy days and (M)ondays always get me (d)own."[1]

F4 is a plausible, although incorrect, symbolization of S3.

(F4) $\forall x[(Rx \ \& \ Mx) \rightarrow Dx]$

(Rx = x is a rainy day, Mx = x is a Monday, Dx = x gets me down) A careful reading of F4 shows that it differs in content from S3. F4 symbolizes (the somewhat less depressed) S4.

(S4) Rainy Mondays always get me down.

The song title can be correctly symbolized by F3.

(F3) $\forall x[(Rx \rightarrow Dx) \ \& \ (Mx \rightarrow Dx)]$

Now F3 and F4 are not equivalent (and for the same reasons that S3 and S4 are not equivalent). S3 and F3 claim that a rainy day gets me down (no matter the day of the week) and also that a Monday gets me down (whatever its weather). Neither of these claims is made by S4 or F4. Now here is a surprising fact: F3 is equivalent to F3'.

(F3') $\forall x[(Rx \ v \ Mx) \rightarrow Dx]$

F3' is another correct symbolization for S3. I am partial to F3' because of its brevity, although I have to admit that F3 tracks better than F3'.
    When I first learned that F3' (with its wedge) represents S3 (with its *and*), I thought I had uncovered a defect in predicate logic. Later I realized that this result is just what you would expect from a *predicate* logic. If you rephrase S3 in terms of predicates the *and* gives way to an *or:*

(S3') Any day that *is-rainy* or *is-a-Monday* gets me down.

We can draw a general moral from the *Rainy Monday* example. The way we discovered that wff F4 did not represent sentence S3 was by reading F4 over and asking the question, "Does this wff make the same claim as is made by this sentence?" If the answer to this question is *no,* you know the symbolization is a "no go." If the answer is *yes,* then the symbolization is acceptable provided that it tracks the sentence well. When you symbolize a sentence that has a form that

---

[1]"Rainy Days and Mondays." Words and music by Paul Williams and Roger Nichols.

is out of the ordinary, you should ask yourself the question mentioned above as a way to check the adequacy of your symbolization.

Domains.   Whenever we treat a sentence or an argument in predicate logic, we employ a *domain*. The domain is the class of objects over which our quantifiers and variables range. In the preceding chapters the domain employed has always been unrestricted; but we can also specify restricted domains. In some cases we can shorten symbolizations (and simplify proofs and additional techniques to be developed later) by adopting a restricted domain. Consider, for example, this sentence:

There are (m)ature (c)hestnut trees on (W)ayah Bald.[2]

If the domain is unrestricted (or restricted to trees), the symbolization for this sentence will be

$\exists x[(Mx \ \& \ Cx) \ \& \ Wx]$

(Wx = x is located on Wayah Bald) If we restrict our domain, we can drop one or more predicate letters and then shorten the symbolization:

Restricted Domain	Symbolization
mature trees	$\exists x(Cx \ \& \ Wx)$
chestnut trees	$\exists x(Mx \ \& \ Wx)$
trees on Wayah Bald	$\exists x(Mx \ \& \ Cx)$
mature chestnut trees	$\exists xWx$
mature trees on Wayah Bald	$\exists xCx$
chestnut trees on Wayah Bald	$\exists xMx$

Obviously a restricted domain is unacceptable if it excludes individuals that are pertinent to the statement in question. So, *Arkansas plumbers* is an unsatisfactory domain to employ when symbolizing "All plumbers are well paid," since the claim made by the statement applies to individuals (like Indiana plumbers) who fall outside the domain. Whatever domain is adopted for one statement in an argument must be used for all of the statements in the argument. Wherever a

---

[2]Because of the chestnut blight (a fungus) that invaded the United States in 1904 and spread rapidly across the country, mature chestnut trees are now very rare.

restricted domain is employed in this book, the constitution of that domain will be specified.

Many students find that their biggest challenge in mastering predicate logic is learning how to symbolize (rather than, for example, learning how to construct proofs). Symbolizing *is* challenging, but it is also satisfying to learn how to do it well. And as you learn to symbolize, you learn more about the logical structure of sentences expressed in English (or any natural language). Consider, as an example, this sign on an Arizona gas-station pump:

> *Arizona checks accepted only with Arizona driver's license and guarantee card.*

Anyone who knows a little English grammar and also something about how the world operates realizes that the sign does not express management's policy. (The policy is to exclude checks drawn on banks in other states as well as checks not supported by sufficient ID, but the statement on the sign if taken literally does not do that.) Armed with the vocabulary and syntax of predicate logic we can express both the claim made by the sentence on the sign and the actual policy, and gain an appreciation for the difference between them:

> $\forall x\{Bx \rightarrow [Cx \rightarrow (Lx \ \& \ Gx)]\}$ (policy expressed on sign)
> $\forall x\{Cx \rightarrow [Bx \ \& \ (Lx \ \& \ Gx)]\}$ (actual policy)

(domain: checks; Bx = x is drawn on an Arizona bank, Cx = x will be accepted, Lx = x is presented with an Arizona driver's license, Gx = x is presented with a guarantee card) Studying the second wff can help you reach a correct English expression of the actual policy:

> *Only an Arizona check accompanied by Arizona driver's license and guarantee card will be accepted.*

Or even clearer:

> *Only Arizona checks accepted, and only with Arizona driver's license and guarantee card.*

I conclude the section with a table of symbolizations of statements not of the *A, E, I,* or *O* variety. Expressions within one cell are logically equivalent. I suggest that you study this table until you understand its contents.

Sentence	Symbolization
Something is (r)ed.	∃xRx
Something isn't red. Not everything is red.	∃x−Rx −∀xRx
Everything is red.	∀xRx
Nothing is red.	∀x−Rx −∃xRx
Something is either (s)oluble or (c)ombustible.	∃x(Sx v Cx)
Something is neither soluble nor combustible.	∃x−(Sx v Cx) ∃x(−Sx & −Cx)
Each thing is either soluble or combustible.	∀x(Sx v Cx)
Each thing is both soluble and combustible.	∀x(Sx & Cx)
Each thing is soluble iff it is combustible.	∀x(Sx ↔ Cx)
Everything insoluble is combustible.	∀x(−Sx → Cx)
Nothing that is insoluble is combustible.	∀x(−Sx → −Cx)
Some (m)ale (R)epublicans are (p)lumbers. Some males are Republican plumbers.	∃x[(Mx & Rx) & Px] ∃x[Mx & (Rx & Px)]
Some male Republicans are not plumbers.	∃x[(Mx & Rx) & −Px]
All males are Republican plumbers.	∀x[Mx → (Rx & Px)]
All male Republicans are plumbers.	∀x[(Mx & Rx) → Px] ∀x[Mx → (Rx → Px)]
All males are either Republicans or plumbers.	∀x[Mx → (Rx v Px)]
Males and Republicans are plumbers.	∀x[(Mx v Rx) → Px]
No male Republicans are plumbers. No males are Republican plumbers.	∀x[(Mx & Rx) → −Px] ∀x[Mx → −(Rx & Px)]

EXERCISES

Instructions for exercises 1, 2 and 4: (1) Symbolize these statements using the suggested abbreviations. (Unless otherwise indicated, predicate letters represent affirmative predicates.) (2) Provide a dictionary for the abbreviating symbols.

1. (a) There are (w)itches.
    *(b) (*Romans*) "All have (s)inned." (domain: people)
    (c) (*physicist Richard Feynman*) "Nobody (u)nderstands quantum mechanics." (domain: people; Ux = x understands quantum mechanics)
    (d) (*cartoon caption*) "Not everyone (w)ants to spend the evening discussing the merits of whole life versus term." (domain: people; Wx = x wants to spend the evening discussing . . .)

(e) (*fan, explaining "double elimination"*) "Each team in the tournament either (l)oses two games or (w)ins the tournament." (domain: teams in the tournament)

*(f) (*lyrics*) "Fellows she can't (g)et are fellows she ain't (m)et." (domain: fellows; Gx = Georgia Brown can get x, Mx = Georgia Brown has met x)

(g) (*Dogbert*) "(P)eople are (i)diots who (d)eserve to be mocked."

(h) People are (i)diots who (d)eserve to be mocked. (domain: people)

(i) (*encyclopedia*) "Some cultivated annuals . . . will (b)lossom only if started under (g)lass. . . ." (domain: cultivated annuals)

*(j) (*philosopher Peter Singer*) "The (c)apacity for suffering and enjoyment is . . . not only necessary, but also sufficient for us to say that a being has (i)nterests. . . ." (domain: beings)

(k) (*logician Gottlob Frege*) "An (o)bject is anything that is not a (f)unction." (This is a definition.)

(l) (*Shakespeare*) "Neither a (b)orrower nor a (l)ender be." (domain: people; Bx = x should be a borrower, Lx = x should be a lender)

(m) (*Sister Louis Gabriel, circa 1917*) "I (k)new everyone in Key West, except (t)ransients." (Give this statement the *weak* interpretation. Domain: people in Key West in 1917; Kx = Sister Gabriel knew x)

*(n) I knew everyone in Key West, except transients. (Give this statement the *strong* interpretation; use dictionary for 1(m).)

2. (a) (K)estrels and sparrow (h)awks are the same bird.

*(b) (*headline*) "Not all of us are (h)unks or (b)abes." (domain: people)

(c) (*newspaper*) "You can't (f)ollow Catholic teachings without (u)nderstanding we have a significant responsibility for God's creations. . . ." (domain: people; Fx = x follows Catholic teachings, Ux = x understands we have . . .)

(d) (*sports story*) "Every (s)tarter got at least one (h)it and scored at least one (r)un."

(e) (*alligator wrestler Joe Wasilewski*) "Any (g)ood alligator wrestler is either missing a (f)inger or missing a (p)iece of a finger." (Gx = x is a good alligator wrestler, Fx = x is missing a finger, Px = x is missing a piece of a finger)

*(f) Some of the (f)ish in the tank are either (c)ardinal tetras or (n)eon tetras. (domain: creatures in the tank)

(g) (*newspaper*) "(G)reyhounds that can't (w)in are (d)estroyed."

(h) (*sportscaster Ron Fraser*) "In the big (l)eagues you'll never see a number (t)hree hitter (b)unt." (Lx = x is a major leaguer)

(i) (*continuation of h*) "But in (c)ollege sometimes they'll do that." (Cx = x is a college baseball player, Tx, Bx)

*(j) (*newspaper*) "Not all comic book (h)eroes are (w)hite or (g)reen."

(k) (*Miriam*) "I skip (c)hurch if I'm not in the (m)ood–when I'm not (d)riving Audrey." (domain: Sundays; Cx = Miriam attends church on x, Mx = Miriam is in the mood for church on x, Dx = Miriam drives Audrey to church on x)

(l) (*IBM attorney David Boies*) "There isn't any (s)ensible human being on the planet–who is not (p)aid by Microsoft–who doesn't (b)elieve that Microsoft has monopoly power." (domain: people; Bx = x believes that Microsoft has monopoly power)

(m) (*logician Geoffrey Hunter*) "A (s)et is (f)inite iff it has only a finite number of (m)embers." (Mx = x has only a finite number of members)

*(n) (*newspaper*) "[The present law] defines a (J)ew as a 'person who is born of a Jewish (m)other or who has (c)onverted.'" (domain: people)

3. Translate each wff into a colloquial English sentence using the dictionary provided.

> domain: people
> Dx = x diets
> Ox = x is obese
> Vx = x is a vegetarian

(a) $\exists xVx$ (e) $\forall x(Ox \leftrightarrow -Vx)$

*(b) $-\forall xOx$ *(f) $\exists x[(Ox \& Vx) \& -Dx]$

(c) $\forall x-Ox$ (g) $\forall x[Ox \rightarrow (Dx \& Vx)]$

(d) $\exists x(Dx \lor Ox)$ (h) $\forall x[(Ox \& Dx) \rightarrow Vx]$

4. (a) (*Section 9.1*) "Statements that are neither (l)ogically true nor cont(r)adictory are *cont(i)ngent*." (This is a definition. domain: statements)

*(b) (*Victor Crawford*[3]) "Only a (l)iar or a (f)ool can . . . call smoking (s)afe." (domain: people)

(c) (*Canadian politician Brian Mulroney*) "I am not ideologically (o)pposed to anything unless it doesn't (w)ork." (domain: policies; Ox = Mulroney is ideologically opposed to x)

(d) (*sign*) "A lot of fellows who (c)omplain about the stupidity of bosses would be (o)ut of a job if the boss were (s)mart." (domain: people; Sx = x's boss is smart)

(e) (*logic text*) "The theorems of S3 are precisely those formulae which are theorems both of S7 and S4." (domain: formulas; Ax = x is a theorem of S3, Bx = x is a theorem of S7, Cx = x is a theorem of S4)

*(f) (*letter to editor*) "Anybody who (b)elieves that sending more spray planes to South America will eliminate or reduce illegal drugs is either (n)aive or has never (r)ead modern history, or both." (domain:

---

[3]Crawford was a tobacco lobbyist who contracted throat cancer and devoted his last years to campaigning against smoking and big tobacco.

people; Bx = x believes that sending . . ., Rx = x has read modern history)

(g) (*marker on cat's grave*) "No, (h)eaven will not ever heaven be; Unless my (c)ats are there to welcome me." (Cx = x includes my cats)

(h) (*Miami-Dade State Attorney Katherine Rundle speaking about those involved in voter fraud*) "Those who (c)heat, (l)ie, or corrupt the election (p)rocess will be held (a)ccountable." (domain: people)

(i) (*historian Joseph Ellis*) "Our (h)eroes . . . are not (g)ods or (s)aints, but (f)lesh-and-blood humans."

*(j) (*newspaper policy*) People are described as "(w)hite" or "(b)lack" only if they are (c)riminal suspects who have not been (a)pprehended. (domain: people; Wx = x is described as "white")

(k) (*newspaper*) "No (R)epublican in the (H)ouse or (S)enate (v)oted for the original bill." (Hx = x is a member of the House, Sx = x is a member of the Senate)

(l) (*newspaper*) "There are . . . (d)octors in the (U)nited States who would try (h)eroin in terminal care if they could employ it (l)egally."

(m) (*Dave Barry's statement of the law of gravity*) "A (d)ropped object will (f)all with an acceleration of 32 feet per second per second, and if it is your (w)allet, it will make every (e)ffort to land in a public toilet."

*(n) (*Plato's "Symposium"*) "(D)runkards and (c)hildren tell the (t)ruth." (domain: people)

5. The eighth amendment to the U.S. Constitution includes this clause:

   (a) . . . *Nor [shall] (c)ruel and (u)nusual punishments [be] (i)nflicted.*

   The Florida constitution includes this clause:

   (b) . . . *Nor [shall] cruel or unusual punishments [be] inflicted.*

   Symbolize both clauses. (domain: punishments; Ux = x is unusual)

   Which clause affords greater protection to citizens. Why?

6. (CHALLENGE) Symbolize using the suggested abbreviations.

   (a) (*TV commercial*) "A (g)reat hamburger is not a great hamburger without Del Monte (c)atsup." (domain: hamburgers)

   (b) (*Indira Gandhi*) "There are two kinds of people: those who do the (w)ork and those who take the (c)redit." (domain: people)

   (c) Sex offenders in Florida prisons get (c)ounseling but only if they (a)sk for it. (domain: sex offenders in Florida prisons)

   (d) (*TV detective*) "The only blood samples found in the (r)oom belonged to either the (s)uspect or the (v)ictim." (domain: blood samples in this fictional realm)

   (e) (*Sartre*) "All that was not (p)resent did not exist." (Px = x was present)

(f) (*road sign in Hell, South Africa*) "Only (h)elicopters and (V)olkswagens (p)ermitted beyond this point."

(g) (*museum sign*) "(B)ats are the only (m)ammals capable of true (f)light."

(h) (*19th century etiquette book*) "Neither (l)adies nor (g)entlemen ever wear gloves at the (t)able, unless their hands . . . are not (f)it to be seen." (Tx = x wears gloves at the table, Fx = x's hands are fit to be seen)

(i) (*U. S. Constitution, Article II, Section I*) "No Person except a natural born (C)itizen . . . shall be eligible to the Office of (P)resident; neither shall any Person be eligible to that Office who shall not have attained to the (A)ge of thirty five Years, and been fourteen Years a (R)esident within the United States." (domain: people)

(j) (*sign in doctor's office*) "(M)edicare patients must (p)ay their $100 calendar-year deductible unless the (s)econdary [insurer] picks those charges up and/or they have paid it to (a)nother physician." (Sx = x's secondary insurer pays the deductible, Ax = x has paid the deductible to another physician)

(k) Individuals who inherited the sickle cell gene from exactly one parent are not subject to ma(l)aria and do not suffer from sickle cell (a)nemia. (domain: people; Mx = x inherited the sickle cell gene from x's mother, Fx = x inherited the sickle cell gene from x's father, Lx = x is subject to malaria, Ax = x has sickle cell anemia)

(l) (*baseball rule*) An (i)nfield fly is a (f)air ball that can be (c)aught by an infielder with ordinary effort, when fi(r)st and (s)econd, or first, second, and (t)hird bases are occupied, before two are out. (domain: fly balls; Cx = x can be caught by an infielder with ordinary effort, Rx = x is hit while first base is occupied, Nx = x is hit when there are no outs, Ox = x is hit when there is one out)

(m) (*baseball rule*) After (t)wo strikes, any subsequent (s)trike constitutes an (o)ut unless either the pitch is hit (f)oul and not (c)aught or the catcher (d)rops the ball and fails to t(a)g the batter or t(h)row the batter out. (domain: pitches to a batter; Tx = x follows two strikes)

7. (CHALLENGE)

   (a) In *The Wizard of Oz*, Glinda (a good witch) asserts:

   > *Only bad witches are ugly.*

   It is clear from the context that she is making claim A1, but her sentence could be used to assert A2. Symbolize both claims.

   (A1) Among (w)itches, only the (b)ad are (u)gly.
   (A2) Among all creatures, only bad witches are ugly.

   (domain: creatures in *The Wizard of Oz*) Note that the amphiboly present in Glinda's sentence cannot be reproduced in a predicate logic wff.

(b) The Shoney's restaurant in Pigeon Forge, Tennessee posted this notice:

No one allowed without shoes or shirts.

Although the intent is clear, the sentence is actually amphibolous. (1) Symbolize the actual policy. (2) Symbolize the other possible meaning. (domain: people; Ax = x is allowed in the restaurant, Ox = x is wearing shoes, Ix = x is wearing a shirt) People in what attire would be treated differently under the two interpretations?

(c) A piece of Florida legislation grants sales tax exemptions to all

groups with an (I)nternal Revenue Code exemption or other (n)on-profit organizations, whose sole and primary (p)urpose is to provide social services.[4]

There are two ways to read this passage. Express them with two wffs: (1) stress the comma, (2) ignore the comma. (domain: Florida organizations; Ex = x is exempt from Florida sales tax) Which groups are treated differently under the two interpretations?

(d) A Florida driver's license exam has a multiple-choice question about the meaning of this sign:

The exam key selects the following answer as correct:

Left turn from left lane only and traffic in adjoining lane may turn left or continue straight ahead.[5]

Of course, this answer is contradictory. The test constructor confused D1 with D2.

(D1) Left turns permitted from left lane only.

(D2) Only left turns permitted from left lane.

Symbolize D1 and D2. (domain: turns; Ix = x is a left turn, Px = x is permitted, Mx = x is made from the left lane)

[4]Michael Ollove, "Bill slices tax breaks of charities," *Miami Herald* (June 11, 1983), p. 1A.

[5]John Keasler, "Driver's license exam: no passing without failure," *Miami News* (November 23, 1971), p. 8-B. Keasler spotted the error.

5.2   Mixed Wffs and Multiple Quantifications

Mixed Wffs.   Some predicate-logic wffs contain dyadic, or two-place, propositional connectives (that is, arrows, ampersands, double arrows, and wedges) that lie outside the scope of any quantifier. I call such wffs *propositional-predicate mixtures,* or *mixed wffs,* for short. Here is an example of a mixed wff:

> Timothy [M]cVeigh will get the (d)eath penalty iff each member of the (j)ury (v)otes for the death penalty.
> Dm ↔ ∀x(Jx → Vx)

The symbol in this wff with the greatest scope is the double arrow. Here are wffs involving other connectives falling outside of the scope of quantifiers:

> (*Eugene Debs*) "While there is a soul in (p)rison anywhere in the world, I am not (f)ree."
> ∃xPx → −Fd
> (domain: people; d = Debs)

> The [l]etter carrier hasn't been (b)y yet or there is no (m)ail for (u)s.
> −Bl v −∃x(Mx & Ux)

> (*newspaper*) "Sally [P]riesand is a (f)emale (r)abbi."
> Fp & Rp

Could we represent the sentence about Ms. Priesand with a pair of wffs?

> Fp, Rp

I suppose we could, but in the interest of uniform symbolization practice let's adopt this convention: One sentence will be represented by one wff.[6]
    On occasion we will use capital letters to represent statements rather than predicates. Here is an example:

> If it rains, no one will (a)ttend the picnic.
> R → ∀x −Ax

(domain: people; R = It rains) How can you tell whether a capital letter in a wff represents a statement or a predicate? If the letter is followed by no individual constant or variable, then the letter represents a statement. If an exercise or example in this text employs a statement letter, I will make that clear by providing a dictionary entry. On occasion a component statement could be symbolized by a statement letter or by a predicate letter and an individual constant. Here is an example:

---

[6]Make an exception to this rule when a premise and the conclusion of an argument are both presented in the same sentence.

The letter carrier has been by.

B (B = The letter carrier has been by)
Bl (l = the letter carrier, Bx = x has been by)

As I make up the dictionary for an argument containing such a statement, how do I decide which symbolization to use? If the argument is valid, I choose the dictionary that produces the briefest sequent that preserves the valid form.

If a wff contains a statement letter and also elements of predicate logic, then I consider it to be a mixed wff. Here is an example involving a statement quoted in a newspaper article:

(S1) *If the tail boom is (s)evered in mid-air, everyone [aboard the helicopter] (d)ies.*
(F1) S → ∀xDx

(domain: people on the helicopter; S = The tailboom is severed in mid-air) Of course, this wff is *mixed* on two counts because it contains both a dyadic connective lying outside the scope of the quantifier and it contains a statement letter. We can change the example somewhat to obtain a wff that counts as mixed on only the second ground.

(S2) It is true of each occupant of the helicopter that if the tail boom is severed in mid-air, that individual dies.
(F2) ∀x(S → Dx)

Quantifier Scope.   One difference between F1 and F2 is that "S →" falls outside the scope of the quantifier in F1 but within the scope of the quantifier in F2. The time has arrived to say more about the concept of *quantifier scope*. The *scope* of a quantifier is the portion of the wff that the quantifier governs. Ordinarily the scope is indicated by a pair of groupers, the left-hand member of which immediately follows the quantifier. The scope consists of the quantifier plus the quantifier-scope groupers and everything located between those groupers. The scope of the quantifier in F3 (and also F5) is the entire wff, while the scope of the quantifier in F4 is the wff fragment preceding the arrow.

(F3) ∃x(Fx & Gx)
(F4) ∃x(Fx & Gx) → Ha
(F5) ∃x[(Fx & Gx) → Ha]

Compare F4 with F5. One difference between them is that the principal logical symbol in F4 is an arrow (that is, F4 is a conditional), while the main symbol in

F5 is a quantifier (F5 is an existential quantification). You may think that F4 and F5 are logically equivalent, but in fact they are not. The difference in quantifier scope accounts for the difference in content between them. I endeavor to explain this mystery in section 13.1. The concept of *quantifier scope* is given a precise definition in section 13.4.

Here are two types of wffs (containing quantifiers) where quantifier-scope groupers are omitted:[7]

1. wffs in which only one predicate lies within the scope of the quantifier, for example: "∃xFx," and
2. wffs in which the first symbol following the quantifier is a dash (whose scope includes the remainder of the wff), for example: "∃x−(Fx & Gx)."

In both cases quantifier-scope groupers are omitted because they are not needed; the scope is clear without them. What is the scope of the quantifier in this wff?

   ∀xFx & Ga

Answer: just the left conjunct. That is because we take the scope of a quantifier to be as small as is consistent with any groupers present. (This is the same principle we use when we determine the scope of a dash.) If we wanted the scope of the quantifier to include the entire wff we would write it as:

   ∀x(Fx & Ga)

We adopt this formation principle regarding quantifier scope:

A formula is a wff only if each variable in it lies within the scope of a quantifier containing that variable.

So, neither of the following formulas counts as a wff:

   ∀x(Fy & Gy)
   ∀xFx & Gx

The second formula fails to be a wff because the last variable does not lie within the scope of the quantifier. The symbolization of any English sentence will (if correct) be a wff. Hence neither of these formulas can symbolize a sentence. And since every line in a proof must be a wff, neither of these formulas could be a line in a correct proof.

When you symbolize a sentence, how do you know whether to make a quantifier or a connective the main symbol (the symbol with greatest scope)? Consider two examples:

   (S6) If *Genesis* is true, then God created everything.
   (F6) G → ∀xCx

---

[7]We will encounter a third type when we reach Chapter Ten.

(S7) Everything is such that if *Genesis* is true, then God created it.
(F7) $\forall x(G \rightarrow Cx)$

(G = *Genesis* is true, Cx = God created x) In S6 the quantifier word *everything* is part of the consequent of the conditional, so clearly the conditional words *if . . . then* have greater scope; hence in F6 the arrow is the main symbol. In S7 the situation is reversed. The conditional words fall within the scope of the quantifier word, so the quantifier is the main symbol in F7. Another clue is that the expression following *then* in S6 is a complete statement, and that is reflected in F6 where the fragment following the arrow could stand alone as a complete wff. By contrast, the expression following *then* in S7 is not a complete statement (the *it* refers to no specific individual but links back to *everything*), and that is reflected in F7 where the fragment following the arrow (*Cx*) cannot stand alone as a wff.

Multiple Quantifications. I call a wff that contains more than one quantifier a *multiple quantification*. Here are some examples:

(*biography*) "Some of his [Gingrich's] ideas (s)ounded odd but not all of them were."
$\exists xSx$ & $-\forall xOx$
(domain: Gingrich's ideas; Sx = x sounds odd, Ox = x is odd)

If some glass bottles are (r)ecyclable, then every glass bottle is recyclable.
$\exists x(Gx$ & $Rx) \rightarrow \forall x(Gx \rightarrow Rx)$
(domain: bottles)

All armadillos in a litter are the same sex.
$\forall xMx \vee \forall xFx$
(domain: armadillos in a given litter; Mx = x is male, Fx = x is female)

(*Windows 95 for Dummies*) "(C)ursors always (b)link steadily; mouse (p)ointers never do."
$\forall x(Cx \rightarrow Bx)$ & $\forall x(Px \rightarrow -Bx)$

Consider these two sentences and their symbolizations:

(S8) (*John Shirkey*) "If anyone is (h)ampered by discrimination, we are all (d)iminished."
(F8) $\exists xHx \rightarrow \forall xDx$

(S9) Anyone who is hampered by discrimination is diminished.
(F9) $\forall x(Hx \rightarrow Dx)$

(domain: people) The two sentences make different claims, so they will be symbolized by different wffs. But does it surprise you that an existential quantifier is used in F8 but not in F9? There are various ways to distinguish these two sentences. The most obvious difference is that S8 is a conditional while S9 is a simple statement. Here is another difference that sheds light on the issue of quantifiers: If you substitute *everyone* for *anyone* in the two sentences you change the content of S8 but not of S9. Conversely, you can substitute *someone* for *anyone* in S8 without changing its content, but not so for S9. When *any* or *anyone* occurs in the antecedent of a conditional it will typically be symbolized by an existential quantifier. If you can substitute *some* for *any* without changing content, then expect to use the existential quantifier.

While *some* and *someone* are generally represented with an existential quantifier, this is not always so. Consider S10 and S11; they make different claims and have different symbolizations.

(S10) If someone is (h)ampered by discrimination, we are all (d)iminished.
(F10) $\exists xHx \rightarrow \forall xDx$

(S11) If someone is hampered by discrimination, he or she is diminished.
(F11) $\forall x(Hx \rightarrow Dx)$

(domain: people) S11 makes a claim about all people (that they are diminished if hampered) and its symbolization is a universal quantification. Why are S10 and S11 symbolized differently? Note that S10 is a conditional connecting complete statements but that S11 is not (in spite of appearances). The pronoun phrase "he or she" in S11 links back to *someone* near the beginning just as the x in F11 links D back to H. In short, S11 is a (disguised) A statement and not a conditional.

All of the multiple quantifications discussed so far have also been mixed wffs. Are all multiple quantifications mixed wffs? No. Here is an example:

$\forall x\exists y(Ax \ \& \ By)$

This wff has *nested* quantifiers, that is, one quantifier lies within the scope of another. We won't encounter another example like this one until we reach Chapter Ten. Note that in this wff two variables (x and y) are employed. That is done to satisfy another formation principle:

A formula is a wff only if no variable in it lies within the scope of two quantifiers containing that variable.

This formula violates the principle:

$\forall x\exists x(Ax \ \& \ Bx)$

Now that we know how to symbolize a rich variety of statement types the next step is to learn how to test for validity arguments containing such statements. In Chapter Six we study formal proofs for such arguments, and in Chapters Seven and Eight we cover two more evaluation methods.

EXERCISES

Instructions for exercises 8 through 10: (1) Symbolize these statements using the suggested abbreviations. (Unless otherwise indicated, predicate letters represent affirmative predicates.) (2) Provide a dictionary for the abbreviating symbols.

8. (a) (*newspaper*) "[I] am a (S)outherner, and I am a (J)ew."

   *(b) Either [M]ichigan State or Wisc[o]nsin will (p)lay for the national championship. (domain: college football teams)

   (c) If Hurricane [B]onnie reaches (l)and, she will do major (d)amage.

   (d) Everyone (p)assed the exam or I am mistaken. (domain: people who took the exam; A = I am mistaken)

   (e) Everyone (p)assed the exam or [I] am (m)istaken. (domain: people who took the exam)

   *(f) If UF plays FSU, then one of them will (l)ose. (P = UF plays FSU, u = UF, f = FSU)

   (g) If everyone (q)uiets down, the bus will depart. (domain: people on the bus; D = The bus will depart)

   (h) (*Carl Hiassen*) "If everybody [who is a politician in Washington, D.C., and] who (c)heated on their spouses (l)eft town, you could safely roll a baby stroller down the middle of Pennsylvania Avenue at rush hour." (domain: Washington politicians; S = You could safely roll a baby stroller down the middle of Pennsylvania Avenue at rush hour)

   (i) (*TV detective*) "If I talk, somebody (d)ies." (domain: people in this fictional realm;[8] T = I talk)

   *(j) There is someone such that if I talk, he or she dies. (Use dictionary for (i).)

   (k) (*college quarterback*) "We have to (w)in all of our games to win the national championship." (domain: the team's games for this season; Wx = we win x, C = We win the national championship)

   (l) It is true of each of our games that we have to win it to win the national championship. (Use dictionary for (k).)

9. (a) (*comic strip character*) "If I'm not (s)afe in my own [h]ome, I'm not safe anywhere." (domain: places in this fictional realm; Sx = I am safe in place x, h = my home)

   *(b) (*manager Jim Leyland*) "If I manage anywhere next year it will be with the [F]lorida Marlins." (domain: major league baseball teams; Lx = Jim Leyland manages team x)

---

[8]Note that we can have *fictional* domains as well as *actual* ones. Don't say that this domain (namely, characters in the TV series) is empty; it contains (fictional, not actual) sleuths, criminals, victims, police officers, cab drivers, etc.

(c) (*bumper sticker*) "SOME DAYS YOU ARE THE BUG; SOME DAYS YOU ARE THE WINDSHIELD" (Bx = x is a day when you are the bug, Wx = x is a day when you are the windshield)

(d) Either everything is (m)ental or everything is (p)hysical.

(e) (*Chevrolet TV ad*) "Nobody's got enough (m)oney and everybody's got enough (w)orries." (domain: people; Mx = x has enough money)

*(f) (*Carolyn Bird*) "College is (g)ood for some people but it is not good for everybody." (domain: people; Gx = college is good for x)

(g) (*Kalahari tribal dictum*) "If one (e)ats, all eat." (domain: tribe members)

(h) (*park naturalist*) "(E)grets have (b)lack legs, and (h)erons have (y)ellow legs."

(i) If everyone were a (v)egetarian, no one would (s)tarve. (domain: people)

*(j) All (b)obcats are (l)ynx, but not all lynx are bobcats.

(k) (*John 3:18*) "He who (b)elieves in him [Jesus] is not (c)ondemned, he who does not believe is condemned already. . . ." (domain: people)

10. (a) If anyone passes the (e)xam, someone will (t)hrow a party. (domain: people)

*(b) If everyone passes the exam, someone will throw a party.

(c) Everyone who passes the exam will throw a party.

(d) There are (b)orrowers iff there are (l)enders. (domain: people)

(e) (*newspaper*) "Someone is going to get (k)illed unless someone (f)ixes the light pole." (domain: people)

*(f) If someone (t)ouches that light pole, he or she will be (k)illed. (domain: people)

(g) (*children's book*) "Everyone [on the beach] wore sun (h)ats and sun-(g)lasses, and everyone used suntan (o)il . . . ." (domain: people at the beach in this story; Hx = x wears a sun hat)

(h) (*Shakespeare*) "Some are (b)orn great, some (a)chieve greatness, and some have greatness (t)hrust upon them." (domain: people)

(i) (*sweatshirt message*) "Lake Wobegon: Where the (w)omen are (s)trong, the (m)en are (g)ood looking, and all of the (c)hildren are (a)bove average." (domain: residents of Lake Wobegon)

*(j) (*Santayana*) "The (y)oung man who has not (w)ept is a (s)avage, and the (o)ld man who will not (l)augh is a (f)ool." (domain: people)

(k) (*Rasputin to Nicholas II*) "[Tsar of the land of Russia, you must know this:] If it was your relations who have (w)rought my death, then no one of your family will remain (a)live for more than two years." (domain: relatives of Nicholas II)

11. Translate each wff into a colloquial English sentence using the dictionary provided.

> domain: people
> Bx = x is Baptist
> Px = x is Protestant
> Fx = x is female
> Mx = x is male
> V = Jesse Ventura is politically correct
> Cx = x is politically correct

> (a) ∀x(Bx → Px)   *(f) ∀x(Fx ∨ Mx)
> *(b) ∃xBx → ∃xPx   (g) ∀xFx ∨ ∀xMx
> (c) ∀xBx → ∀xPx   (h) V → ∀xCx
> (d) ∃xFx & ∃xMx   (i) ∀x(V → Cx)
> (e) ∃x(Fx & Mx)

12. (CHALLENGE) Symbolize using the suggested abbreviations.

(a) (*syllabus*) "Only some homework (a)ssignments will be (c)ollected."

(b) (*letter to editor about treatment of homosexuals*) "There are (C)hristian and (J)ewish congregations that are not (f)illed with hate." (Cx = x is a Christian congregation, Jx = x is a Jewish congregation)

(c) (*this chapter*) "Every *(A), (E), (I),* or *(O)* statement contains (t)wo predicates, but some statements having two predicates do not exhibit any of these four forms." (domain: statements)

(d) (*Carl Hempel*) "It is neither necessary nor sufficient for the scientific (a)dequacy of an explanation that it should (r)educe the explicandum to ideas with which we are already familiar." (domain: explanations; Ax = x is scientifically adequate, Rx = x reduces the explicandum . . .)

(e) (*book review*) "If (g)ood (i)ntroductory books are (l)ucidly written, then if . . . [*P*]*erception* is an introductory book it cannot be counted a good one." (domain: books)

(f) (*Bob Griese and Brent Mussberger*) "No (P)ac-Ten or (B)ig-Ten team will play in the [2002] (R)ose Bowl [this year–for the first time in 55 years] . . . unless one of them is ranked (o)ne or (t)wo [in the final BCS standings]." (domain: 2001 college football teams)

(g) (*Julius Caesar*) "The (D)ruids are exempt from (m)ilitary service, and do not pay (t)axes like the rest of the Gauls." (domain: Gauls; Mx = x is required to serve in the military)

(h) (*novel*) ". . . He [Vance] was a (k)ind (m)an and, like all kind people, (p)leasant to be with and mildly (d)epressed." (domain: people in this fictional realm; v = Vance)

6

Intermediate Proofs

6.1 Intermediate Proofs

We need to be able to construct proofs for valid sequents containing wffs of the kinds discussed in the preceding chapter. Happily the proof system set out in Chapters Three and Four is adequate to the task without any additions or changes. All we need to do here is issue a warning and offer some strategic advice.

The warning is the reminder that our rules apply to entire lines and not merely parts of lines, and that the logical symbol of greatest scope in a wff determines the rule(s) that may be applied to the wff. For example:

wff	*applicable rule*	*inapplicable rule*
(F1) $\forall x(Fx \ \& \ Gx)$	$\forall O$	$\& O$
(F2) $\forall xFx \ \& \ \forall xGx$	$\& O$	$\forall O$

Here is a proof that F2 entails F1:

1	(1)	$\forall xFx \ \& \ \forall xGx$	A
2	(2)	$-\forall x(Fx \ \& \ Gx)$	PA
2	(3)	$\exists x-(Fx \ \& \ Gx)$	2 QE
1	(4)	$\forall xFx$	1 &O
1	(5)	$\forall xGx$	1 &O
2	(6)	$-(Fa \ \& \ Ga)$	3 $\exists$O
1	(7)	Fa	4 $\forall$O

1	(8)	Ga	5 ∀O
1,2	(9)	−Ga	6,7 CA
1,2	(10)	Ga & −Ga	8,9 &I
1	(11)	∀x(Fx & Gx)	2-10 −O

We use the &O Rule to divide line 1 into its parts so that we may apply the ∀O Rule to the parts.

This proof establishes that F1 entails F2:

1	(1)	∀x(Fx & Gx)	A	
2	(2)	−∀xFx	PA	
2	(3)	∃x−Fx	2 QE	
2	(4)	−Fb	3 ∃O	
1	(5)	Fb & Gb	1 ∀O	Subproof 1
1	(6)	Fb	5 & O	
1,2	(7)	Fb & −Fb	6,4 &I	
1	(8)	∀xFx	2-7 −O	
9	(9)	−∀xGx	PA	
9	(10)	∃x−Gx	9 QE	
9	(11)	−Gc	10 ∃O	
1	(12)	Fc & Gc	1 ∀O	Subproof 2
1	(13)	Gc	12 &O	
1,9	(14)	Gc & −Gc	13,11 &I	
1	(15)	∀xGx	9-14 −O	
1	(16)	∀xFx & ∀xGx	8,15 &I	

This proof divides into two subproofs, as indicated. The first establishes that F1 entails the left conjunct of F2, and the second (isomorphic to the first) shows that F1 entails the right conjunct of F2. Then all that remains to do is to bring those conjuncts together on line 16. Note that the ∀O Rule is applied twice to line 1, once on line 5 and again on 12. This is legitimate. And it was necessary to do this because when it came time to apply the ∃O Rule on line 11, the restriction on the rule prevented me from instantiating to *b*. The only way to get to the standard contradiction on line 14 was to return to line 1 and instantiate it a second time to a different dummy name.

Many sequents have conditional conclusions; proofs for such sequents usually involve the Arrow In strategy. Here is an example inspired by a *Peanuts* cartoon:

> If everybody (a)greed with Lucy, they'd all be (r)ight—because anyone who agrees with Lucy is right.
>
> ∀x(Ax → Rx) ⊢ ∀xAx → ∀xRx

1	(1)	$\forall x(Ax \rightarrow Rx)$	A
2	(2)	$\forall xAx$	PA
3	(3)	$-\forall xRx$	PA
3	(4)	$\exists x-Rx$	3 QE
3	(5)	$-Rd$	4 $\exists$O
1	(6)	$Ad \rightarrow Rd$	1 $\forall$O
2	(7)	Ad	2 $\forall$O
1,2	(8)	Rd	6,7 $\rightarrow$O
1,2,3	(9)	$Rd \ \& \ -Rd$	8,5 &I
1,2	(10)	$\forall xRx$	3-9 $-$O
1	(11)	$\forall xAx \rightarrow \forall xRx$	2-10 $\rightarrow$I

Subproof 2 } Subproof 1

The provisional assumption on line 2 (and the goal wff on line 10) are dictated by the Arrow In strategy, while the provisional assumption on line 3 is made in accordance with the Dash Out strategy.

If a sequent has a conditional premise you might provisionally assume, or endeavor to deduce, either its antecedent (so that a step of Arrow Out can be taken) or the negation of its consequent (to set up a Modus Tollens move). Here is an example.

> If even one child is (r)owdy, every child will serve (d)etention. Hence, every rowdy child will serve detention.

> $\exists xRx \rightarrow \forall xDx \vdash \forall x(Rx \rightarrow Dx)$

The following proofs involve different strategies.

1	(1)	$\exists xRx \rightarrow \forall xDx$	A
2	(2)	$-\forall x(Rx \rightarrow Dx)$	PA
2	(3)	$\exists x-(Rx \rightarrow Dx)$	2 QE
2	(4)	$-(Re \rightarrow De)$	3 $\exists$O
2	(5)	$Re \ \& \ -De$	4 AR
2	(6)	Re	5 &O
2	(7)	$\exists xRx$	6 $\exists$I
1,2	(8)	$\forall xDx$	1,7 $\rightarrow$O
1,2	(9)	De	8 $\forall$O
2	(10)	$-De$	5 &O
1,2	(11)	$De \ \& \ -De$	9,10 &I
1	(12)	$\forall x(Rx \rightarrow Dx)$	2-11 $-$O

1	(1)	$\exists xRx \rightarrow \forall xDx$	A
2	(2)	$-\forall x(Rx \rightarrow Dx)$	PA
3	(3)	$-\forall xDx$	PA

1,3	(4)	$-\exists xRx$	1,3 MT
2	(5)	$\exists x-(Rx \rightarrow Dx)$	2 QE
1,3	(6)	$\forall x-Rx$	4 QE
2	(7)	$-(Rf \rightarrow Df)$	5 $\exists$O
1,3	(8)	$-Rf$	6 $\forall$O
2	(9)	$Rf \& -Df$	7 AR
2	(10)	Rf	9 &O
1,2,3	(11)	$Rf \& -Rf$	10,8 &I
1,2	(12)	$\forall xDx$	3-11 $-$O
1,2	(13)	Df	12 $\forall$O
2	(14)	$-Df$	9 &O
1,2	(15)	$Df \& -Df$	13,14 &I
1	(16)	$\forall x(Rx \rightarrow Dx)$	2-15 $-$O

In the first proof the strategy is to deduce (on line 7) the wff that matches the antecedent of line 1, allowing for an Arrow Out step on line 8. In the second proof the strategy is to make a provisional assumption (on line 3) that will permit a Modus Tollens step (on line 4). The first proof is shorter because it involves an $\exists$I move, and that typically shortens a proof by four lines. The idea in each proof is to make a move involving line 1 that is appropriate for a conditional wff ($\rightarrow$O or MT).

If a sequent has a disjunctive conclusion, try the Dash Out–DeMorgan's Law strategy; that is, provisionally assume the negation of the conclusion and then apply the DM Rule. For a sequent with a disjunctive premise line you could use the Wedge Out strategy, or provisionally assume, or try to deduce, the negation of one of the disjuncts (to set up a Disjunctive Argument move).

The following table reveals some interesting entailment relationships. Entailment (between wffs on a row) is indicated by the double-shafted arrows.

$\exists x(Ax \& Bx)$	$\Rightarrow$	$\exists xAx \& \exists xBx$
$\exists x(Ax \vee Bx)$	$\Leftarrow$ $\Rightarrow$	$\exists xAx \vee \exists xBx$
$\forall x(Ax \& Bx)$	$\Leftarrow$ $\Rightarrow$	$\forall xAx \& \forall xBx$
$\forall x(Ax \vee Bx)$	$\Leftarrow$	$\forall xAx \vee \forall xBx$

The table shows mutual entailment (that is, logical equivalence) where the existential quantifier and the wedge are associated, and the same where the universal quantifier and the ampersand are associated. This stems from the affinity that exists between the existential quantifier and the wedge (and between the universal quantifier and the ampersand). Note the closeness in content of S3 and S4 (and of S5 and S6).

(S3) Some integer is (p)rime.   (F3) ∃xPx
(S4) Either 1 is prime or 2 is prime or ...   (F4) Po v (Pt v ...)

(S5) Every integer is (s)elf-identical.   (F5) ∀xSx
(S6) 1 is self-identical and 2 is   (F6) So & (St & ...)
      self-identical and ...

EXERCISES

1. Complete the following proofs. Every assumption has been identified.

(a) 1   (1) ∀x[Hx → (Ix & Jx)]   A
     2   (2) −∀x(−Jx → −Hx)   PA
     2   (3)   2 QE
     2   (4) −(−Ja → −Ha)   3 ∃O
     1   (5)   1 ∀O
     2   (6)   4 AR
     2   (7)   6 &O
     2   (8)   7 DN
     1,2   (9)   5,8 →O
     1,2   (10) Ja   9 &O
     2   (11)   6 &O
     1,2   (12)   10,11 &I
     1   (13) ∀x(−Jx → −Hx)   2-12 −O

*(b) 1   (1) ∀x(Ax → Bx)   A
      2   (2) ∃xAx   PA
            (3) Ac
            (4) Ac → Bc
            (5) Bc
            (6) ∃xBx
            (7) ∃xAx → ∃xBx

(c) 1   (1) ∃x(Mx & Lx)   A
     1   (2) Md & Ld
     3   (3)   PA
     3   (4) ∀x−Mx
     3   (5)   4 ∀O
     1   (6)   2 &O
     1,3   (7) Md & −Md

1	(8)		3-7 —O
9	(9)	—∃xLx	PA
9	(10)		9 QE
9	(11)	—Ld	
1	(12)		2 &O
1,9	(13)	Ld & —Ld	
1	(14)		9-13 —O
1	(15)	∃xMx & ∃xLx	

Note: To practice proof construction without the need for prior symbolization, see the Chapter Six practice problems in the Proofs section of "PredLogic."

Instructions: Symbolize arguments (where necessary) on one horizontal line, using the suggested abbreviations. Construct a proof for each sequent.

2. [G]od can (b)urn a rock. Therefore, it is false that nobody can do that.
   (domain: inhabitants–both divine and mortal–of this comic strip world)

By permission of Johnny Hart and Creators Syndicate, Inc.

*3. A woman in a small Maine town mowed her lawn topless, and a neighbor complained that she was behaving indecently.[1] The town manager rejected the complaint using this argument:

> [According to Maine law] (i)ndecent behavior involves displaying (g)enitalia in public or committing (s)exual acts in public. Thus, the act of [t]opless lawn mowing is not indecent behavior, because it does not involve displaying genitalia and it does not involve committing sex acts.

Treat the first premise as a (legal) definition.

[1]"Maine town OKs topless lawn mowing," *Miami Herald* (November 5, 1998), p. 26A.

4. April reasons as follows:

> If someone (s)ays that it is OK for April to go outside, then she may go out. [A]pril says that it is OK for April to go out. So, April may go out.

(domain: inhabitants of this comic strip world; $Sx = x$ says that it is OK for April to go outside, $M = $ April may go out, $a = $ April)

© Lynn Johnston Productions, Inc./
Dist. by United Feature Syndicate, Inc.

5. Some years ago youths stoned Yosemite park rangers and their horses during a demonstration. A park spokesperson argued that the demonstration was planned.[2] Part of his reasoning:

> At least some of the rocks (t)hrown were (b)rought to the park. Proof: Some of the thrown rocks were (s)andstone. No sandstone rocks are (n)ative to Yosemite. Any rocks that are not native to Yosemite were brought into the park.

(domain: rocks)

6. The Florida High School Activities Association (FHSAA) gave the Berkshire School the "death penalty" for recruiting violations. The school was ejected from the group, and all schools in the association were forbidden to play Berkshire in any sport. Newspaper sports stories[3] traced the consequence for Berkshire:

> No (F)HSAA school will (p)lay Berkshire. Every other high school in the state is a member of FHSAA. So, no other Florida high school will play Berkshire.

(domain: Florida high schools other than Berkshire; $Px = x$ is a school that will play Berkshire)

---

[2]"Yosemite denies brutality story," *Miami Herald* (August 4, 1970), p. 4A.

[3]Stephen F. Holder, "Berkshire thrown out of FHSAA," *Miami Herald* (May 17, 2000), p. 1D, and Pedro F. Fonteboa, "Banned but not broken," *Miami Herald* (January 16, 2001), p. 8C.

*7. Some students at East High School in Salt Lake City asked the school board to authorize a gay–straight student alliance at their school. In response the board banished all extracurricular clubs at all of the city's high schools.[4] Their "reasoning":

> [By federal law] we will either (a)llow all clubs or no clubs. We won't allow the [G]ay–Straight Student Alliance. Therefore, we will allow no clubs.

(domain: Salt Lake City high school extracurricular clubs; Ax = x is approved by the school board)

8. Philosopher Peter Unger writes:

> *Now, first, if someone, anyone,* knows *that there are rocks, then the person* can know *the following quite exotic thing: there is* no *evil scientist deceiving him into* falsely *believing that there are rocks.... Now, as we have agreed, if you know* that there are rocks, *then you* can know *that there is no scientist doing this to you. But no one can ever* know *that this exotic situation does not obtain.... That is our second premise, and it is also very difficult to deny. So, thirdly, as a consequence of these two premises, we have our skeptical conclusion: you never* know *that there are rocks.*[5]

(domain: people; Rx = x knows that there are rocks, Sx = x can know that there is no evil scientist deceiving people into falsely believing that there are rocks[6])

9. An interviewer asked *X-Files* co-star Gillian Anderson whether she would direct another episode of the series. She replied,

> *... I'm not crazy about writing a script again during the season.... On the other hand, I can't imagine directing an episode that wasn't mine, so if I am going to direct again on this show, I would just have to bite the bullet and try to write another one.*[7]

A simplified version of her argument:

> If I (d)irect an episode I will (w)rite an episode, because I won't direct an episode I haven't written.

(domain: future *X-Files* episodes; Dx = Anderson directs x, Wx = Anderson writes x)

10. This table shows interesting entailment patterns involving the quantifiers and the arrow. Entailment between adjacent wffs is represented by arrows.

---

[4]"Rather than OK gay group, school board bans all clubs," *Miami Herald* (February 22, 1996), p. 9A.

[5]*Ignorance: A Case for Scepticism* (Oxford: Clarendon Press, 1975), pp. 7 & 8.

[6]This assignment of meaning to the predicate *S* somewhat distorts Unger's argument. In section 9.3 I will explain why this distortion was forced upon us.

[7]"Gillian: Ready for more 'X'," *Miami Herald* (April 11, 2000), p. 4A.

$$(\text{F1}) \; \exists x A x \rightarrow \forall x B x$$
$$\Downarrow$$

$$(\text{F2}) \; \forall x (A x \rightarrow B x)$$
$$\Downarrow \qquad\qquad \Downarrow$$

$$(\text{F3}) \; \forall x A x \rightarrow \forall x B x \qquad (\text{F4}) \; \exists x A x \rightarrow \exists x B x$$
$$\Downarrow \qquad\qquad\qquad\qquad \Downarrow$$

$$(\text{F5}) \; \forall x A x \rightarrow \exists x B x \;\; \Leftrightarrow \;\; (\text{F6}) \; \exists x (A x \rightarrow B x)$$

When I constructed a proof (in this chapter) for the Lucy example I was showing that F2 entails F3. When you worked exercise 1(b) you showed that F2 entails F4. Now establish three more results:

(a) F3 entails F5.

*(b) F6 entails F5.

(c) F1 entails F2.

11. Numbers 12:3: "Moses was ... the most humble person on earth."

> No (h)umble person would (c)laim to be the most humble person on earth. If Moses wrote Numbers 12:3, then he claimed just that. If [M]oses was not humble, then Numbers 12:3 is not true. Therefore, either Numbers 12:3 is not true or it was not written by Moses.

(domain: people; Cx = x claims to be the most humble person on earth, W = Moses wrote Numbers 12:3, T = Numbers 12:3 is true)

12. A newspaper story[8] about a confrontation between government soldiers and guerrillas in Peru contains this argument:

> All of the (r)ebels were (k)illed. Some of the rebels (s)urrendered. Anyone who surrenders and is killed is (e)xecuted. Thus, some of the rebels were executed.

*13. Philosopher Peter Singer writes:

> *So, the researcher's central dilemma exists in an especially acute form in psychology: either the animal is not like us, in which case there is no reason for performing the experiment; or else the animal is like us, in which case we ought not to perform on the animal an experiment that would be considered outrageous if performed on one of us.*[9]

---

[8]Tim Johnson and Juan O. Tamayo, "Hostage-takers in Peru were reportedly shot after capture," *Miami Herald* (April 25, 1997), p. 14A.

[9]*Animal Liberation*, new revised edition (New York: Avon Books, Inc., 1990), p. 52.

His argument reformatted:

> It is useless to perform psychological experiments on animals that are not (l)ike humans. It is immoral to perform such experiments on animals that are like humans. So, for any animal, it is either useless or immoral to perform a psychological experiment on it.

(domain: animals; Ux = it is useful to perform a psychological experiment on x, Lx = x is like a human, Mx = it is moral to perform a psychological experiment on x)

14. In Chapter Five I discussed the symbolization of S1 and S2.

> (S1) No (L)utheran (r)ock climbers play (b)ridge.
> (F1) $\forall x[(Lx \ \& \ Rx) \rightarrow -Bx]$

> (S2) No Lutherans are rock climbers who play bridge.
> (F2) $\forall x[Lx \rightarrow -(Rx \ \& \ Bx)]$

(a) Prove that S1 entails S2.

(b) Prove that S2 entails S1.

Also in Chapter Five I offered two symbolizations for "(R)ainy Days and (M)ondays always Get Me (D)own."

> (F3) $\forall x[(Rx \rightarrow Dx) \ \& \ (Mx \rightarrow Dx)]$
> (F3′) $\forall x[(Rx \lor Mx) \rightarrow Dx]$

(c) Prove that F3 entails F3′.

(Exercise 26 concerns the entailment of F3 by F3′.)

15. From Chapter Two:

> *Let's define a singular statement as a statement containing one or more singular terms. We shall call a statement that has no singular terms a general statement. (Does it follow from these definitions that every statement is either singular or general? Do the definitions imply that no statement is both?)*

*(a) Show that the two definitions entail that every statement is either (s)ingular or (g)eneral.

(b) Show that the definitions entail that no statement is both singular and general.

(domain: statements; Cx = x contains one or more singular terms)

16. The movie *Clue* contains this bit of dialogue (paraphrased):

> *Splitting up into pairs means one of us will be paired with the killer, which means that someone will die. When someone dies, we'll learn who the killer is.*

The reasoning:

> If we split into pairs, then someone will be (p)aired with the killer. Anyone who is paired with the killer will (d)ie. If someone dies, we'll learn who the killer is. Therefore, if we split into pairs, we'll learn the identity of the killer.

(domain: people in the mansion in this fictional realm; S = We split into pairs, Px = x is paired with the killer, Dx = x dies, I = We learn the identity of the killer)

17. When Monica Lewinsky and President Clinton first gave conflicting accounts about their relationship, one could have reasoned as follows:

> Someone is not telling the truth, because it is not the case that [L]ewinsky and [C]linton are both telling the (t)ruth.

(Tx = x is telling the truth)

*18. In issue 21 of the *Dilbert Newsletter,* Scott Adams advances this argument related to the (then impending) impeachment of President Clinton for lying:

> Everyone in the line of presidential succession is a (l)iar. Hence, if you (i)mpeach all the liars in the line, you impeach everybody in the line.

(domain: officials in the line of presidential succession)

19. Smudgie's kittens are anatomically identical. If so, then either all of them are (m)ales or all are (f)emales. All (c)alico kittens are females. There is a calico in the litter. No kitten is both male and female. Therefore, all (S)mudgie's kittens are female.

(domain: kittens; I = Smudgie's kittens are anatomically identical)

20. An astronomer reasons:

> Something is a ho(l)e iff it is a hollow (p)lace in a solid mass or an ope(n)ing through something. *(B)lack holes* are neither. It follows that black holes are not holes.[10]

21. In panel seven of the following comic, Curtis advances this argument:

> The people in the building who (w)ork are too (b)usy to circulate a petition, and the people who don't are too (l)azy to do it. If everyone in the building is either too busy or too lazy to carry a petition, then there will be no petition. Hence, there will be no petition.

(domain: inhabitants of this comic strip world who live in Curtis' building; P = There will be a petition)

---

[10]Neil F. Comins, "Get the Hole Story," *Astronomy,* April 2001, p. 52.

Reprinted with special permission of King Features Syndicate.

*22. TV public service announcement:

> *If it's not safe to be a Jew everywhere on earth, it's not safe to be a Jew anywhere. And if it is not safe to be a Jew, it is not safe to be a human.* [11]

Interpret the second statement to mean "If it is not safe to be a (J)ew somewhere, then it is not safe to be a human there." The unstated conclusion is "If it is not safe to be a Jew everywhere, then it is not safe to be a human anywhere." (domain: locations; Jx = it is safe to be a Jew in location x, Hx = it is safe to be a human in location x)

23. (CHALLENGE) A sports story posted on the Internet concerning the 2000 NCAA men's Division One basketball tournament begins:

> *A Big Ten team will play for the national championship. Michigan State earns a trip to the Final Four by beating Iowa State. . . . Earlier, eighth-seeded Wisconsin advances to the Final Four. . . .* [12]

Suppressed parts of the argument are brought to the surface in this reformulation:

> Michigan State will play Wisconsin in a semifinal game. If so, then one of those teams will play for the (n)ational championship. It follows that a Big (T)en team will play for the national championship, as both of these teams are Big Ten teams.

(P = Michigan State will play Wisconsin in a semifinal game, m = the Michigan State team, o = the Wisconsin team, Nx = x plays for the national championship, Tx = x is a Big Ten team)

[11] Broadcast by NBC on April 16, 1978.

[12] "Men's Tournament," *AOL Sports* (March 26, 2000).

24. (CHALLENGE) The table below was displayed near the end of this chapter. Two of the entailments were validated in the text and one is the subject of exercise 1(c).

∃x(Ax & Bx)		⇒	∃xAx & ∃xBx
∃x(Ax ∨ Bx)	⇐	⇒	∃xAx ∨ ∃xBx
∀x(Ax & Bx)	⇐	⇒	∀xAx & ∀xBx
∀x(Ax ∨ Bx)		⇐	∀xAx ∨ ∀xBx

Establish the remaining three entailments:

(a) ∃x(Ax ∨ Bx) ⊢ ∃xAx ∨ ∃xBx

(b) ∃xAx ∨ ∃xBx ⊢ ∃x(Ax ∨ Bx)

(c) ∀xAx ∨ ∀xBx ⊢ ∀x(Ax ∨ Bx)

25. (CHALLENGE) Establish two more results from the table in exercise 10:

(a) F4 entails F6.   ∃xAx → ∃xBx ⊢ ∃x(Ax → Bx)

(b) F5 entails F6.   ∀xAx → ∃xBx ⊢ ∃x(Ax → Bx)

26. (CHALLENGE)

∀x[(Rx ∨ Mx) → Dx] ⊢ ∀x[(Rx → Dx) & (Mx → Dx)]

7

Counterexamples

7.1 Actual CEXes

So far we have developed a technique for establishing the **validity** of arguments (the method of formal proof), but we have not yet explained a technique
for establishing **invalidity**. You realize, of course, that failing to complete a
proof for a sequent is no proof of invalidity. Your failure to finish the proof
could be due to lack of inspiration, rather than to a defect in the sequent under
evaluation. In this chapter I present a logical device that will demonstrate invalidity: the method of counterexamples. This method has great scope; it applies
not only to every invalid predicate argument, but to any invalid argument in
any branch of deductive logic.

There are two versions of this technique for establishing invalidity: **actual
counterexamples** and **possible-world counterexamples**. When you apply
the first method to some argument (call it the *target* argument), you create an
analogous argument (the counterexample) that has the same logical form as the
target but has (all) true premises and a false conclusion. We know from the definition of *validity* that any such argument is invalid. We also know that if two arguments have the same logical form and one of them is invalid, they are both
invalid, since being either valid or invalid is strictly a matter of form. Therefore,
producing a well-crafted counterexample (or *CEX*,[1] for short) constitutes a

---

[1]You can decide how to pronounce my abbreviation *CEX.* Here are three possibilities: "sea-
ee-eks," "kex," and "sex."

proof of the invalidity of the target argument. I will illustrate the technique. Imagine that you offer me this bit of faulty reasoning:

> *Good philosophical papers are always argumentative. My philosophy paper on Plato is argumentative. And, therefore, it is a good one.*

I could respond:

> *You might as well argue: All Episcopalians are Protestants. Jesse Jackson is a Protestant. And, therefore, he is an Episcopalian.*

We know that my CEX about Jackson is invalid because it has true premises and a false conclusion. It follows that your argument about philosophy papers is also invalid since it has the same form. Q.E.D.

One part of this reasoning seems soft, namely the claim that the target and the CEX have the same form. We haven't demonstrated that. But we could establish that by showing that the two arguments can be correctly symbolized with the same sequent:

symbolization:	$\forall x(Gx \to Ax)$, $Ap \vdash Gp$
target dictionary:	domain: philosophy papers; $Gx = x$ is good, $Ax = x$ is argumentative, $p =$ the paper on Plato
CEX dictionary:	domain: people; $Gx = x$ is Episcopalian, $Ax = x$ is Protestant, $p =$ Jesse Jackson

Here is a faulty argument drawn from a book review,[2] together with an invalidating CEX:

1. **target:**	No machine is free. Any machine is incapable of determining the truth of Gödel statements. Some people can determine the truth of Gödel statements. This proves that some people are free.
2. **target dictionary:**	$Mx = x$ is a machine, $Fx = x$ is free, $Gx = x$ can determine the truth of Gödel statements, $Px = x$ is a person
3. **symbolization:**	$\forall x(Mx \to -Fx)$, $\forall x(Mx \to -Gx)$, $\exists x(Px \,\&\, Gx) \vdash \exists x(Px \,\&\, Fx)$
4. **CEX dictionary:**	domain: animals; $Mx = x$ is a cardinal, $Fx = x$ is a cat, $Gx = x$ is black, $Px = x$ is a dog

---

[2] *Choice*, June 1971, p. 560.

5. CEX: No cardinal is a cat. (T)
                               No cardinal is black. (T)
                               Some dogs are black. (T)
                               This proves that some dogs are cats. (F)

Inventing the CEX is a creative endeavor, and it may involve some trial-and-error work. For example, your first attempt may produce an argument that does not exhibit the necessary pattern of truth values (all true premises and a false conclusion). Here are some tips that should help you devise satisfactory CEXes: (1) Choose a domain that divides neatly into subclasses. *People, animals,* and *integers* make good domains. It is easy to divide people into religious or political groups, regions of residence, gender, etc. The animal kingdom can be divided into nested subclasses, for example, *mammals, felines, tigers,* etc. The set of integers subdivides into such categories as *positive, even, prime, greater than 7,* and so forth. (2) Generally it helps to focus attention first on the conclusion of the CEX, making sure that you secure a false statement; then you can work on devising true premises. But sometimes you will find that it is impossible to devise a satisfactory CEX using the conclusion you have adopted; in that case you have to scrap the conclusion and start over.

The method of actual CEXes is subject to four requirements; two are logical, one material, and one epistemic. The logical requirements are (1) the domain you select must have at least one member (that's not much of a limitation), and (2) if there are individual constants in the sequent, they must denote members of the chosen domain. For example, if your domain is *Canadians,* you cannot let the constant *a* denote George W. Bush since he is not a Canadian. (On the other hand, it is permissible to give a predicate a meaning such that the predicate applies to nothing in the domain. So, when the domain is *Canadians* you are free to assign the meaning "is a Mexican" to any of the predicates.) (3) The material requirement is obvious: each premise of the CEX must be true and the conclusion has to be false. (4) The epistemic requirement is that the premises and conclusion of the CEX you create must treat matters of common knowledge. Otherwise, although the CEX will establish invalidity to *your* satisfaction, it will not do the same for others (for instance, the teacher grading your work). For example, if "My sister plays lacrosse" is a statement in your CEX, you will know the truth value of the statement, but most others will not.

Here are a few fine points to bear in mind: (a) If the target argument satisfies the four requirements listed in the previous paragraph, it can serve as its own CEX! (b) Two or more predicates can be assigned the same meaning in your CEX, and two or more individual constants may designate the same individual. (c) The target and CEX domains may be the same. (d) A given predicate letter can have the same meaning in both the CEX and target dictionaries, and a given individual constant can identify the same individual. (e) You can specify a domain either by providing its name or by listing its members; when doing the latter it is customary to use braces. Here are two ways to specify the same domain: "prime numbers less than 10," "$\{2, 3, 5, 7\}$."

Even when the sequent symbolizing a target argument includes a mixed wff or a multiple quantification, the technique remains the same. Here is an example:

1. **target:**	No proposition with factual content is necessary. Therefore, either all mathematical propositions lack necessity or they all lack factual content.[3]
2. **target dictionary:**	domain: propositions; $Fx = x$ has factual content, $Nx = x$ is necessary, $Mx = x$ is mathematical
3. **symbolization:**	$\forall x(Fx \rightarrow -Nx) \vdash \forall x(Mx \rightarrow -Nx) \vee \forall x(Mx \rightarrow -Fx)$
4. **CEX dictionary:**	domain: integers; $Fx = x$ is odd, $Nx = x$ is even, $Mx = x$ is prime
5. **CEX:**	No odd integer is even. (T) Thus, either no primes are even or no primes are odd. (F)

Why is the conclusion false? Because both of its disjuncts are false. The left disjunct is false since 2 is an even prime, and the right disjunct is false because 3 (or any larger prime) is an odd prime. When you construct CEXes for problems that involve mixed wffs you should bear in mind the principles of propositional logic (such as that a disjunction is false iff both disjuncts are false, or that a conditional is false iff it has a true antecedent and a false consequent).

You can also use the method to demonstrate the invalidity of a sequent in the absence of a target argument expressed in English. Constructing a CEX for this sequent requires ingenuity.

1. **sequent:**	$\forall xFx \rightarrow P \vdash \forall x(Fx \rightarrow P)$
2. **CEX dictionary:**	domain: people; $Fx = x$ is red headed, $P =$ Everyone is red headed
3. **CEX:**	If everyone is red headed, then everyone is red headed. (T) Therefore, it is true of each and every person that if he or she is red headed, then everyone is red headed. (F)

---

[3]This argument is advanced by A. J. Ayer in *Language, Truth and Logic* (Harmondsworth, Middlesex: Penguin Books, Ltd., 1971), p. 97. Ayer may have assumed the premise "If even one mathematical proposition is necessary, then they all are." Adding that premise transforms the argument into a valid one.

(Note that the meaning we assign to the statement letter *P* in this CEX dictionary is a statement.) It is obvious that the premise of this CEX is true, but less evident that the conclusion is false. Here is a way to see that the conclusion really is false. Is it true of the prop comedian Carrot Top (a.k.a. Scott Thompson) that if he is red headed then everyone is? Of course not. Although Carrot Top is red headed, not everyone is; so this conditional is false. But since it is not true of Carrot Top that if he is red headed then everyone is, then it is not true of everyone that if he or she is red headed, then everyone is. If this puzzles you, remember that just as "x is true of Carrot Top" follows from "x is true of everyone," so "it is not the case that x is true of everyone" follows from "it is not the case that x is true of Carrot Top."

EXERCISES

Instructions: Symbolize arguments (where necessary) and establish invalidity by constructing actual CEXes.

1. (a) $\exists xFx \vdash Fa$
    *(b) $Fa \vdash \forall xFx$
    (c) $\exists xFx \vdash \forall xFx$

2. Prove that *A* and *O* statements are not validly convertible.
    (a) $\forall x(Fx \rightarrow Gx) \vdash \forall x(Gx \rightarrow Fx)$
    (b) $\exists x(Fx \ \& -Gx) \vdash \exists x(Gx \ \& -Fx)$

Note: For additional practice in constructing CEXes without the need for prior symbolization, see the practice problems in the CEX section of "PredLogic."

*3. Part of an answer to an exam question about Plato's ethics:

> *[C]ourage is a type of (k)nowledge. Since courage is a (v)irtue, all virtues must be some type of knowledge.*

4. In a campaign speech made March 8, 2000,[4] presidential candidate George W. Bush said, "If people are happy with the status quo in Washington, then [they should] vote for Al Gore." This argument is suggested:

> Voters (h)appy with the status quo should vote for (G)ore. Hence, voters not happy with the status quo should not vote for Gore.

(domain: American voters)

---

[4]The sentence quoted was broadcast that evening on "NBC Nightly News."

5. Huck Finn reasons:

> *Jim said bees wouldn't sting idiots; but I didn't believe that, because I had tried them lots of times myself, and they wouldn't sting me.*[5]

Huck's argument appears to be:

It is false that bees won't sting idiots. My reasons: Bees won't (s)ting me. I am not an (i)diot.

(domain: people in *The Adventures of Huckleberry Finn;* Sx = bees will sting x, h = Huck Finn, Ix = x is an idiot) The second premise is unstated.

6. When I lecture on the free-will problem in Introduction to Philosophy, I explain the various positions with the help of syllogisms. Not surprisingly when my students write about the issue on exams, they also use syllogisms. However, some of the ones they construct are invalid. Here are some examples found in their exams. Use this dictionary: domain: acts; Cx = x is caused, Fx = x is free, Hx = x is performed by a human, Px = x is predictable, Dx = x is determined.

(a) No caused acts are free.
    Some human acts are not caused.
    So, some human acts are free.

*(b) All free acts are uncaused.
    Not all human acts are caused.
    So, human acts are free.

(c) Some caused acts are free.
    All human acts are caused.
    Thus, some human acts are free.

(d) Some human acts are predictable.
    All determined acts are predictable.
    So, all human acts are determined.

(e) Some human acts are free.
    No caused acts are free.
    Therefore, no human acts are caused.

*7. All (h)ealthy diets contain significant amounts of (p)rotein. All diets that include (m)eat contain significant amounts of protein. Hence, all healthy diets include meat.

(domain: diets)

8. One question on an exam in Contemporary Moral Issues asked students to argue either for or against the thesis that it is always wrong to kill infants. One student defended the thesis with an argument that I present in "bare-bones" fashion:

---

[5]Mark Twain, *Adventures of Huckleberry Finn* (Berkeley and Los Angeles: University of California Press, 1985), p. 55.

> It is wrong to kill any infant that can have a (p)roductive life.
> Every infant with (D)own's Syndrome can have a productive life.
> Thus, it is wrong to kill any infant.

(domain: infants; Wx = it is wrong to kill x)

9. Crunchy offers this explanation for not laughing:

> If something is (f)unny I'll laugh. Nothing is funny. So, I don't laugh.

(domain: events in this comic strip world; L = I'll laugh)

JUMP START reprinted by permission of United Feature Syndicate, Inc.

10. A student in a Philosophy of Religion class told about a group of people who had a mass religious experience, and then reasoned in this way:

   (a) Each person in the group either (l)ied, (h)allucinated, or had a (g)enuine religious experience. They were not all liars. And they were not all hallucinating. It follows that they all had a genuine religious experience.

   (domain: people in the group)

   *(b) Prove invalid the argument that results when you weaken the conclusion of (a) to "Some had a genuine religious experience."

11. (CHALLENGE) A nasty cartoon boss lambastes an older worker with this argument:

> [H]erman, you are not (p)roductive. Therefore, if people should (r)etire only if they are no longer productive, then you should retire.

12. (CHALLENGE) A manuscript for a logic textbook contains this passage:

> *A (s)ound argument, then, is a (v)alid argument whose premises are all (t)rue. It follows that an unsound argument [that is, an argument that is not sound] is a valid argument whose premises are not all true.*

Both sentences are definitions. (domain: arguments)

13. (MAJOR CHALLENGE)

$$\exists x(Fx \to P) \vdash \exists xFx \to P$$

7.2 Possible-World CEXes

Bob Dole appears to advance this argument in a TV commercial for Viagra:[6]

> A medical checkup for ED takes courage.
> Everything worthwhile takes courage.
> So, a medical checkup for ED is worthwhile.

We can establish the invalidity of this argument using the technique presented in the preceding section:

target dictionary:	domain: events; Mx = x is a medical checkup for ED, Cx = x takes courage, Wx = x is worthwhile
symbolization:	$\forall x(Mx \rightarrow Cx), \forall x(Wx \rightarrow Cx) \vdash \forall x(Mx \rightarrow Wx)$
CEX dictionary:	domain: people; Mx = x is Lutheran, Cx = x is Protestant, Wx = x is Methodist
CEX:	All Lutherans are Protestants. (T)
	All Methodists are Protestants. (T)
	So, all Lutherans are Methodists. (F)

Here is another way that we could prove the target argument invalid. Imagine that there is a barn somewhere (call it *Farmer Logik's barn*) that contains exactly two animals: a white chicken and a white duck. Let those two animals make up the domain for our CEX. We continue as follows:

CEX dictionary:	Mx = x is a chicken, Cx = x is white, Wx = x is a duck
CEX:	All chickens (in the barn) are white. (T)
	All ducks are white. (T)
	So, all chickens are ducks. (F)

There may or may not be a barn like the one we have described that contains just two animals of the species and colors we have stipulated. But it turns out not to matter whether there is, for such a collection of animals is surely possible. So, we have shown that it is *possible* for the premises of the CEX to be true and the conclusion false. And that is all that is required in order to establish invalidity, for in a valid argument such a combination is not even possible. We call this method the technique of *possible-world CEXes* because the domain we chose and the facts about it that we stipulated constitute a very small possible world.

Why should we take this approach rather than the one laid out in the preceding section? One practical reason is that this approach lends itself well to a computer environment, and specifically to the tutorial program *PredLogic*. It is much easier to program a computer to register the description of a possible domain whose members have certain specified properties, than to program a

---

[6]Broadcast in March, 1999.

computer so it can determine whether such a domain corresponds to anything in reality. And it is easy to represent graphically on a computer screen the information about a possible world like Farmer Logik's barn.

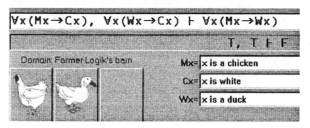

Note on the line beneath the sequent the depiction of the truth values of the wffs when they are interpreted as applying to the possible situation portrayed.

There is another practical reason for employing the possible-world approach to at least some CEX problems. When a target argument is complex it may be easier to devise a possible-world refutation than an actual CEX. When you create a possible-world CEX you don't have to worry about whether the analogue argument you create has the crucial truth values in the actual world. It is good enough if it has the crucial truth values in the possible world you have invented. Consider, for example, this argument that a newspaper story[7] seems to advance:

> One is a (J)ew iff one's (m)other is a Jew or one has (c)onverted to Judaism according to Orthodox standards.[8] Every Jew is (e)ligible to apply for Israeli citizenship. It follows that (A)mericans whose mothers are not Jewish and who have not converted to Judaism according to Orthodox standards [although they have converted under Reform or Conservative standards] are not eligible to apply for Israeli citizenship.
>
> $\forall x[Jx \leftrightarrow (Mx \lor Cx)], \forall x(Jx \rightarrow Ex) \vdash \forall x\{[Ax \,\&\, (-Mx \,\&\, -Cx)] \rightarrow -Ex\}$

It would probably take a lot of ingenuity to construct an actual CEX refutation of this argument; it is easier to create a possible-world CEX that does the trick:

$\forall x[Jx \leftrightarrow (Mx \lor Cx)], \forall x(Jx \rightarrow Ex) \vdash \forall x\{[Ax \,\&\, (-Mx \,\&\, -Cx)] \rightarrow -Ex\}$

T, T ⊢ F

Domain: Farmer Logik's barn

Jx=	x is a bird
Mx=	x is a chicken
Cx=	x is a duck
Ex=	x is white
Ax=	x is a sheep

---

[7]"Orthodox group: Other Jews 'not Jewish'," *Miami Herald* (March 22, 1997), p. 10A.

[8]This is a feature of strict religious law in Israel.

One element that is missing from the above is the English-language statement of the CEX, but we can supply that:

CEX: Every bird (in the barn) is either a chicken or a duck. (T)
All birds are white. (T)
So, no sheep that is not a chicken and not a duck is white. (F)

The conclusion is false because there is a white sheep in the domain.

Recall the four requirements that apply to the method of actual CEXes? The two logical requirements (that the domain have at least one member and that constants denote members of the domain) apply also to this method. For the new method we add a third logical requirement: the world depicted must be possible, that is, its description must involve no logical contradiction. The so-called material requirement that applied to the actual CEX method, the requirement that the premises be true and the conclusion false of the actual world, is replaced by the requirement that the premises of the CEX be true and the conclusion false of the possible world described. Finally, the epistemic requirement drops out (assuming you have provided a full description of the relevant facts) because your description provides the needed information about truth values to someone examining your work.

I should show you how graphic CEXes handle individual constants. This CEX refutes the argument about philosophy papers that was displayed at the beginning of the chapter. By placing the letter p in the second cell we indicate that the duck is individual p.

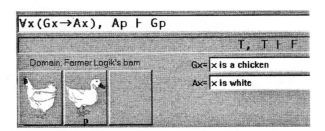

CEX: Every chicken (in the barn) is white. (T)
Individual p is white. (T)
So, individual p is a chicken. (F)

Just as failing to complete a proof is no demonstration of invalidity, failure to construct a successful CEX (whether actual or possible-world) is no demonstration of validity. Logicians call the proof and CEX methods *non-effective*, where an *effective* method is one that gives (in a finite number of steps) a definite answer of *valid* or *invalid* for any sequent. In the next chapter we will study a method, *truth trees,* that is effective for sequents employing the vocabulary that we have developed to this point.[9]

EXERCISES

Instructions: Symbolize arguments (where necessary) and establish invalidity by constructing possible-world CEXes. (It is not essential that you use the program, "PredLogic," but it will be convenient. If you do use the program and print your work, remember to add the English version of each CEX.)

14. (a) $\exists xFx, \exists xGx \vdash \exists x(Fx \ \& \ Gx)$

   *(b) $\forall x(Fx \lor Gx) \vdash \forall xFx \lor \forall xGx$

   (c) $-\forall xFx \vdash \forall x-Fx$

15. In the fifth and sixth panels of the following cartoon the lawyer offers an explanation in the form of a valid argument. We'll skip that argument since we are now focusing on invalidity.

   (a) In the next-to-last panel the King puts forward this argument:

   > It is false that all the world loves a funny man because I [the King] am not (f)unny, yet I am (l)oved.

   (b) At the end of the strip the lawyer appears to be thinking of this argument:

   > The [K]ing is neither (f)unny nor (l)oved. Thus, it is true that all the world loves a funny man.

   (domain for both problems: inhabitants of Id; k = the King)

By permission of Johnny Hart and Creators Syndicate, Inc.

[9]The method of *logic diagrams* is also an effective technique for a restricted range of sequents, namely sequents containing no mixed wffs, no multiple quantifications, and no relational predicates. This method is explained in the document *diagrams.pdf* contained on the *PredLogic* CD-ROM packaged with this book.

16. Here are more arguments from Introduction to Philosophy exams. The first four syllogisms were contained in responses to the question *Could a robot have free will?*

   *(a) We (h)umans are all (a)ctive. But since (r)obots are not human, they are not active.

   (b) Some (e)vents are not (c)aused.
   All (r)obot acts are events.
   So, some robot acts are not caused.

   (c) All c(y)bernetic acts are (c)aused.
   All (e)vents are caused.
   Therefore, all cybernetic acts are events.

   (d) Some (r)obot acts are not (c)aused.
   No (f)ree acts are caused.
   So, some robot acts are free.

   *(e) All (h)uman acts are (c)aused [acts].
   All human acts are (e)vents.
   So, all caused acts are events.

17. A proof that (p)ropositions are not mind-(d)ependent: The (l)aws of physics are propositions. The laws of physics will (h)old when all human minds have disappeared. Nothing that holds when all human minds have disappeared is mind-dependent.

18. In Plato's *Phaedo*[10] Socrates advances, and Cebes accepts, this inference:

   Every (l)ive (b)ody has a (s)oul. Hence, every body that has a soul is alive.

19. Philosopher William James appears to advance the following argument in *Pragmatism*:[11]

   (a) If no (t)rue ideas are (g)ood, then we will not have the idea that truth is precious. But, since we do have that idea, it follows that good ideas are true and vice versa.

   (domain: ideas; P = We have the idea that truth is precious)

   *(b) Prove invalid the argument that results when you weaken the conclusion of (a) to "Good ideas are true *or* vice versa."

20. (CHALLENGE) A logic exercise book presents this as a valid sequent:

   $(\forall xCx \lor \forall xMx) \rightarrow \forall x - Dx, \exists x(Dx \& Ex) \vdash \exists x - (Cx \lor Mx)$

21. (CHALLENGE) The author of an LSAT study guide believes that statements 1 through 7 together entail 8.[12] Show that he is wrong.

[10]105c–105d. *The Last Days of Socrates*, trans. Hugh Tredennick (Baltimore: Penguin Books, 1989), p. 167.

[11](Indianapolis, Ind.: Hackett Publishing Company, 1981), p. 37.

[12]Karl Weber, *How To Prepare For the New Law School Admission Test* (New York: Harcourt Brace Jovanovich, Publishers, 1983), pp. 69, 70 & 116.

1. None of those on the (l)acrosse team are also on the field (h)ockey team.
2. All of those on the (p)olo team are also on the field hockey team.
3. Some of those on the field hockey team are also on the (b)adminton team.
4. None of those on the lacrosse team are also on the badminton team.
5. All of those on the (c)ricket team are also on either the slow-pitch (s)oftball team or the lacrosse team, but not both.
6. Some of those on the cricket team are also on the field hockey team.
7. All of those on the badminton team are also on the polo team.
8. Some of those on the cricket team are not on the polo team.

(domain: members of a college's athletic teams)

22. (CHALLENGE) This table was featured in an exercise in the preceding chapter. Non-entailment between adjacent wffs is shown by the absence of arrows pointing in the appropriate direction.

$$(F1)\ \exists xAx \rightarrow \forall xBx$$
$$\Downarrow$$
$$(F2)\ \forall x(Ax \rightarrow Bx)$$
$$\Downarrow \qquad\qquad \Downarrow$$
$$(F3)\ \forall xAx \rightarrow \forall xBx \qquad (F4)\ \exists xAx \rightarrow \exists xBx$$
$$\Downarrow \qquad\qquad \Downarrow$$
$$(F5)\ \forall xAx \rightarrow \exists xBx \ \Leftrightarrow\ (F6)\ \exists x(Ax \rightarrow Bx)$$

Establish these results:

(a) F2 does not entail F1.
(b) F3 does not entail F2.
(c) F3 does not entail F4.
(d) F4 does not entail F2.
(e) F4 does not entail F3.
(f) F5 does not entail F3.
(g) F6 does not entail F4.

23. (CHALLENGE) In the summer of 1991 prospects for Arab-Israeli peace talks were slim. This argument attempts to provide a summary of the situation:

[I]srael will not pa(r)ticipate in the talks if any Pa(l)estinians from (E)ast Jerusalem participate. No Palestinians will participate unless some Palestinians from East Jerusalem participate. No (A)rab state will participate unless some Palestinians participate. It follows that neither Israel nor any Arab state will participate in the talks.

8

Truth Trees'

8.1 Constructing Trees

The truth-tree method in predicate logic is grafted onto the propositional-logic truth-tree technique in much the same way that the predicate proof technique is built upon the propositional proof system. Just as we have a left rule and a right rule for each propositional connective (see page 280), we also have left and right rules for both quantifiers. The four quantifier tree rules are remarkably similar, differing mainly in the conditions that are imposed. We begin by considering the two left-hand (or truth-side) rules.

The Universal Quantifier Left Rule ($\forall$L):

$$+\forall x Ax \mid$$
$$Ac \mid$$

("$\forall x Ax$" represents any universal quantification and "Ac" represents any instance of the quantification.)

The Existential Quantifier Left Rule ($\exists$L):

$$\checkmark \exists x Ax \mid$$
$$Ac \mid$$

("$\exists x Ax$" represents any existential quantification and "Ac" represents any instance of the quantification.)

c is new to the branch

There are only two differences between these two rules (beyond the fact that they concern different quantifiers): (1) they employ different *dispatch* marks,

---

'The technique explained in this chapter treats two-sided trees; one side represents truth, the other falsity. Some logicians prefer a different format that may be labeled *one-sided trees* because it represents wffs as true, but not as false. That technique is explained in an alternate version of Chapter 8 included on the CD-ROM packaged with this book (one-sided-trees.pdf).

and (2) only the ∃L Rule is burdened with a restriction. The significance of the **plus** dispatch mark (used in the ∀L Rule) is that it is permissible to return to the wff at a later point in tree construction and apply the rule to it again; the significance of the **check mark** (used in the ∃L Rule) is that you may not apply the rule again to that wff. No doubt you have noticed the similarity between the ∀L tree rule and the ∀O proof rule, and between the ∃L tree rule and the ∃O proof rule. That is to be expected because there is a close analogy between making deductions in a proof and decomposing wffs located on the left (truth) side of a tree branch. The justifications provided in Chapter Three for the ∀O and ∃O proof rules apply also to the left-hand tree rules.

This tree illustrates the proper employment of the ∀L and ∃L rules:

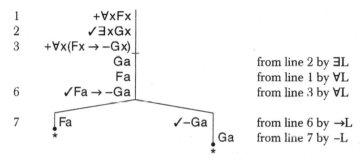

1	+∀xFx	
2	✓∃xGx	
3	+∀x(Fx → −Gx)	
	Ga	from line 2 by ∃L
	Fa	from line 1 by ∀L
6	✓Fa → −Ga	from line 3 by ∀L
7	Fa ✓−Ga	from line 6 by →L
	* Ga	from line 7 by −L
	*	

The column of line numbers on the left and the column of justifications on the right have been added to help you understand the tree; they are not part of the tree itself. The short horizontal line crossing the trunk beneath the third wff separates the initial wffs from the rest. I apply the ∃L Rule first because it carries the restriction that the constant introduced must be new to the branch. Note that the logical symbol in the wff on line 3 that has the greatest scope is the universal quantifier and not the arrow; hence the ∀L Rule may be applied to line 3 but the →L Rule may not. The left branch closes because "Fa" appears both on the left and the right sides of the branch, and the right branch closes because "Ga" occurs on both sides of the branch. The two asterisks (or stars) indicate that both branches have closed. Because all of the branches close, the tree itself is closed.

There are only two more rules to add; these rules apply to quantifications positioned on the right (or falsity) side of branches.

The Universal Quantifier Right Rule (∀R):

∀x𝒜x✓
𝒜c

c **is new to the branch**

The Existential Quantifier Right Rule (∃R):

∃x𝒜x+
𝒜c

As was the case with the left-hand quantifier rules, there are two differences between these two rules: they employ different dispatch marks, and the ∀R Rule (but not the ∃R Rule) comes with a restriction. Notice that these features are reversed between the left-hand and right-hand rules. That is, it is the ∃L and ∀R rules that get the check mark and the restriction, while the ∀L and ∃R rules employ the plus mark. Why the flip flop? As you know, writing a wff on the left side of a branch represents the wff as true, while placing it on the right signifies falsity. This means that placing "∃xAx" on the left side is tantamount to placing "−∃xAx" on the right, but the latter wff is equivalent to "∀x−Ax." Thus, an existential quantification on the left amounts to a universal quantification on the right (with a dash added following the quantifier), and, of course, a universal quantification on the left is tantamount to an existential quantification on the right. That is why the restriction that the constant be new to the branch applies to both the ∃L Rule and the ∀R Rule.

Consider two small trees:

<pre>
1   │∃xFx+
     Fb │
3   │Fb   from line 1 by ∃R
         *
</pre>

Because the ∃R Rule has no restrictions, we could use any constant on line 3, but obviously we should select *b* since that will allow us to close the tree.

<pre>
1   │∀xFx✓
     Fb │
3   │Fc   from line 1 by ∀R
         o
</pre>

Because the ∀R Rule is restricted we cannot instantiate to *b* on line 3, but must choose another constant. The tree ends on line 3 because there are no more moves to make. Because the wff on line 1 has a check mark (rather than a plus), we cannot return and make another move from it. The branch and the tree are open because no wff appears on both sides of the branch. An "o" at the tip of the branch marks it as open.[2]

Why is the ∃R Rule sound? Because if "∃xFx" is false (as is assumed when it is written on the right side of the branch) then nothing *F*s, and if that is so, then any wff of the form "*Fa*" will also be false. Hence, we are entitled to write any such wff on the falsity side of the branch. Why is the ∀R Rule sound? Because if "∀xFx" is false (as is assumed), then there is some individual that doesn't *F*, and we can represent that individual (whose name is presumably not known to us) by a constant that is new to the branch, that is, by a dummy name.

---

[2]In propositional trees we indicate that a branch is open by *not* marking it with a star. In predicate logic we need a mark to signify openness because there is a third possibility (beyond being open and closed). This possibility is explained in Chapter Twelve.

Hence, we are entitled to add "Fc" on the falsity side of the branch (so long as *c* is a dummy name).

8.2 Testing Sequents

Let's evaluate this argument:

> Any car with (p)ainted bumpers has a serious design (f)law.[3] All (n)ew cars have painted bumpers. Hence, all new cars exhibit a serious design flaw.

> $\forall x(Px \rightarrow Fx), \forall x(Nx \rightarrow Px) \vdash \forall x(Nx \rightarrow Fx)$

(domain: cars) As you recall from your study of propositional logic, the tree test proceeds as follows: We assume the premises of the sequent to be true (by writing them on the left side of the tree trunk) and the conclusion false (by placing it on the right of the trunk). Next we see whether this assumption leads to a contradiction, which would be shown by closure of the tree. The assumption (about truth values) is a contradiction iff the sequent is valid. So, the sequent is valid if the tree closes, and it is invalid if the tree remains open. This tree establishes the validity of the argument about bumpers:

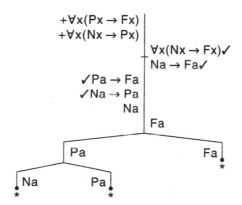

In a Chapter Three exercise I mentioned this argument that seems to be suggested by a sign in the "Big Bugs" traveling museum exhibit:

> (A)rachnids have (e)ight legs. (S)corpions have eight legs. Hence, scorpions are arachnids.

> $\forall x(Ax \rightarrow Ex), \forall x(Sx \rightarrow Ex) \vdash \forall x(Sx \rightarrow Ax)$

---

[3]You can verify this premise by walking through a parking lot examining bumpers. One purpose of auto bumpers is to protect the front and back of a car from the dings and nicks that occur in parking. A painted bumper cannot protect *itself* from dings and nicks.

This tree proves invalidity:

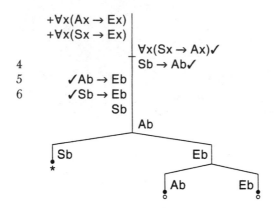

Why did I dispatch line 6 before line 5? Because I realized that this would reduce branching; I saw that one branch would close immediately. Had I dispatched the lines in the other order, the tree would contain four branches. A
tree with four branches would not be less correct, just less elegant and more
work to construct. I dispatched line 4 before 6 for the same reason.

Next I will construct a tree for this foolish argument:

> Some mammals are (b)ears. Some mammals are (g)iraffes. It follows
> that some bears are giraffes.
>
> ∃xBx, ∃xGx ⊢ ∃x(Bx & Gx)

(domain: mammals)

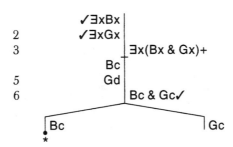

(This tree is not yet complete. That is why the right branch tip is unmarked.)
When I decompose line 2 (on line 5) I am forced by the restriction on the ∃L
Rule to avoid *c* and select another constant. When I decompose line 3 (on line 6)
I should choose either *c* or *d;* obviously I cannot use both of those constants in

the wff on line 6. Arbitrarily I choose *c* for line 6. No wff occurs on both sides of the right branch. Am I entitled to mark that branch open at this point and declare the tree to be open and the sequent invalid? No. We must adopt the following principle (call it the *Plus Principle*):

> **If an open branch contains a quantification marked with a plus that has not yet been instantiated to some constant that occurs on that branch, then the quantification must be instantiated to that constant before the branch may be marked open.**

Apply the Plus Principle to the partially completed tree above. The quantification on line 3 (with its plus dispatch mark) has not been instantiated to *d*, a constant that occurs on the branch. So, we must continue the tree:

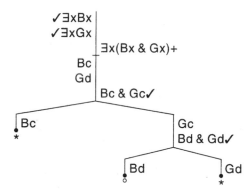

I can show why the Plus Principle is essential by constructing a tree for another argument. In 1985 Philadelphia police dropped a bomb from a helicopter on a city housing development, resulting in an inferno that destroyed 61 row houses and took 11 lives. A civil suit was brought against the city by a survivor and relatives of the victims. Their attorney, interviewed on ABC News,[4] said:

> *We will show that the [b]omb and the [f]ire were uncontrollable forces, and an uncontrollable force ... is unreasonable force.*

We supply the unstated conclusion and then symbolize her argument like this:

$$-Cb \ \& \ -Cf, \forall x(-Cx \rightarrow -Rx) \vdash -Rb \ \& \ -Rf$$

---

[4]Broadcast April 3, 1996. The plaintiffs won a $1.5 million judgement.

(In the interest of simplicity, I use two premise wffs instead of one lengthy conjunctive wff. domain: forces; Cx = x is controllable, Rx = x is reasonable) The tree for this sequent:

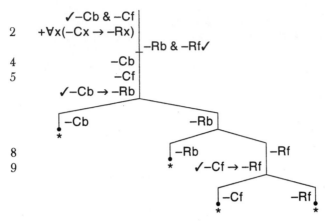

If it weren't for the Plus Principle I might have stopped the tree prematurely at line 8, marking the right-hand branch open, and judged the sequent to be invalid. But the sequent is valid. This becomes clear after I decompose the wff on line 2 for a second time, instantiating to f on line 9. One oddity of this tree is that it contains a number of negations (for example, those on lines 4 and 5) that are never decomposed. The tree closes even without decomposing them. It wouldn't be a mistake to decompose those wffs, but doing so would make the tree less elegant.

A final sample tree illustrates how we treat mixed wffs.

$$\exists xAx \rightarrow \exists xBx \vdash \forall xAx \rightarrow \forall xBx$$

```
1    ✓∃xAx → ∃xBx
2                 ∀xAx → ∀xBx✓
3         +∀xAx
                 ∀xBx✓
                 Be
            Ae
      ┌─────────────┐
   ∃xAx+          ✓∃xBx
   Ae               Bf
    *               Af
                     ∘
```

As line 1 is a conditional, the only rule that may be applied to it is →L; it would be a mistake to apply ∃L. Similar comments apply to line 2. Because an f appears on the right branch I am required by the Plus Principle to re-instantiate the (plus-marked) wff on line 3 to that constant. The tree is open, showing the sequent to be invalid.

There is a connection between the truth tree and CEX techniques. Each open branch of a tree points the way to a possible-world CEX. Collect the undispatched truth-side wffs from the open branch and add the negation of each undispatched falsity-side wff. For the open branch above, that would be the set {Ae, Bf, Af, −Be}. The domain for the CEX will be the set {e, f}. The facts about the domain are those asserted and denied by the four wffs (plus any additional facts entailed by those facts). The CEX:

> If something *As*, then something *Bs*. (T)
> So, if everything *As*, then everything *Bs*. (F)

Why is the premise true? Because individual *f Bs*, something *Bs*; so the consequent of the premise is true, and that makes the entire premise true. Because *e* and *f* exhaust the domain and they both *A*, the antecedent of the conclusion is true. And since *e* doesn't *B*, the consequent of the conclusion is false; so the conclusion is false. And what is the connection between the CEX technique and a tree that closes? The tree shows that no counterexample can be constructed for the sequent. Had counterexamples been possible, the tree technique would have created one.

It will be helpful to bring together in one place the main principles that govern the construction of predicate truth trees:

1. **Postpone branching as long as possible.**
2. **Apply ∃L and ∀R before either ∀L or ∃R (whenever possible).**
3. **When applying ∀L and ∃R, instantiate to constants already present on the branch (whenever possible).**
4. **A move made from a given wff must be made on every open branch on which that wff appears.**
5. **(The Plus Principle) If an open branch contains a quantification marked with a plus that has not yet been instantiated to some constant that occurs on that branch, then the quantification must be instantiated to that constant before the branch may be marked open.**

The first three principles are *elegance* principles. If you violate them, you will create inefficient (and ugly) trees that may still be correct. The last two principles are different. Violate one of them, and the tree you construct will be wrong and may give you an incorrect evaluation of the sequent under examination.

When is a truth tree incomplete? When there is a wff on some open branch that is capable of decomposition but has not been decomposed. Also, if principle 5 above is violated, the tree is not complete.

EXERCISES

1. Complete the following truth trees. Remember to insert dispatch marks ("✓" and "+") and to mark each branch open ("○") or closed ("*"). Identify each tree as *open* or *closed*.

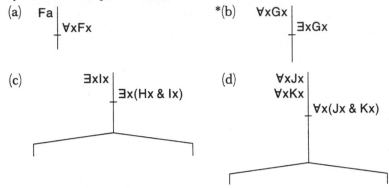

(a)   Fa
      │
      │ ∀xFx
      ┴

*(b)   ∀xGx
       │
       │ ∃xGx
       │

(c)   ∃xIx
           │
           │ ∃x(Hx & Ix)
           ┴
     ┌─────────┴─────────┐

(d)   ∀xJx
       ∀xKx
           │
           │ ∀x(Jx & Kx)
           ┴
     ┌─────────┴─────────┐

Note: For additional practice in testing sequents by trees without the need for prior symbolization, see the practice problems in the truth trees section of "PredLogic."

Instructions: Symbolize and test by the truth-tree method. Indicate whether the sequents are valid or invalid.

2. (a) By the third panel in the "Dilbert" strip the boss's inference has been revealed as:

   Someone (s)ays our web site is ugly. Therefore, everyone says that.

   *(b) Ming uses the following argument to refute the claim made (in the first panel) by the boss.

   Some Tibetan (m)onk does not (s)ay that our web site is ugly.
   Hence, it is false that everyone says that it is ugly.

(domain for both arguments: people in Dilbert's world)

DILBERT reprinted by permission of United Feature Syndicate, Inc.

3. An LSAT study guide[5] regards the following reasoning as valid:

   Some (C) are (F). Thus, some C are not F.

4. Sunny makes two inferences:

   (a) Any creature with long (e)yelashes is a (g)irl. The [c]ow depicted on the milk carton has long eyelashes. Therefore, it is a girl.

   (b) All (c)ows are (g)irls. So, all girls are cows.

   (domain: creatures in this comic strip world)

JUMP START reprinted by permission of United Feature Syndicate, Inc.

*5. If any of this week's Leno shows is a (r)erun, then they are all reruns. [L]ast night's show was; hence, [t]onight's program will be also.

   (domain: this week's Leno shows)

6. In March of 1997 a sports pickup failed to negotiate a curve in Winona, Minnesota, passed over the Mississippi River dike, and plunged through the ice into the river. Sadly, the five occupants drowned. Relatives of the victims sued the three Winona bars where they had been drinking before the accident. It was crucial to the legal case to establish that the driver of the truck was intoxicated and had been drinking at the bars, but the investigating police could not determine who had driven the truck. Therefore, this argument came into play:

   All of the truck occupants were (i)ntoxicated. All had consumed alcohol at the three (b)ars. Some occupant (d)rove the truck. It follows that someone who was intoxicated and had consumed alcohol at the three bars drove the truck.

   (domain: occupants of the truck)

7. A student who lost $190 in the university library posted a notice asking that $150 of it be returned. A librarian criticized the notice with this argument:

   Anyone who finds the money will return either (a)ll of it or (n)one of it. Proof: anyone who is (h)onest and finds the money will return it all. And any dishonest finder will return none of the money.

   (domain: finders of the money)

[5]Karl Weber, *How To Prepare For the New Law School Admission Test* (New York: Harcourt Brace Jovanovich, Publishers, 1983), p. 116.

8. An argument advanced in an LSAT study guide:[6]

> All of those on the cricket team are also on either the slow-pitch (s)oft-ball team or the (l)acrosse team, but not both. So, some cricket players are slow-pitch softball players.

(domain: cricket players)

*9. The "Dilbert" strip suggests this argument:

> The astrologer's prediction is true iff someone is plotting to (r)ip the boss off. Therefore, the prediction is true since the [a]strologer is plotting to rip off the boss.

(domain: Dilbert's world; T = The astrologer's prediction is true)

DILBERT reprinted by permission of United Feature Syndicate, Inc.

10. (a) If every jury member has been (b)ribed, then all of them will vote (a)cquittal. Thus, every jury member who has been bribed will vote acquittal.
    (b) Every jury member who has been bribed will vote acquittal. So, if every jury member has been bribed, then all of them will vote acquittal.

(domain: jury members)

11. Philosopher Peter Singer writes:

> *The capacity for suffering and enjoying things is a prerequisite for having interests at all, a condition that must be satisfied before we can speak of interests in any meaningful way. It would be nonsense to say that it would not be in the interests of a stone to be kicked along the road by a schoolboy. A stone does not have interests because it cannot suffer. Nothing that we can do to it could possibly make any difference to its welfare. A mouse, on the other hand, does have an interest in not being tormented, because it will suffer if it is.*[7]

---

[6]Weber, *Ibid.*, pp. 69 & 116.

[7]"All Animals Are Equal," reprinted in *The Right Thing to Do: Basic Readings in Moral Philosophy*, 2nd ed., ed. by James Rachels (Boston et al: McGraw-Hill College, 1999), p. 213. Published originally in *Annual Proceedings of the Center for Philosophical Exchange*, 1, no. 5 (1974), 103–111.

Singer seems to be advancing two arguments:

(a) Having the capacity for s(u)ffering is a necessary condition for having (i)nterests. A s(t)one does not have interests because it cannot suffer.

*(b) Having the capacity for suffering is a necessary condition for having interests. A (m)ouse does have interests because it can suffer.

(c) Test the argument that results when you replace the first premise of (b) with "Having the capacity for suffering is a necessary and sufficient condition for having interests." (Presumably Singer would accept this premise.)

12. James Wattengel writes in a letter to *Scientific American*:[8]

> *A missile defense system against nuclear or other mass-destruction warheads has to be 100 percent reliable to be successful. . . . I don't know of any other machine or system in the civilian or military world that has to perform to this extreme degree.*

His argument:

A (n)uclear missile defense system will be (s)uccessful only if it is 100% (r)eliable. But no system is 100% reliable. Therefore, no nuclear missile defense system will be successful.

(domain: systems; Nx = x is a nuclear missile defense system)

13. Descartes thought that the human soul was connected to the body at the pineal gland. One could use the following argument in support of this view:

The [p]ineal gland is an organ in the human body where the soul and body intersect. Proof: There is an organ in the human body where the soul joins the body. Any organ where the human body and the soul are joined is one that nonhuman animals lack. Nonhuman animals do not possess the pineal gland.

(Ox = x is an organ in the human body where the soul meets the body, Ax = nonhuman animals possess x) The third premise is false but was believed by Descartes.

*14. When a South Florida home was burgled, the Cuban-American owner reasoned that the thief was another Cuban-American:[9]

Someone took both the (t)elevision set and the St. Lazarus (i)con. Therefore, the TV and the icon were stolen by a (C)uban-American since only a Cuban-American would take the icon.

(domain: people; Tx = x stole the TV, Ix = x stole the icon)

[8]"Debating Defense" (December 1999), p. 14.

[9]Hilda Inclan, "I signed away kids, influence was bad," *Miami News* (May 9, 1974) p. 6-A.

15. This dialogue between Vincent Vega (John Travolta) and Jules Winnfield (Samuel L. Jackson) in the movie *Pulp Fiction*[10] contains three arguments. I number some of the speeches in order to refer to them.

VINCENT: *Want some bacon?*

JULES: *Naw, man, I don't eat pork.* [2]

VINCENT: *Are you Jewish?*

JULES: *I ain't Jewish, I just don't dig on swine, that's all.*

VINCENT: *Why not?*

JULES: *Pigs are filthy animals. I don't eat filthy animals.* [6]

VINCENT: *Yeah, but bacon tastes good. Pork chops taste good.*

JULES: *Hey—sewer rat may taste like pumpkin pie, but I'll never know 'cause I wouldn't eat the filthy motherfuckers. Pigs sleep and root in shit. That's a filthy animal. I ain't eating nothin' that ain't got sense enough to disregard its own feces.* [8]

VINCENT: *How about a dog? A dog eats his own feces.* [9]

JULES: *I don't eat dog either.*

VINCENT: *Yeah, but do you consider a dog to be a filthy animal?* [11]

JULES: *I wouldn't go so far as to call a dog filthy, but they're definitely dirty. But—dog's got personality; personality goes a long way.*

VINCENT: *So by that rationale, if a pig had a better personality, he'd cease to be a filthy animal? Is that true?* [13]

JULES: *Well, we'd have to be talkin' 'bout one charmin' motherfuckin' pig. I mean, he'd have to be ten times more charming than that Arnold on Green Acres, you know what I'm sayin'?*

The first argument is put forth by Jules in speeches 2, 6, and 8:

(a) All p(i)gs (s)leep and root in shit. I don't (e)at animals that do that. So, I don't eat pigs.

(Sx = x sleeps and roots in shit, Ex = I (Jules) eat x) The second argument is advanced by Vincent in speeches 9 and 11:

(b) (D)ogs e(a)t their own feces. Dogs are not (f)ilthy animals. Hence, it is false that all animals who eat their own feces are filthy.

(c) Test the argument that results when you replace the first premise of (b) with "Some dogs eat their own feces."

(Puzzled by the fact that one of the preceding two arguments is invalid? Section 9.2 treats this matter.) The third argument is also Vincent's,

[10]© 1994 by Miramax Film Corporation.

although it employs a premise suggested by Jules; this argument is expressed in speech 13:

*(d) Animals with (g)ood personality aren't (f)ilthy. Thus, if a p(i)g had a good personality, it wouldn't be filthy.

(domain for all arguments: animals)

16. (a) Any integer (l)arger than zero is (p)ositive. And any integer (s)maller than zero is (n)egative. But z[e]ro is neither larger than nor smaller than itself. Consequently, zero is neither positive nor negative.

  (b) Any positive integer is larger than zero. And any negative integer is smaller than zero. But zero is neither larger than nor smaller than itself. Consequently, zero is neither positive nor negative.

(domain: integers; Lx = x is larger than zero, Sx = x is smaller than zero, e = zero)

17. Philosopher R. E. Allen writes:[11]

> ... *Whatever is (r)ed is (e)xtended; whatever is extended is (l)ocatable with respect to any other thing which is extended; (m)irror images are not so locatable; therefore, they are neither extended nor red.*

(Lx = x is locatable with respect to any other thing which is extended) I suggest that you treat each of the first three clauses as a separate premise.

18. Another version of the argument about Smudgie's kittens:

*(a) Smudgie's kittens are anatomically identical. If so, then either all of them are (m)ales or all are (f)emales. All (c)alico kittens are females. There is a calico in the litter. Every kitten is either male or female. Thus, all (S)mudgie's kittens are female.

(domain: kittens; I = Smudgie's kittens are anatomically identical)

  (b) Test the argument that results when you replace the last premise of (a) with "No kitten is both male and female." (This is the argument in Chapter 6, exercise 19.)

19. (SEMI-CHALLENGE) A criticism of the naive view that all words are names:

  (a) If every (w)ord is a (n)ame, then every (s)entence (c)ontaining more than one word is a (l)ist. No lists have (t)ruth values. It follows that some words are not names since some sentences have truth values.

  (b) Test the argument that results when you replace the last premise of (a) with "Some sentences containing more than one word have truth values."

[11]"Participation and Predication in Plato's Middle Dialogues," *The Philosophical Review*, LXIX (1960), n. 13, p. 154.

9

Property-Logic Refinements

I wrap up the treatment of property logic by discussing three topics: (1) evaluating statements, (2) penevalidity, and (3) intensionality.

9.1 Statements

To this point our focus has mainly been on evaluating arguments, but statements also can be logically evaluated. Statements and their symbolizations can be divided into three classes: logical truths, contradictions, and contingencies. *Logical truths* are statements having a form that makes falsity logically impossible, while *contradictions* are statements whose form makes truth logically impossible. Statements that are neither logically true nor contradictory are *contingent*.

We can demonstrate logical truth by proof or truth tree. Consider this statement made by former University of North Carolina football coach Mack Brown:

> *If we can't (b)eat [F]lorida State, we can't win all of our games.*
> $-Bf \rightarrow -\forall xBx$

(domain: UNC's football opponents for the season; Bx = UNC beats x) Deriving this wff free of all assumptions shows that it is a logical truth.

1	(1)	$-Bf$	PA
1	(2)	$\exists x-Bx$	1 $\exists I$

1 (3) $-\forall xBx$ 2 QE
  (4) $-Bf \rightarrow -\forall xBx$ 1-3 $\rightarrow$I

Line 4 depends on the assumption on line 1–less line 1, that is, it depends on no assumptions. Only a logical truth can be derived free of all assumptions. Another way to prove that the wff is logically true is to place it on the falsity (right) side of a truth-tree trunk and show that the tree closes. This indicates that the wff logically cannot be false.

$$
\begin{array}{l}
|\,-Bf \rightarrow -\forall xBx\checkmark \\
\checkmark -Bf \\
|\,-\forall xBx\checkmark \\
|\,Bf \\
+\forall xBx \\
Bf \\
*
\end{array}
$$

Now let's consider a logical contradiction:

Everyone is (c)ruel, although no one is cruel.
$\forall xCx \ \& \ \forall x-Cx$

(domain: people) One way to show that this wff is a contradiction is to derive a standard contradiction from it.

(1) $\forall xCx \ \& \ \forall x-Cx$ A
(2) $\forall xCx$ 1 &O
(3) $\forall x-Cx$ 1 &O
(4) Ca 2 $\forall$O
(5) $-Ca$ 3 $\forall$O
(6) $Ca \ \& \ -Ca$ 4,5 &I

Since only a contradiction entails a contradiction, any wff (the wff on line 1, for example) that entails a standard contradiction (like the wff on line 6) must be contradictory.

Another way to establish that this wff is a contradiction is to place it on the truth (left) side of a tree trunk and show that the tree closes.

$$
\begin{array}{r}
\checkmark \forall xCx \ \& \ \forall x-Cx\,| \\
+\forall xCx \\
+\forall x-Cx \\
Ca \\
\checkmark -Ca \\
|\,Ca \\
*
\end{array}
$$

*(b) Either everything is red or everything is not red.

(c) Everything is red, although this [p]en is not red.

2. (a) Someone is (f)emale, but not everyone is.

(b) Someone is female, although no one is.

*(c) If everyone is female, then someone is.

(domain: people)

3. (a) If there are (M)uslim (p)lumbers, then there are Muslims and plumbers.

(b) If there are Muslims and plumbers, then there are Muslim plumbers.

(c) [J]ones is a Muslim plumber, although there are no plumbers.

4. *(a) (*Yogi Berra*) "I really didn't (s)ay everything I said." (Sx = Yogi Berra said x)

(b) (*headline*) "Ki(d)s who ki(l)l are kids."

(c) (*saying*) "You're d(a)mned if you d(o) and damned if you don't." (domain: people in the jam in question; Ax = x suffers unpleasant consequences, Ox = x performs the action in question)

5. (CHALLENGE) Devise a logically true statement whose logical truth cannot be demonstrated in our system as so far developed. Devise a contradictory statement whose contradictoriness cannot be demonstrated in our system. (Do not pattern your answers on the examples provided in section 9.1.)

6. (CHALLENGE)

(a) Prove by the proof and truth-tree methods that the symbolization of this sentence is a logical truth:

There is someone such that if he or she makes a (d)onation to charity, then everyone makes such a donation.

(domain: people)

(b) Should we regard the English sentence as logically true? Defend your answer.

9.2 Penevalidity

Consider this syllogism (we'll call it "Baldcypress"):

Every (b)aldcypress tree is a (c)onifer (bears cones).
Every baldcypress tree is (d)eciduous (sheds leaves or needles).
Therefore, some conifers are deciduous.

$\forall x(Bx \to Cx), \forall x(Bx \to Dx) \vdash \exists x(Cx \& Dx)$

(domain: trees) Seems like a good argument, right? But what about this syllogism concerning the students in PHI 210, Symbolic Logic (call it "Cheaters")?

Every student who is (c)aught cheating on the final will (f)ail the course.
Every student who is caught cheating on the final will be referred to the (h)onor council.
Thus, some students who fail the course will be referred to the honor council.

$$\forall x(Cx \rightarrow Fx), \forall x(Cx \rightarrow Hx) \vdash \exists x(Fx \ \& \ Hx)$$

"Cheaters" seems suspect. If no one fails PHI 210 the conclusion will be false, but the premises might be true nevertheless. Suppose the premise statements appear in the course syllabus and suppose also that the teacher is the kind of person who scrupulously keeps her syllabus commitments. In that case the premises would seem to be true even if no student is caught cheating. So, it looks like it is possible for the premises of "Cheaters" to be true while the conclusion is false, and if that is possible, then "Cheaters" is invalid. But doesn't "Baldcypress" have the same form as "Cheaters"? After all, the two arguments are symbolized in the same way. So, maybe the initial intuition that "Baldcypress" is a good argument was mistaken. In this section we will try to get clearer about this matter.

Let's begin by demonstrating by truth tree that the sequent that symbolizes "Baldcypress" is invalid.

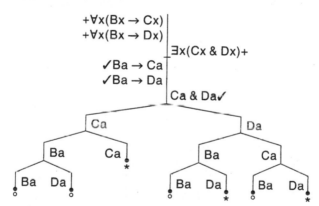

More than half of the branches are open.

Logicians are confronted with a basic decision about how to interpret general subject–predicate[2] statements. Let's focus on these two statements:

(S1) All baldcypress trees are conifers.
(S2) Some baldcypress trees are conifers.

The issue is which, if either, of these two statements entails S3.

(S3) There are baldcypress trees.

[2]Note that this is the grammarian's, and not the logician's, sense of *predicate*.

There are four possible positions one can take:

1. Both S1 and S2 entail S3.
2. Neither of them entails S3.
3. S1 entails S3, but S2 does not.
4. S2 entails S3, but S1 does not.

So far as I know, no one has ever found the third position plausible; we can safely ignore it and concentrate on the remaining three positions.

The system of logic we have set out endorses the fourth view; most contemporary logicians adopt this position. As you know, we symbolize S1 through S3 as follows:

(F1) $\forall x(Bx \rightarrow Cx)$
(F2) $\exists x(Bx \ \& \ Cx)$
(F3) $\exists xBx$

(Bx = x is a baldcypress tree, Cx = x is a conifer) It is easy to show by proof or truth tree that F2 entails F3.

(1)	$\exists x(Bx \ \& \ Cx)$	A	
(2)	Bd & Cd	1 $\exists$O	
(3)	Bd	2 &O	
(4)	$\exists xBx$	3 $\exists$I	

$\checkmark\exists x(Bx \ \& \ Cx)$ |
$\qquad\qquad\qquad$ $\exists xBx+$
$\checkmark$Be & Ce ⌐
$\qquad$ Be
$\qquad$ Ce
$\qquad\qquad$ Be
$\qquad\qquad$ *

It is also easy to show by truth tree or CEX that F1 does not entail F3.

$+\forall x(Bx \rightarrow Cx)$ |
$\qquad\qquad\qquad$ $\exists xBx+$
$\checkmark$Bf $\rightarrow$ Cf ⌐
$\qquad\qquad$ Bf
|
Bf $\qquad\qquad\qquad\qquad$ Cf
o $\qquad\qquad\qquad\qquad\quad$ o

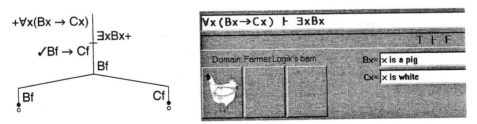

CEX: All pigs (in the barn) are white. (T)
$\qquad\qquad$ So, there is a pig. (F)

If you are puzzled by the fact that F1 has a true interpretation in the CEX, bear in mind that F1 is equivalent to F1′.

(F1′) $\forall x(-Bx \lor Cx)$

F1′ is true (in this interpretation) iff every resident of the barn (that is, the chicken) is either not a pig or is white. (In fact, the chicken is *both* not a pig *and* white!) We call subject–predicate statements (like the premise in the CEX above) whose subject term refers to nothing, *vacuous* statements. Using reasoning like the above we can show that all vacuous universal statements are true (according to our system of logic).

The wffs we have chosen to symbolize S1 and S2 make clear how we are interpreting those statements. Statements R1 and R2 express the literal readings of F1 and F2.

(S1) All baldcypress trees are conifers.
(F1) $\forall x(Bx \rightarrow Cx)$
(R1) For any individual, if it is a baldcypress tree, then it is a conifer.

(S2) Some baldcypress trees are conifers.
(F2) $\exists x(Bx \ \& \ Cx)$
(R2) There exists an individual that is a baldcypress tree and a conifer.

It is evident that F1 gives a *hypothetical* (that is, a *conditional*) interpretation to S1. On this interpretation S1 claims that *if* anything is a baldcypress tree it is a conifer, but it does not claim that anything is a baldcypress tree. By contrast, F2 gives an *existential* (or *categorical*) interpretation to S2. Under our interpretation, S2 claims that something is a baldcypress tree and goes on to say that it is also a conifer. Logicians introduce the technical term *existential import* to summarize the situation. The standard position in logic is that S1 lacks existential import, while S2 has existential import. We can define the technical term like this:

A general subject–predicate statement has existential import iff it entails the existence of something referred to by its subject term.

The standard view in logic is that universal subject–predicate statements (including *A* and *E* statements) lack existential import and that existential subject–predicate statements (including *I* and *O* statements) possess it.

The reason why "Baldcypress" is invalid (according to the standard view) is that its conclusion makes an existential claim while its premises make no existential claims. The premises are *A* statements and hence lack existential import. The conclusion is an *I* statement and accordingly has existential import. That is a recipe for invalidity. It is logically possible that there are no baldcypress trees and no deciduous conifers. In that situation "Baldcypress" would have true premises and a false conclusion (according to the view being described). At the beginning of the section we proved "Baldcypress" to be invalid by truth tree. We can establish the same result by CEX.

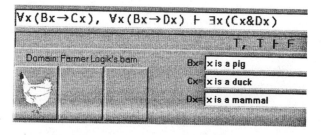

> **CEX:**   All pigs (in the barn) are ducks. (T)
> All pigs are mammals. (T)
> So, some ducks are mammals. (F)

The premises are vacuously true because there are no pigs in the barn. The conclusion is false because there is no duck (in the barn). What is the chicken doing? Satisfying the logical restriction on the CEX method that the domain not be empty. Every argument whose premises all lack existential import and whose conclusion has it will be invalid. So, every argument whose premises are all *A* and *E* statements and whose conclusion is an *I* or an *O* (or the negation of an *A* or an *E*) will be invalid.

Note that if we add a simple existential premise, S3, to "Baldcypress" we transform it into a valid argument:

(S3) There are baldcypress trees.

Once we add that premise the CEX above fails. There is no pig in the barn, so S3 is false. And if we add a pig we falsify the first premise. The validity of the argument that results from adding S3 as a premise can be shown by truth tree or proof. We can call "Baldcypress" a *penevalid* [3] argument, defining *penevalidity* in this way:

> **A penevalid argument is an invalid argument that can be transformed into a valid one by the addition of a single one-predicate existential premise.**

"Baldcypress" is an instance of a penevalid syllogistic form. There are eight other penevalid syllogistic forms (plus an infinite variety of penevalid non-syllogistic argument forms). Contemporary logicians recognize 15 valid syllogism forms while medieval logicians held out for 24. The difference, of course, lies in the nine penevalid forms.

Now we can explain why the second argument from *Pulp Fiction* is invalid.

> Dogs eat their own feces.
> Dogs are not filthy animals.
> So, it is false that all animals who eat their own feces are filthy.

The premises lack existential import. The conclusion is equivalent to an *O* statement, so it has existential import. The argument, then, is penevalid. One way to transform it into a valid argument is to add the auxiliary premise, "There are dogs." Another way is to replace the first premise with "Some dogs eat their own feces," a statement that has existential import.

When confronted with a penevalid argument, how do we determine which predicate will appear in the existential premise that will transform the

---

[3]The prefix *pene-* means "almost." (A *peninsula* is "almost an island [*insula*].")

invalid argument into a valid one? In the case of "Baldcypress," how did we know that the needed premise is "There are baldcypress trees," and not "There are conifers" or "There are deciduous trees"? If you answer, "Because *baldcypress trees* is the subject term in the premises," you answer too quickly. In many penevalid syllogisms the two premises have different subject terms; how then do you tell? And in one penevalid syllogism form the crucial predicate is not the subject term of either premise. One way to determine the predicate for the auxilliary existential premise is to begin a proof or truth tree for the penevalid sequent and see what additional premise will enable you to reach the conclusion of the proof or close every branch on the tree.

I have explained the view about existential import that has been adopted by most logicians. But is this position the best one to adopt? I think that it is, and I will defend it now. It is clear that we regard some *A* statements as lacking existential import. Consider this principle of physics as an example:

(S4) All moving objects subject to no forces continue to move in a straight line.

We take S4 to be a truth even though we know that there are no moving objects subject to no forces. (Every object is subject to gravitational pulls, for example.) It would be puzzling if some *A* statements possess existential import and others do not. When I utter S1 ("All baldcypress trees are conifers.") in conversation with you, we both take it for granted that baldcypress trees exist, but I am not *asserting* that they exist. If I were making that assertion, I would be making a *double* assertion: (1) that baldcypress trees exist and (2) that if a tree is a bald-cypress it is a conifer. Notice that on this view the negation of S1 (S5) would be equivalent to the disjunction S6. That seems farfetched.

(S5) It is false that all baldcypress trees are conifers.
(S6) Either there are no baldcypress trees or some baldcypress trees are not conifers.

It seems even clearer that we regard *E* statements as lacking existential import. Statement S7 is an obvious truth, but then if conversion is valid for *E* statements, and it surely seems to be, we must count S8 as a truth as well, even though there are no circle squarers.[4]

(S7) No geometricians are circle squarers.
(S8) No circle squarers are geometricians.

---

[4] An ancient geometric problem: given an arbitrary circle, construct a square having the same area using only a straight edge and a compass that cannot hold a setting. There is a mathematical proof that this problem cannot be solved. By a *circle squarer* I mean a person who has solved the problem.

I mentioned near the beginning of this section that there are four possible positions relating to the existential-import issue. I've been defending the "standard view," and another view is quite implausible; so two views remain to consider:

1. Both *A* and *I* statements have existential import.
2. Neither of them has existential import.

We'll consider them in turn. Since the first view ascribes existential import to *I* statements it presumably will ascribe it to *O*'s as well. Consider two *A* and *O* statements that have the same subjects and (grammatical) predicates, S1 and S9, for example.

(S1) All baldcypress trees are conifers.
(S9) Some baldcypress trees are not conifers.

It seems clear that these are contradictory statements; each claims exactly what the other denies. But if they both have existential import, then they could both be false. Consider what would happen if a blight wiped out all baldcypress trees. Two statements that can both be false are by definition not contradictory.

The problem with the second view lies in the denial that *I* statements have such import. When you assert "Some conifers are deciduous" what claim could you possibly be making if you are not saying that there is at least one conifer that is deciduous? Until someone can give us a sensible non-existential interpretation for *I* statements, we are justified in rejecting the second view. What about the proposal that "Some conifers are deciduous" really means "If conifers exist, then there are conifers that are deciduous"? If *I*'s and *E*'s with the same subjects and predicates are contradictory (as they certainly seem to be), then this view implies the implausible position that *E* statements are actually conjunctions. "No conifers are deciduous" would amount to "Conifers exist, but there aren't any deciduous conifers." Furthermore, why would you deny existential import to *A* statements and confer it on *E*'s?

I have tried to show that the standard view is the best of the lot, but it isn't without drawbacks. One problematic aspect of this view is that it holds that all vacuous universal subject–predicate statements are true, whatever their subject matter. While vacuous statement S4 (the physics principle) seems obviously true, it is less plausible to say the same about S10.

(S10) All (g)hosts are (b)ody-builders.

Logicians who embrace the standard view on existential import and who deny the existence of ghosts are required to say that S10 is true. The validity of the following sequent is easily shown by proof or truth tree.

$$-\exists xGx \vdash \forall x(Gx \rightarrow Bx)$$

If you hold the premise true and the sequent valid you are forced to agree that the conclusion is true. How can one defend that result? By noting:

> *Statement S10 just means that **if** any individual is a ghost, then it is also a body-builder. And that just means that each individual either isn't a ghost or is a body-builder. And that's true!*

But a defender of the standard position must admit that most people unconta-minated by logic will regard S10 as false.

EXERCISES

Instructions for exercises 7 through 13: Each argument is penevalid. (1) Symbolize it and establish its invalidity by constructing a CEX and a truth tree. (2) Identify the one-predicate existential supplementary premise that will transform the argument into a valid one. (3) Establish the validity of the augmented argument by constructing a proof and a truth tree.

7. (a) All (L)utherans are (P)rotestants. Hence, some Protestants are Lutherans.

    *(b) No (a)ntelopes are (l)izards. Thus, some antelopes are not lizards.

8. A biology professor presented this argument in a lecture:

    > (F)latworms are not (v)ertebrates, but they exhibit (b)ilateral symmetry. Therefore, it is false that only vertebrates exhibit this kind of symmetry.

9. Garrison Keillor writes:

    > *Cats are intended to teach us that not everything in nature has a function.*[5]

    Keillor's quip appears to advance this argument:

    > Not everything in nature has a (f)unction because (c)ats have no function.

    (domain: natural things)

10. All the area (c)oordinators attended the (b)anquet. Everyone at the banquet made a (p)ledge. Thus, some of those who pledged are area coordinators.

    (domain: people)

*11. This penevalid syllogism is an instance of the least plausible of all pene-valid syllogism forms. Even those not initiated into the mysteries of logic

---

[5]Quoted in "365 Cats Calendar" (New York: Workman Publishing, Inc., 1995), page for Jan-uary 24, 1996.

are likely to regard the premises of this syllogism as true and its conclusion as false.

> All (g)eometers are (m)athematicians. No mathematicians are (c)ircle squarers. So, some circle squarers are not geometers.

12. An argument considered by Bertrand Russell:[6]

> All (h)umans are (e)vil. Nothing evil is (p)art of God. Thus, the thesis [of pantheism] that everything is part of God is false.

13. A philosopher visiting the University of Miami employed this argument in a lecture:

> All (p)hysical events can be explained in purely physical (t)erms. No event of (e)xtra-sensory perception is explicable in purely physical terms. Every ESP event is a (m)ental event. This proves that some mental events are not physical events.

(domain: events; $Tx = x$ can be explained in purely physical terms) The crucial existential assumption is controversial, to say the least.

14. Symbolize each argument and establish its validity by constructing a proof and a truth tree.
    (a) There are no (g)hosts. Hence, all ghosts are (b)ody-builders.
    *(b) All (g)hosts are (b)ody-builders. No ghosts are body-builders. Therefore, there are no ghosts.

15. (CHALLENGE)
    (a) Symbolize exercise 7(b) using *antelopes* as the domain and eliminating the predicate letter A.
    (b) Establish the validity of the resulting sequent by constructing a proof and a truth tree.
    (c) Explain why sequent 7(b) is merely penevalid while sequent 15 is valid.

9.3 Intensional Contexts

Consider this argument ("Killer Sister"):

> Brian Burch believes that all murderers should be executed.
> Brian's sister Clarissa is a murderer.
> Therefore, Brian believes that Clarissa should be executed.

The evidence for premise one is that Brian proclaims this view with fervor to anyone who will listen, and he is not the sort of person who lies. Now Brian has no idea that Clarissa is a murderer. (In fact no one besides Clarissa even suspects this, for she is an apparently upright citizen who has committed the "perfect"

---

[6] *Religion and Science* (New York: Henry Holt and Company, Inc., 1935), pp. 193–94.

crime.) Believing Clarissa to be guilty of no crime, Brian does not believe that she should be executed. (Even if he later learned that Clarissa is a murderer, he still would not believe that she should be executed because he loves her dearly; rather he would then either be forced to give up the belief mentioned in the first premise or remain inconsistent.) The premises of "Killer Sister" are true and the conclusion is false. There could hardly be a clearer case of invalidity. But it appears that we can symbolize "Killer Sister" with a valid sequent:

$$\forall x(Mx \rightarrow Bx), Mc \vdash Bc$$

(domain: people; Mx = x is a murderer, Bx = Brian believes that x should be executed, c = Clarissa) It is easy to prove that this sequent is valid, by constructing a truth tree, for example. How are we to explain this seeming paradox? The answer we must give is that the sequent is not a satisfactory symbolization of the argument expressed in English. One purpose of this section is to explain why the symbolization is defective.

Logicians distinguish between the *extension* and the *intension*[7] of a singular term, a term like "George W. Bush" or "the oldest woman in Wyoming." The extension of the latter term is the aged individual it denotes, while its intension is the meaning of the expression. In a similar way, logicians distinguish between the extension and intension of a predicate, like "is a pilot." The extension of that expression is the class of all aviators, while the intension is the property of being an aviator.

A system of predicate logic is labeled *extensional* iff individual constants (and also predicate letters) can be substituted for one another in a wff without changing its truth value—**when the two symbols have the same extension.** A system of predicate logic that is not extensional is called *intensional.* The logic presented in this book, which is the standard predicate logic, is extensional. A sequent having the following form will be provable in our system:

$$\forall x(Fx \leftrightarrow Gx) \vdash (\ldots F \ldots) \leftrightarrow (\ldots G \ldots)$$

(where "$(\ldots F \ldots)$" represents any wff containing the predicate letter F and "$(\ldots G \ldots)$" represents the result of replacing that letter by G). The premise in this sequent schema represents the claim that F and G have the same extension, and the conclusion corresponds to the claim that F can be substituted for G in some wff without a change in truth value.

Most sentences in a natural language (such as English) function extensionally. For instance, because Clarissa killed John Hooker, the following two sentences must have the same truth value, whether it be truth or falsity:

---

[7]Differentiate between *intension* (with an *s*) and *intention* (with two *t*'s). The first word (when used in logic) means "meaning or property," while the second term, of course, means something like "end," "purpose," etc.

>Clarissa ate breakfast at Denny's this morning.
>
>John Hooker's killer ate breakfast at Denny's this morning.

The sole difference between the sentences is that they contain different singular terms that have the same extension. The same holds for extensionally equivalent predicates for most natural-language sentences. Consider these examples:

>Fred carved an equilateral triangle in the teacher's desk.
>
>Fred carved an equiangular triangle in the teacher's desk.

Because the predicates "is an equilateral triangle" and "is an equiangular triangle" have the same extension, those two sentences must have the same truth value. Our logic is equipped to deal with sentences like the four displayed in this paragraph.

The problem is that some natural-language sentences are **not** extensional. Think about these sentences:

>(S1) Brian believes that Clarissa ate breakfast at Denny's this morning.
>
>(S2) Brian believes that John Hooker's killer ate breakfast at Denny's this morning.

The sole difference between S1 and S2 is that where one contains the term "Clarissa" the other has the term "John Hooker's killer." Remember that these terms refer to the same individual (that is, have the same extension). Nevertheless, S1 is true (Brian was sitting across the table from Clarissa at Denny's this morning), while S2 is false. Brian believes that Hooker's killer is in the state penitentiary, where indeed the man falsely convicted of Hooker's murder languishes in a cell. Logicians describe this situation by saying that the words "Brian believes that" create an *intensional context* for the singular terms that follow them in S1 and S2. Our logic should not be applied to sentences like S1 and S2.

Not only singular terms but also predicates can occur in intensional contexts. Consider these sentences:

>(S3) Brian believes that all equiangular triangles have 60 degree angles.
>
>(S4) Brian believes that all equilateral triangles have 60 degree angles.

Brian is not much good at geometry, and while he knows that the angles in an equiangular triangle are 60 degrees, he is under the misapprehension that the angles of an equilateral triangle measure 75 degrees. (He doesn't realize that a triangle is equiangular iff it is equilateral, and he is unaware that the sum of the angles of a triangle must total 180 degrees.) So, S3 is true and S4 false in spite of the fact that the predicates "is an equiangular triangle" and "is an equilateral triangle" are extensionally equivalent. While the predicates have the same extension, they have different intensions (they refer to different properties: *having equal angles* and *having equal sides*). So, again we cannot apply our logic to statements like S3 or S4.

How do we recognize expressions that create intensional contexts? This is not a simple matter,[8] but for our purposes this principle will suffice:

When providing dictionary entries for predicates in an extensional predicate logic (such as ours), never permit a variable to follow the word *that*.[9]

For example, all of the following dictionary entries are illicit for an extensional system of logic:

Kx = Smith knows that x is red
Hx = Smith hopes that x loves him
Cx = Smith claims that x is addicted to drugs
Px = it is possible that x is married
Nx = it is necessary that x is married
Px = it is permitted that x carry a weapon
Ox = it is obligatory that x carry a weapon

An argument that can be symbolized only by employing a dictionary entry like one of these is an argument that goes beyond the scope of our system of logic. That shows why we cannot successfully treat "Killer Sister" in our system. There are logics, called (appropriately enough) *intensional logics,* in which that argument may be treated satisfactorily. Of course, it will be ruled invalid in such a logic.

An exercise in Chapter Six concerned an argument by philosopher Peter Unger that included this premise:

(S5) If you know that there are rocks, then you can know that there is no evil scientist deceiving you to falsely believe that there are rocks.

Your first attempt at symbolizing this statement might be:

(F5) $\forall x(Rx \rightarrow Sx)$

---

[8]A fuller account is provided in Chapter Six of Robert E. Rodes, Jr., and Howard Pospesel, *Premises and Conclusions: Symbolic Logic for Legal Analysis* (Upper Saddle River, New Jersey: Prentice-Hall, Inc., 1997).

[9]While this principle is roughly on the mark, it is not theoretically sound. There are two problems with it: (1) it rules out some dictionary entries that ought not to be excluded, for example, "it is the case that x is red," and (2) it accepts some entries that should be excluded, for example, "Brian believes x to be the murderer."

domain: people

Rx = x knows that there are rocks

Sx = x can know that there is no evil scientist deceiving x into falsely believing that there are rocks

The dictionary entry for *R* is all right, but the entry for *S* is illicit because the last occurrence of *x* falls within the intensional context created by the words "knows that." In order to avoid this problem I supplied a slightly different interpretation for *S*:

Sx = x can know that there is no evil scientist deceiving people into falsely believing that there are rocks

The price paid was that now F5 does not represent Unger's exact premise but rather this similar statement:

(S5′) If you know that there are rocks, then you can know that there is no evil scientist deceiving *people* to falsely believe that there are rocks.

However, this change does not materially affect the philosophical argument in question, so I was able to bring Unger's argument into the extensional fold.

EXERCISES

Instructions for exercises 16 through 20: Identify the dictionary entries that fall outside the scope of our extensional logic.

16. It is necessarily true that any number evenly divisible by two is even. So, it is necessarily true that the number of states making up the United States is even since the number of states making up the United States is evenly divisible by two.

    (domain: numbers; Dx = x is evenly divisible by two, Ex = it is neces-
    sarily true that x is even, n = the number of states making up the United
    States)

*17. Fergus read in the dictionary that a person who collects butterflies is a lepi-
    dopterist. Lionel collects butterflies. Hence, Fergus read in the dictionary that
    Lionel is a lepidopterist.

    (domain: people; Lx = Fergus read in the dictionary that x is a lepidop-
    terist, Bx = x collects butterflies, l = Lionel)

18. Section 8501 specifies that only licensed surveyors residing in the county are
    eligible for the post of County Surveyor. All of the licensed surveyors residing in
    the county are white males. If section 8501 specifies that only white males are
    eligible for the post of County Surveyor, then section 8501 is unconstitutional.
    This proves that section 8501 is unconstitutional.

(domain: people; Sx = section 8501 specifies that x is eligible for the post of County Surveyor, Lx = x is a licensed surveyor, Rx = x resides in the county, Wx = x is white, Mx = x is male, C = Section 8501 is constitutional)

19. Henry intentionally donned his red striped tie. His red striped tie has a spot. Thus, Henry intentionally donned a tie with a spot.

   (domain: Henry's neckties; Ix = Henry intended that Henry don x; r = Henry's red striped tie, Sx = x has a spot)

20. (CHALLENGE)

   Viola plans to purchase a bicycle. Therefore, there is a bike that Viola plans to buy.

   (Px = Viola plans to make it true that she buys x, Bx = x is a bike) Is this English argument valid? Defend your answer.

10

Relational Symbolization

We encountered this argument (call it "Jurassic Park") in Chapter One:

> Two dinosaurs can breed only if one is female and one is not.
> All of the dinosaurs in Jurassic Park are female.
> So, the dinosaurs in Jurassic Park can't breed.

We cannot analyze "Jurassic Park" satisfactorily using only the resources of logic that have been explained so far. That is because it involves the notion of one creature *breeding with* another. Breeding is a relation and not a property. Consider a second argument ("Sheila"):

> Everyone loves Sheila.
> Hence, Sheila loves someone.

You probably recognize this as the argument version of a logically true statement discussed in section 9.1. "Sheila" is valid because the premise entails "Sheila loves Sheila," and that statement in turn entails the conclusion. (The preceding sentence expresses another argument that will be an exercise in section 13.3.) The validity of "Sheila" cannot be shown (without adding a supplementary premise) in the logic of properties that we have learned so far. We could try to symbolize "Sheila" in one of these ways (or by using some combination of the two):

As ⊢ Bs   (Ax = everyone loves x, s = Sheila, Bx = x loves someone)

∀xCx ⊢ ∃xDx   (Cx = x loves Sheila, Dx = Sheila loves x)

These sequents are invalid and therefore do not adequately represent the valid argument expressed in English. The problem here is the same as the one encountered with the dinosaur argument. Loving (like breeding) is a relation that holds between individuals. In order to treat "Jurassic Park" and "Sheila" satisfactorily we will need to extend our logic to encompass relations. This chapter is concerned with the symbolization of statements involving relations. Chapters Eleven and Twelve extend to relational arguments the evaluation methods already mastered for property arguments, and Chapter Thirteen discusses some of the finer points of relational logic.

10.1   Symbolizing Relational Statements

All of the predicates discussed in earlier chapters have been *property* predicates. A property predicate denotes a property (characteristic, quality, feature, aspect) that an individual may possess or exhibit. A property predicate and *one* singular term juxtaposed (in a suitable order) form a statement. For example, S1 results from placing together the singular term 'Jesse Ventura' and the property predicate 'is bald'.

(S1) Jesse Ventura is bald.

A *relational* predicate denotes a relation that can hold between *two* (or more) individuals. A relational predicate and two (or more) singular terms juxtaposed (in a suitable order) will form a statement. S2 results from placing together the singular terms 'Coral Gables' and 'Key West' and the relational predicate 'is larger than'.

(S2) Coral Gables is larger than Key West.

Relational predicates (like property predicates) are abbreviated by capital letters. But whereas a property-predicate letter is always followed by one lowercase letter (individual constant or variable), a relational predicate letter is always followed by two (or more) lower-case letters. S2 will be symbolized with F2.

(S2) [C]oral Gables is {l}arger than [K]ey West.
(F2) Lck

Often I will use braces to identify the letter to be used in abbreviating a relational predicate (like 'is larger than'). A *dyadic* relational predicate is one that can be transformed into a statement by the addition of *two* singular terms, for example, "is larger than." Most of the relational predicates we will consider are dyadic (or two-place), but now and then we will meet three- and four-place predicates. There is no maximum number of places that a predicate can involve. S3 contains the three-place predicate 'borrows … from'.

(S3) [J]im {b^3}orrowed the [h]acksaw from [C]armen.
(F3) Bjhc

When the relational predicate involves more than two places, I indicate this with a superscripted numeral within the braces.

English relational statements are sometimes expressed in the "active voice" (as in S4) and sometimes in the "passive voice" (as in S5).

(S4) [C]arol {l}oves [S]tewart.
(S5) Stewart is loved by Carol.

We adopt the convention that relational-predicate letters abbreviate predicates expressed in the active voice. For example, *L* abbreviates 'loves', not 'is loved by'. So, both S4 and S5 are symbolized by F4.

(F4) Lcs

F6 symbolizes neither S4 nor S5; it does represent S6.

(F6) Lsc
(S6) Stewart loves Carol.

As you can see, the order in which lower-case letters follow a relational-predicate letter is crucial.

Many relational symbolizations involve quantifiers. Examples:

Someone {h}ates [M]ax.	∃xHxm
Max hates everyone.	∀xHmx
Max hates no one.	∀x−Hmx *or* −∃xHmx
Someone hates himself or herself.	∃xHxx

(domain: people) Some relational statements are symbolized by multiple quantifications.

(S7) Someone hates somebody.   (F7) ∃x∃yHxy
(S8) Everyone hates everybody.   (F8) ∀x∀yHxy

Two different variable letters are required in the symbolization of S7 and S8. F9 is not an acceptable symbolization of S7.

(F9) ∃x∃xHxx

F9 is not even well formed; it violates the rule (stated first in section 5.2) that no variable in a wff may fall within the scope of two quantifiers containing that variable. Three of the four occurrences of the variable in F9 lie within the scope of two quantifiers containing x.

Special problems arise when relational symbolizations involve both universal and existential quantifiers.

(S10) There is a person who hates everybody.   (F10) $\exists x \forall y Hxy$

There is a person who is hated by everybody. $\exists x \forall y Hyx$

Everybody hates at least one person. $\forall x \exists y Hxy$

(S11) Each person is hated by at least one person.   (F11) $\forall x \exists y Hyx$

No two of these four English sentences are logically equivalent, and (of course) no two of the four wffs that symbolize them are equivalent. Not only is the order of variables following the predicate letter crucial (as was noted above), the order of the quantifiers is equally significant (when one is universal and one existential). If we transpose the quantifiers in any of these four wffs, we radically change the content of the wff. For example, by switching the quantifiers in F10 we produce F12.

(F12) $\forall y \exists x Hxy$

F12 does *not* symbolize S10; rather, it symbolizes S11. (F11 and F12 are logically equivalent. Note that if you systematically interchange two variables in a wff, for example, substituting x for y and vice versa, the resulting wff will be equivalent to the original. F11 and F12 are instances of this.) We will further study this matter of quantifier order in section 13.2.

Relational statements commonly contain both property predicates and relational predicates. S13 is an example:

(S13) There is a (c)at who {f}ears no (d)ogs.

Until you develop proficiency in relational symbolization it may be a good idea to symbolize a sentence like S13 in stages, replacing at each step a bit of English with the corresponding abbreviations or logic symbols.

(S13) There is a (c)at who {f}ears no (d)ogs.

There is an x such that x is a cat and x fears no dogs.

There is an x such that x is a cat, and for any y if y is a dog then x does not fear y.

$\exists x[Cx$ & for any y if y is a dog then x does not fear y]

(F13) $\exists x[Cx \ \& \ \forall y(Dy \rightarrow -Fxy)]$

Close study of the table below will teach you much about relational symbolization. The sentences in each box are equivalent and so are the wffs in each box. A sentence may be symbolized by any wff in its box; generally the top wff in each box "tracks" the sentences best. No two sentences in different boxes are equivalent, and, of course, no two wffs in different boxes are equivalent.

Eight Relational Symbolizations

Sentence	Symbolization
Every (t)hief can {p}ick some (l)ock. Any thief can pick some lock or other.	∀x[Tx → ∃y(Ly & Pxy)]
Every thief can pick every lock. Any thief can pick any lock. All thieves can pick all locks.	∀x[Tx → ∀y(Ly → Pxy)] ∀x∀y[(Tx & Ly) → Pxy]
There is a thief who can pick every lock. There is a thief who can pick all locks. Some thief can pick all locks.	∃x[Tx & ∀y(Ly → Pxy)]
There is a thief who can pick some lock. Some thief can pick some lock.	∃x[Tx & ∃y(Ly & Pxy)] ∃x∃y[(Tx & Ly) & Pxy]
There is a thief who can't pick any lock. There is a thief who can pick no locks. Some thief can't pick any lock.	∃x[Tx & ∀y(Ly → −Pxy)] ∃x[Tx & −∃y(Ly & Pxy)]
There is a thief who can't pick every lock. There is a thief who can't pick all locks. Some thief can't pick every lock.	∃x[Tx & −∀y(Ly → Pxy)] ∃x[Tx & ∃y(Ly & −Pxy)] ∃x∃y[(Tx & Ly) & −Pxy]
No thief can pick every lock. No thief can pick all locks.	∀x[Tx → −∀y(Ly → Pxy)] ∀x[Tx → ∃y(Ly & −Pxy)] −∃x[Tx & ∀y(Ly → Pxy)]
No thief can pick any lock. Every thief can pick no locks.	∀x[Tx → ∀y(Ly → −Pxy)] ∀x∀y[(Tx & Ly) → −Pxy] −∃x[Tx & ∃y(Ly & Pxy)] −∃x∃y[(Tx & Ly) & Pxy]

Focusing on the the affirmative examples in this table and the first symbolizations offered for them, you will notice these patterns:

Each *A* *R*'s some *B*.	∀x[Ax → ∃y(By & Rxy)]
Each *A* *R*'s every *B*.	∀x[Ax → ∀y(By → Rxy)]
There is an *A* that *R*'s every *B*.	∃x[Ax & ∀y(By → Rxy)]
There is an *A* that *R*'s some *B*.	∃x[Ax & ∃y(By & Rxy)]

Notice that these four wffs (indeed all the wffs in the table above) observe the customary correlation of universal quantifiers with arrows and existential quantifiers with ampersands.

In the next table I provide more examples of relational symbolization. I recommend studying each example until it makes good sense. Any two wffs in one cell are logically equivalent.

Ten More Relational Symbolizations

Sentence	Symbolization	Dictionary
[P]olio is {c}aused by a (v)irus.	$\exists x(Vx \ \& \ Cxp)$ $\exists x(Cxp \ \& \ Vx)$	
(*Poor Richard*) "[G]od {h}elps them that help themselves."	$\forall x(Hxx \rightarrow Hgx)$	domain: people
(*Children's book*) "[B]enjy {l}oved every-body in his family and they all loved him."	$\forall xLbx \ \& \ \forall xLxb$ $\forall x(Lbx \ \& \ Lxb)$	domain: members of Benjy's family
Both U[M] and [F]SU {s}cored in every (q)uarter.	$\forall x[Qx \rightarrow (Smx \ \& \ Sfx)]$	$Sxy = x$ scored in y
(*quip*) "People who (s)nore always {f}all asleep first."	$\forall x\forall y\{[Bxy \ \& \ (Sx \ \& \ -Sy)] \rightarrow Fxy\}$	domain: people; $Bxy = x$ is bedmate of y, $Fxy = x$ falls asleep before y
All male humans (a)live now are {d}escended from one male human	$\exists x\forall y(Ay \rightarrow Dyx)$	domain: male humans
(*sign about snakes on a trail in Everglades N.P.*) "Don't {t}read on me and I won't {h}arm you."	$\forall x\forall y[(Ux \ \& \ Sy) \rightarrow (-Txy \rightarrow -Hyx)]$	$Ux = x$ is a human, $Sx = x$ is a snake
(*A.A. principle*) "Only a (d)runk can {h}elp another drunk."	$\forall x\forall y[(Dx \ \& \ Hyx) \rightarrow Dy]$ $\forall x[\exists y(Dy \ \& \ Hxy) \rightarrow Dx]$[1]	
If you {t}rust everyone, then you haven't {m}et everybody.	$\forall x(\forall yTxy \rightarrow -\forall yMxy)$	domain: people
Every (l)ichen is {c³}omposed of (f)ungi and (a)lgae.	$\forall x\{Lx \rightarrow \exists y\exists z[(Fy \ \& \ Az) \ \& \ Cxyz]\}$	$Cxyz = x$ is composed of y and z

---

[1]These two wffs may not appear to be equivalent, but they are. This matter is discussed in section 13.1.

As in earlier chapters, quantifications with two or more predicates require quantifier-scope groupers. However, when two quantifiers in such a wff have the same scope (except that the first quantifier precedes the scope of the second), only one pair of quantifier-scope groupers is used. For example, the following formula is punctuated correctly:

$\forall x \forall y (Rxy \rightarrow Ryx)$

There are more examples in the table above.

Now we are equipped to symbolize "Jurassic Park":

Two dinosaurs can {b}reed only if one is (f)emale and one is not.
All of the dinosaurs in (J)urassic Park are female.
So, the dinosaurs in Jurassic Park can't breed.

$\forall x \forall y \{Bxy \rightarrow [(Fx \,\&\, -Fy) \lor (-Fx \,\&\, Fy)]\}, \forall x(Jx \rightarrow Fx)$
$\vdash \forall x \forall y[(Jx \,\&\, Jy) \rightarrow -Bxy]$

(domain: dinosaurs; Bxy = x can breed with y, Fx = x is female, Jx = x is located in Jurassic Park) We need the wedge in the symbolization of the first premise because the first creature considered could be female and the second male, or vice versa. The first premise may also be (equivalently) symbolized:

$\forall x \forall y[Bxy \rightarrow (Fx \leftrightarrow -Fy)]$

In the following chapter we will establish the validity of "Jurassic Park."

Some English relational sentences are amphibolous; S14 is an example.

(S14) Some thief can pick any lock.

A person who utters S14 may have in mind the claim expressed by S15 or the one conveyed by S16.

(S15) There is a thief who can pick every lock.

(F15) $\exists x[Tx \,\&\, \forall y(Ly \rightarrow Pxy)]$

(S16) Any lock can be picked by at least one thief.

(F16) $\forall x[Lx \rightarrow \exists y(Ty \,\&\, Pyx)]$

S15 entails, but is not entailed by, S16. S15 asserts the existence of an omni-competent lock picker; S16 does not. It is a noteworthy fact about predicate logic that no symbolization of S14 will preserve its amphiboly. In a language of wffs, this sort of ambiguity does not occur. Consider another example; S17 was part of a TV public-service announcement.

(S17) Someone knows about every child that's neglected.

S17 could be construed as equivalent to S18 or S19; but we all view it as synonymous with S18, probably because S19 is so obviously false.

(S18) Each case of child (n)eglect is   (F18) $\forall x[Nx \rightarrow \exists y(Py \, \& \, Kyx)]$
       {k}nown by at least one (p)erson.

(S19) There is a person who knows of   (F19) $\exists x[Px \, \& \forall y(Ny \rightarrow Kxy)]$
       all cases of child neglect.

(Nx = x is a case of child neglect, Kxy = x knows about y) No wff retains the ambiguity inherent in S17.

Chief Seattle expressed this aphorism, "What happens to beasts will happen to man." The general drift of his remark is evident, but if you try to formulate the thought with precision you discover four possible interpretations:

Whatever h{a}ppens to any (b)east $\forall x[\exists y(By \, \& \, Axy) \rightarrow \exists y(Uy \, \& \, Axy)]$
will happen to some h(u)man.

Whatever happens to any beast $\forall x[\exists y(By \, \& \, Axy) \rightarrow \forall y(Uy \rightarrow Axy)]$
will happen to every human.

Whatever happens to every beast $\forall x[\forall y(By \rightarrow Axy) \rightarrow \exists y(Uy \, \& \, Axy)]$
will happen to some human.

Whatever happens to every beast $\forall x[\forall y(By \rightarrow Axy) \rightarrow \forall y(Uy \rightarrow Axy)]$
will happen to every human.

Notice that the left bracket is properly positioned in each of these wffs. That placement shows that the initial quantifier has the entire wff in its scope, while the scope of the next quantifier is much smaller (ending with the first right-hand parenthesis).

EXERCISES

1. Symbolize statements (a) through (f) using a domain of persons.

   (a) [F]red {l}oves [A]lice.   (d) There is a person who loves everyone.

   *(b) Fred loves someone.   (e) Each person loves someone or other.

   (c) Everyone loves Alice.   *(f) Everybody loves everybody.

Translate wffs (g) through (m) into colloquial English sentences using this dictionary: domain: persons; Lxy = x loves y.

(g) ∃x∃yLxy

*(h) ∃xLxx

(i) ∃x∀yLyx

(j) ∀x∃yLyx

(k) ∃x∀y−Lxy

*(l) ∃x−∀yLxy

(m) −∃x∀yLxy

2. Symbolize statements (a) through (d).

(a) Some (p)erson {k}nows some (s)ong.

*(b) There is a person who knows every song.

(c) Every person knows at least one song.

(d) Every person knows every song.

Translate wffs (e) through (i) into colloquial English sentences using this dictionary: Px = x is a person, Kxy = x knows y, Sx = x is a song.

(e) ∃x[Px & ∀y(Sy → −Kxy)]

*(f) ∀x[Px → ∀y(Sy → −Kxy)]

(g) ∀x∀y[(Px & Sy) → −Kxy]

(h) ∃x[Px & −∀y(Sy → Kxy)]

(i) ∀x[Px → −∀y(Sy → Kxy)]

Instructions for exercises 3 through 5: (1) Symbolize using the suggested abbreviations. (2) Provide a dictionary for the abbreviating symbols.

3. Use people as the domain if no other domain is stipulated.

(a) (*newspaper*) "[In today's society], everybody {s}ues everybody."

*(b) (*book title*) "Everything is somewhere." (unrestricted domain; Lxy = x is located in place y)

(c) (*children's book*) "[G]eorgie never {s}cared anybody."

(d) (*newspaper*) "Not everyone {l}oves [K]ato Kaelin."

(e) (*sign in gas station*) "No one can {p}lease everybody."

*(f) Everyone {k}nows at least one (p)olitician.

(g) Every (p)olitician {k}nows at least one person.

(h) (*student newspaper*) "Everyone who goes to UM {k}nows someone [at UM] who uses (m)arijuana. (domain: UM students)

(i) (*Boswell*) "One does not {l}ike those whom one has greatly {i}njured."

*(j) (*Samuel Johnson*) "Every man {k}nows some whom he cannot induce himself to {t}rust." (Txy = x can induce himself or herself to trust y)

(k) (*radio newscast*) "Everyone in H(u)ntsville {k}new at least some of the h(o)stages." (Ux = x is a resident of Huntsville)

4.   (a) (*sign*) "Shoplifting is stealing." (Ax = x is an instance of shoplifting, Bx = x is an instance of stealing)

  *(b) Shoplifting is stealing. (Cxy = x shoplifts y, Dxy = x steals y)

  (c) Shoplifting is stealing. (Exyz = x shoplifts item y belonging to z, Fxyz = x steals item y from z)

  (d) (*newspaper, during a gas crisis*) "Everybody {l}oves a man who has (g)asoline for sale." (domain: people; Gx = x has gasoline for sale)

  (e) (*Snoopy*) "In all my life, I've never {k}issed a (c)at!" (s = Snoopy)

  *(f) (*Goethe*) "No one {d}eceives you unless you deceive yourself." (domain: people)

  (g) [M]iami-Dade County government is not {p}ermitted to do business with any (f)irm that {d}oes business with [C]uba. (Pxy = x is permitted to do business with y, Dxy = x does business with y)

  (h) (*poster*) "Every (l)iving thing is our {r}elation." (Hx = x is a human, Rxy = x is related to y)

  (i) (*Thule catalog*) "All (p)roducts are not {a}vailable in all (c)ountries." (Px = x is a Thule product, Axy = x is available in y)

  *(j) (*Dean Martin's theme song*) "Everybody {l^3}oves somebody sometime." (Px = x is a person, Lxyz = x loves y at time z)

  (k) ("*Shout*" *ad*) "No (p)roduct {g}ets out all (s)tains." (Px = x is a stain-removal product)

5.   (a) (*newspaper*) "No two nations who have (M)cDonald's franchises have ever {w}arred against each other." (Symbolize the likely intended claim. domain: nations; Wxy = x wars against y)

  *(b) (*newspaper*) "A h(e)althy (w)olf has never {a}ttacked a h(u)man in North America." (domain: creatures in North America)

  (c) (*Florida law*) "Anyone committing a (f)elony that involves a (d)eath can be charged with {m}urder" (Px = x is a person, Cxy = x commits y, Dx = x involves a death, Mxy = x can be charged with murder in connection with y)

  (d) (*children's book*) "In all (F)rance there was no (m)ouse more {b}eloved than [A]natole." (domain: creatures in this fictional realm; Fx = x resides in France, Bxy = x is more beloved than y)

  (e) (*book*) "Other whales are a{f}raid of (k)iller whales." (domain: whales; Fxy = x fears y)

  *(f) (*bumper sticker*) "ANY (D)AY {S}PENT ABOVE GROUND IS A {G}OOD ONE." (Px = x is a person, Sxy = x is above ground during y, Gxy = x is good for y)

  (g) (*Internet humor*) "{I}nside every (f)at book there is a t(h)in book t{r}ying to get out." (domain: books; Rxy = x is trying to get out of y)

(h) (*headline*) "{G}randkids considered {d}ependents only if both parents are dead." (domain: people; Gxy = x is a grandchild of y, Dxy = x is a dependent of y, Mx = x's mother is dead, Fx = x's father is dead)

(i) There is a (s)chool with only (b)lack {p}upils. (Pxy = x is a pupil in y)

*(j) (*newspaper*) "No two nations who have (M)cDonald's franchises have ever {w}arred against each other." (Construe the sentence strictly. domain: nations; Wxy = x wars against y)

(k) (*dialogue from "It's a Wonderful Life"*) "No man is a f(a)ilure who has f{r}iends." (domain: people; Rxy = x is a friend of y)

(l) (*Garfield, commenting on a movie monster that devoured Tokyo*) "Anything that {e}ats everything can't be all (b)ad." (Bx = x is all bad)

(m) A home run is a (g)rand slam iff every (b)ase is {o}ccupied when it is hit. (domain: home runs; Oxy = x is occupied when y is hit)

6. In an episode of *The Simpsons*, Moe, the bartender, muses that "Old people are no good at everything." Symbolize these four possible meanings:

    (a) No (o)ld (p)eople are {g}ood at anything.

    *(b) No old people are good at everything.

    (c) Not all old people are good at something.

    (d) Not all old people are good at everything.

    (Gxy = x is good at y)

7. A logic-text manuscript contained these sample symbolizations:

    (S1) Some (p)erson {h}as all the (c)hips.
    (F1X) ∀x[Cx → ∃y(Py & Hyx)]

    (S2) No (p)erson {h}as any (m)oney.
    (F2X) ∀x[Mx → ∃y(Py & −Hyx)]

    (S3) No (p)erson {h}as all the (c)hips.
    (F3X) ∀x∀y[(Px & Cy) → −Hxy]

All of these symbolizations are mistaken!

    *(a) Prove that F1X is a mistaken symbolization for S1 by describing a situation in which S1 and F1X have different truth values.

    (b) Provide the correct symbolization for S1.

    (c) Translate F1X into a colloquial English sentence.

    (d) Prove that F2X is a mistaken symbolization for S2 by describing a situation in which S2 and F2X have different truth values.

    *(e) Provide the correct symbolization for S2.

    (f) Translate F2X into a colloquial English sentence.

(g) Prove that F3X is a mistaken symbolization for S3 by describing a situation in which S3 and F3X have different truth values.

(h) Provide the correct symbolization for S3.

*(i) Translate F3X into a colloquial English sentence.

Instructions for exercises 8 and 9: Symbolize using the suggested abbreviations.

8. (SEMI-CHALLENGE)

   (a) (*Gautama*) "A man is not (n)oble if he {i}njures (l)iving creatures." (Px = x is a person)

   (b) (*"Dear Abby"*) "No one can be {h}appy with a (s)lob but another slob." (domain: people; Hxy = x lives happily with y)

   (c) (*R. M. Hare*) "No single statement can be made in (i)nterpretation of Plato which some (s)cholars will not {d}ispute" (Ix = x is a statement of Platonic interpretation, Dxy = x will dispute y)

   (d) Every person who commits suicide commits homicide. (domain: people; Kxy = x kills y)

   (e) (*Dennis Miller*) "[In view of all the deadly computer viruses that have been spreading lately, *Weekend Update* would like to remind you that] when you {l}ink up to another computer, you're linking up to every computer that that computer has ever linked up to." (Don't symbolize the bracketed text. domain: computers; c = your computer, Lxy = x links up to y)

   (f) (*dictionary*) "{G}randdaughter: a {d}aughter of one's {s}on or daughter." (domain: people)

   (g) (*newspaper, commenting on drug mules*) "[It is a terrible risk to take.] A p(e)llet (l)eaks and a swallower d(i)es." (Rx = x is a person, Ex = x is a drug pellet, Sxy = x swallows y)

   (h) (*quip*) "A (c)losed (m)outh {g}athers no (f)eet."

   (i) (*Dagwood Bumstead's mailman*) "Mailmen have mailmen too." (domain: people; Mxy = x is y's letter carrier)

   (j) (*park ranger*) "Every (s)pider in the park is h{a}rmful to some creature, but only some of them are harmful to h[u]mans." (domain: species in the park; Sx = x is a species of spider, Axy = members of species x have the capacity to harm members of species y, u = the human species)

9. (CHALLENGE) Symbolize using the suggested abbreviations.

   (a) (*headline*) "No single {c}ure covers all of Latin America's fiscal (a)fflictions." (Ax = x is a Latin American fiscal affliction, Cxy = x cures y)

(b) (*Seattle city attorney*) "If you {b}ooze and cr{u}ise you lose … your (l)icense and your c(a)r." (Sx = x is a Seattleite, Bxy = x drinks at time y, Ux = x drives at time y, Lx = x loses x's license, Ax = x loses x's car)

(c) (*faculty senate chair*) "Everyone who {v}olunteered to serve on some (c)ommittee has been {a}ssigned to some committee [although not necessarily the committee requested]." (Don't symbolize the bracketed text. Px = x is a person, Vxy = x volunteers to serve on y, Axy = x has been assigned to y)

(d) (*ACLU slogan*) "What may be done to one may be done to all." (Dxy = x may be done to y, Px = x is a person)

(e) (*proverb*) "Wa{s}te not, wa{n}t not." (Px = x is a person, Sxy = x wastes y, Nxy = x is in need of y)

(f) (*aphorism*) "Any (l)awyer who represents himself has a (f)ool for a {c}lient" (Symbolize literally. domain: people; Cxy = x is a client of y)

(g) (*aphorism*) "Any lawyer who represents himself has a fool for a client." (Symbolize the gist. Use dictionary for (f).)

(h) (*magazine ad*) "Some c(h)ildren {w}ear nothing but Florence (E)iseman c(l)othes." (Wxy = x wears y, Ex = x is manufactured by Florence Eiseman, Lx = x is an article of clothing)

(i) Each c(h)ild of mine who {o}wns a c(a)r owns at least one (S)aturn. (Hx = x is a child of mine)

(j) (*comic strip*) "Every mother has the right to give advice to any mother's child." (domain: people; Mxy = x is mother of y, Rxy = x has the right to give advice to y)

(k) Everyone (n)amed *Pospesel* (spelled with two *e*'s) either lived in (O)swego, New York, or has an {a}ncestor who lived there, or is {m}arried to someone who has an ancestor who lived there. (domain: people)

(l) ("*Dilbert*" *character Catbert*) "Any e(m)ployee who {s^3}its in a company (c)hair while {h}aving a personal thought will be e(x)ecuted by security." (Sxyz = x sits in y at time z, Hxy = x has a personal thought at time y)

(m) (*Geoffrey Hunter*) "So far as logic and mathematics are concerned, whatever can be said in some existing natural language or other can be said in some one existing natural language." (Lx = x pertains to logic, Mx = x pertains to mathematics, Sxy = x can be said in y, Nx = x is a natural language)

10. (CHALLENGE) Sign posted near an apartment-complex pool: "Non-breakable containers can only be used in pool area."

  (a) Symbolize the claim expressed by the sentence when it is construed strictly.

  (b) Symbolize the claim the sign maker intended to express.

(Bx = x is breakable, Cx = x is a container, Mxy = x may be used in location y, Px = x is in the pool area)

11. (CHALLENGE) Philosopher Hans Reichenbach discusses this sentence, apparently unaware that it is amphibolous.

> *If any two men either {l}ove each other or {h}ate each other, then either there is a man who loves all men or for every man there exists some man whom he hates.*[2]

(domain: men) One meaning is logically true, the other contingent.

(a) Symbolize the logically true meaning.

(b) Symbolize the contingent meaning.

12. (CHALLENGE) Sign in a 7-Eleven convenience store: "Colder beer than ours ... there ain't." Two putative symbolizations:

(F1) $\forall x \forall y[(Sx \,\&\, -Sy) \rightarrow Cxy]$
(F2) $\forall x \forall y[(Sx \,\&\, -Sy) \rightarrow -Cyx]$

(domain: beer; Sx = x is sold at a 7-Eleven store, Cxy = x is colder than y) One of these wffs correctly symbolizes the sign, the other does not. (a) Which one is correct? (b) Why is the other incorrect?

Two of my logic students offered F4 and F5 as symbolizations of S3.

(S3) There are no smallest particles of matter.
(F4) $-\exists x[Mx \,\&\, \forall y(My \rightarrow Sxy)]$
(F5) $-\exists x[Mx \,\&\, \forall y(My \rightarrow -Syx)]$

(Sxy = x is smaller than y) One of these symbolizations is correct and one is not. (c) Which one is correct? (d) Why is the other incorrect?

(WARNING: Questions (e) through (g) are quite tough.) F7 and F8 are plausible symbolizations for S6:

(S6) Every (w)oman at the (t)able was {s}erved a roll {b}efore any (m)an at the table was served a roll.

(Tx = x was at the table, Sxy = x was served a roll at time y)

(F7) $\forall x \forall y\{[(Wx \,\&\, Tx) \,\&\, (My \,\&\, Ty)] \rightarrow \exists z[Sxz \,\&\, \forall w(Syw \rightarrow Bzw)]\}$
(F8) $\forall x[(Wx \,\&\, Tx) \rightarrow \exists y(Sxy \,\&\, \forall z \forall w\{[(Mz \,\&\, Tz) \,\&\, Szw] \rightarrow Byw\})]$

F7 and F8 are not equivalent wffs. (e) Cite a wff that is either entailed by only one of these wffs or entails only one of these wffs. Because F7 and F8 are not equivalent, it is reasonable to suppose that one is a better symbolization of S6 than the other. (f) Which is better? (g) Why is it better?

[2]*The Rise of Scientific Philosophy* (Berkeley and Los Angeles, Calif.: University of California Press, 1958), p. 223.

11

Relational Proofs

11.1 Relational Proofs

At the beginning of the movie *Dracula's Daughter,*[1] the old professor kills Count Dracula by driving a wooden stake through his heart. His younger colleague, not realizing that the victim is a vampire, is aghast, and offers to speak on the old man's behalf at the trial that he anticipates will occur.

YOUNG PROFESSOR:	*I'll tell the court you're insane.*
OLD PROFESSOR:	*But I'm not insane.*
YOUNG PROFESSOR:	*Then you are guilty of murder!*
OLD PROFESSOR:	*You can't murder a man who has been dead for 500 years.*

The old man advances a relational argument:

No one can {m}urder a person who has been dead (f)ive hundred years. Count [D]racula has been dead that long. Therefore, [I] have not murdered him.

$\forall x(Fx \rightarrow \forall y - Myx)$, Fd $\vdash -Mid$

(domain: people in this fictional realm; Mxy = x murders y, Fx = x has been dead 500 years, i = the old professor) A proof of validity is easily constructed:

(1) $\forall x(Fx \rightarrow \forall y - Myx)$ A
(2) Fd   A

---

[1]Universal Studios (1936), directed by Lambert Hillyer.

$$(3) \quad Fd \rightarrow \forall y-Myd \qquad \qquad 1 \; \forall O$$
$$(4) \quad \forall y-Myd \qquad \qquad 3,2 \rightarrow O$$
$$(5) \quad -Mid \qquad \qquad 4 \; \forall O$$

The first line in this proof is a quantification containing two quantifiers; such wffs are common in relational proofs. In order to accommodate this new wrinkle we need to slightly revise our definition of *instance*. This is the only change we are required to make in order to extend our proof mechanism to relational arguments.

> **An instance of a quantification is a wff that results from (a) deleting the *initial* quantifier (as well as groupers showing the scope of the quantifier) and (b) replacing each of the remaining occurrences of the *initial quantifier* variable by the same individual constant.**

(The new elements in the definition are italicized.) Line 3 in the proof above was constructed in compliance with this definition. The initial quantifier on line 1 is dropped, and the occurrences of that variable (x) are replaced by a constant (d). The two y's appearing in line 1 are untouched in the move to line 3. For additional examples of the extended definition of *instance*, note that F2 is an instance of F1, while neither F3 nor F4 is an instance of F1. Be sure that you understand why.

(F1) $\forall x \exists y Rxy$
(F2) $\exists y Ray$
(F3) Rab
(F4) $\forall x Rxa$

Matters can be somewhat confusing when the instantiating constant also appears in the quantification. This happens (twice) when we construct a proof for "Sheila" (an argument introduced at the beginning of Chapter Ten):

> Everyone loves Sheila.
> So, Sheila loves someone.
>
> $\forall x Lxs \vdash \exists x Lsx$

$$(1) \quad \forall x Lxs \qquad A$$
$$(2) \quad Lss \qquad \quad 1 \; \forall O$$
$$(3) \quad \exists x Lsx \qquad 2 \; \exists I$$

One might suppose that since s occurs in line 1 it cannot serve as the instantiating constant on line 2, but this is not so; nothing in the definition of *instance* precludes this move. Similarly, even though s occurs on line 3, it may also serve as the instantial constant on line 2 (relative to the $\exists I$ move). In relational proofs, as before, when you instantiate a variable, every occurrence of that variable must be replaced by the same individual constant. This principle was respected in the proof above.

Of course, on line 2 of the proof above I could have selected some other constant for my instance; so I could have begun the proof like this:

(1) ∀xLxs   A
(2) Las   1 ∀O

The problem with selecting *a* is that I cannot move from line 2 to the conclusion of the sequent. The move from line 2 to the conclusion can be made only if line 2 is an instance of "∃xLsx" and any instance of this wff will have an *s* in the spot immediately following the *L*. That realization is what prompted me to select *s* as the instance in the move from line 1 to line 2. This proof illustrates a fact: **the most challenging aspect of relational proofs is selecting instantiating constants wisely.** In the proofs that follow I will give my reasons for selecting various constants as I invoke the ∀O and ∃O Rules.

In the "Grade School Confidential" episode of *The Simpsons*,[2] principal Seymour Skinner is accused of having had sexual relations with teacher Edna Krabappel. When Skinner is confronted by school superintendent Chalmers, Skinner is adamant that he is a virgin. Chalmers replies,

> *Well, Seymour, it's clear you have been falsely accused, because no one anywhere ever would pretend to be a 44-year-old virgin.*

The superintendent's argument in formal dress:

> Sey[m]our is (f)orty-four and he (c)laims to be a virgin. No one who is 44 and is not a (v)irgin would claim to be one. A virgin has had {s}ex with no one. It follows that Seymour has not had sex with [E]dna.
>
> Fm & Cm, ∀x[(Fx & −Vx) → −Cx], ∀x(Vx → ∀y−Sxy) ⊢ −Sme

(domain: people in the Simpsons' world; Cx = x claims to be a virgin, Vx = x is a virgin, Sxy = x has had sexual relations with y) I construct a proof for this argument and supply some commentary:

(1) Fm & Cm   A
(2) ∀x[(Fx & −Vx) → −Cx]   A
(3) ∀x(Vx → ∀y−Sxy)   A
(4) (Fm & −Vm) → −Cm   2 ∀O   I chose *m* for the instance on line 4 because it occurs after *F* (and also *C*) on line 1.

[2]April 6, 1997.

(5) Vm → ∀y−Smy   3 ∀O   I chose *m* for the instance on line 5 because it occurs after *V* on line 4. (Remember that ∀O may not be applied to line 5 because it is not a quantification.)

(6) Cm   1 &O
(7) Cm → −(Fm & −Vm)   4 CN
(8) −(Fm & −Vm)   7,6 →O
(9) Fm   1 &O
(10) Fm → Vm   8 AR
(11) Vm   10,9 →O
(12) ∀y−Smy   5,11 →O
(13) −Sme   12 ∀O

Next let's construct a proof for "Jurassic Park," which may be symbolized:

$$\forall x \forall y[Bxy \rightarrow (Fx \leftrightarrow -Fy)], \forall x(Jx \rightarrow Fx) \vdash \forall x \forall y[(Jx \& Jy) \rightarrow -Bxy]$$

Because the conclusion is a universal quantification we will adopt the Dash Out proof strategy, so the first three lines of the proof will be:

1   (1) ∀x∀y[Bxy → (Fx ↔ −Fy)]   A
2   (2) ∀x(Jx → Fx)   A
3   (3) −∀x∀y[(Jx & Jy) → −Bxy]   PA

The next move should be a step of QE:

3   (4) ∃x−∀y[(Jx & Jy) → −Bxy]   3 QE

Our first quantifier-instantiation move should be made from line 4 (rather than line 1 or 2) because, as always, we want to make ∃O moves as early in the proof as possible.

3   (5) −∀y[(Ja & Jy) → −Bay]   4 ∃O

Of course, any instantiating constant will do here as well as any other. Next we apply QE to line 5 and ∃O to line 6:

3   (6) ∃x−[(Ja & Jy) → −Bay]   5 QE
3   (7) −[(Ja & Jc) → −Bac]   6 ∃O

On line 7 we can instantiate to any constant except *a*. Now we should apply ∀O to lines 1 and 2. The trick will be to instantiate wisely. It makes sense to start with line 1 because that line contains the predicate letter *B* and line 7 indicates what constants should follow that letter (and in what order).

1	(8) ∀y[Bay → (Fa ↔ −Fy)]	1 ∀O
1	(9) Bac → (Fa ↔ −Fc)	8 ∀O

At this point it will be useful to make some propositional moves.

3	(10) (Ja & Jc) & − −Bac	7 AR
3	(11) Ja & Jc	10 &O
3	(12) Ja	11 &O
3	(13) Jc	11 &O
3	(14) − −Bac	10 &O
3	(15) Bac	14 DN
1,3	(16) Fa ↔ −Fc	9,15 →O

In the wff on line 16, the predicate letter *F* is associated with both *a* and *c*, so it seems smart to instantiate line 2 to both constants, in two separate instantiations, of course.

2	(17) Ja → Fa	2 ∀O
2	(18) Jc → Fc	2 ∀O
2,3	(19) Fa	17,12 →O
2,3	(20) Fc	18,13 →O
1,3	(21) Fa → −Fc	16 ↔O
1,2,3	(22) −Fc	21,19 →O
1,2,3	(23) Fc & −Fc	20,22 &I
1,2	(24) ∀x∀y[(Jx & Jy) → −Bxy]	3-23 −O

Note that the same constant has to occur in both conjuncts of line 23 in order for it to qualify as a standard contradiction. For example, there is nothing contradictory about "Fa & −Fc" I rewrite the proof sans the commentary clutter.

1	(1) ∀x∀y[Bxy → (Fx ↔ −Fy)]	A
2	(2) ∀x(Jx → Fx)	A
3	(3) −∀x∀y[(Jx & Jy) → −Bxy]	PA
3	(4) ∃x−∀y[(Jx & Jy) → −Bxy]	3 QE
3	(5) −∀y[(Ja & Jy) → −Bay]	4 ∃O
3	(6) ∃x−[(Ja & Jy) → −Bay]	5 QE

3	(7)	$-[(Ja \& Jc) \rightarrow -Bac]$	6 ∃O
1	(8)	$\forall y[Bay \rightarrow (Fa \leftrightarrow -Fy)]$	1 ∀O
1	(9)	$Bac \rightarrow (Fa \leftrightarrow -Fc)$	8 ∀O
3	(10)	$(Ja \& Jc) \& --Bac$	7 AR
3	(11)	$Ja \& Jc$	10 &O
3	(12)	Ja	11 &O
3	(13)	Jc	11 &O
3	(14)	$--Bac$	10 &O
3	(15)	Bac	14 DN
1,3	(16)	$Fa \leftrightarrow -Fc$	9,15 →O
2	(17)	$Ja \rightarrow Fa$	2 ∀O
2	(18)	$Jc \rightarrow Fc$	2 ∀O
2,3	(19)	Fa	17,12 →O
2,3	(20)	Fc	18,13 →O
1,3	(21)	$Fa \rightarrow -Fc$	16 ↔O
1,2,3	(22)	$-Fc$	21,19 →O
1,2,3	(23)	$Fc \& -Fc$	20,22 &I
1,2	(24)	$\forall x \forall y[(Jx \& Jy) \rightarrow -Bxy]$	3-23 −O

Next we will construct a proof for this argument:

(M)ushrooms are (f)ungi. So, anyone who {e}ats mushrooms eats fungi.

$$\forall x(Mx \rightarrow Fx) \vdash \forall x\{Px \rightarrow [\exists y(My \& Exy) \rightarrow \exists y(Fy \& Exy)]\}$$

(Px = x is a person) The nineteenth-century mathematician-logician Augustus DeMorgan (after whom the familiar rule of inference is named) used an argument of this form to show the limitations of syllogistic logic, pointing out that its validity could not be established in the traditional system of logic.

1	(1)	$\forall x(Mx \rightarrow Fx)$	A
2	(2)	$-\forall x\{Px \rightarrow [\exists y(My \& Exy) \rightarrow \exists y(Fy \& Exy)]\}$	PA
2	(3)	$\exists x-\{Px \rightarrow [\exists y(My \& Exy) \rightarrow \exists y(Fy \& Exy)]\}$	2 QE
2	(4)	$-\{Pb \rightarrow [\exists y(My \& Eby) \rightarrow \exists y(Fy \& Eby)]\}$	3 ∃O
2	(5)	$Pb \& -[\exists y(My \& Eby) \rightarrow \exists y(Fy \& Eby)]$	4 AR
2	(6)	$-[\exists y(My \& Eby) \rightarrow \exists y(Fy \& Eby)]$	5 &O
2	(7)	$\exists y(My \& Eby) \& -\exists y(Fy \& Eby)$	6 AR
2	(8)	$\exists y(My \& Eby)$	7 &O
2	(9)	$Mc \& Ebc$	8 ∃O

The strategy up to this point has been to make ∃O moves as early in the proof as possible. We should choose *c* as our instantiating constant on line 10 because that forges a link with line 9.

1	(10)	Mc → Fc	1 ∀O
2	(11)	−∃y(Fy & Eby)	7 &O
2	(12)	∀y−(Fy & Eby)	11 QE
2	(13)	−(Fc & Ebc)	12 ∀O

I selected *c* on line 13 because of the pattern of constants on lines 9 and 10. The remainder of the proof is entirely propositional.

2	(14)	Mc	9 &O
1,2	(15)	Fc	10,14 →O
1,2	(16)	−Ebc	13,15 CA
2	(17)	Ebc	9 &O
1,2	(18)	Ebc & −Ebc	17, 16 &I
1	(19)	∀x{Px → [∃y(My & Exy) → ∃y(Fy & Exy)]}	2-18 −O

Proofs for relational arguments are often longer than proofs for property arguments, as the last two proofs have illustrated. These three shortcuts will help shorten many relational proofs:

∀O shortcut: When a quantification begins with two or more contiguous universal quantifiers, you may instantiate all of them in one step of ∀O.

∃O shortcut: When a quantification begins with two or more contiguous existential quantifiers, you may instantiate all of them in one step of ∃O.

∃I shortcut: When a quantification begins with two or more contiguous existential quantifiers, you may derive it in one step of ∃I (from the appropriate instantial wff).

Of course when you take the ∃O shortcut each instantiating constant must be a different dummy name new to the proof so as to satisfy the restriction on the ∃O Rule. These three shortcuts are illustrated in the following proof:

(1)	∀x∀yRxy	A
(2)	∃x∃ySxy	A
(3)	Sab	2 ∃O

(4) Rba	1 ∀O
(5) Rba & Sab	4,3 &I
(6) ∃x∃y(Rxy & Syx)	5 ∃I

How did I select the constants for line 4? By looking ahead to line 5, which in turn was constructed with an eye on lines 3 and 6. (As you know, many proofs are best invented by working from both top and bottom toward the middle.) If we were asked to justify any of the shortcuts introduced in this paragraph, we could show in any proof where it is used how we could reach the same wff by a longer route. Note that the ∀O shortcut does not apply to any of the following wffs because the universal quantifiers are not contiguous:

∀x∃y∀zRxyz

∀x−∀ySxy

∀x(∀yTyx → Fx)

Similar points apply to the other shortcuts.

EXERCISES

1. Complete the following proofs. Every assumption has been identified.

(a) 1   (1) ∀x∀yRxy   A
         (2)   PA
         (3)   2 QE
         (4) −Raa
         (5)   1 ∀O
         (6)   5,4 &I
         (7) ∀xRxx   2-6 −O

*(b) 1   (1) ∃x∀y−Syx   A
          (2) −∀x−∀ySxy   PA
          (3) ∃x− −∀ySxy
          (4) ∀y−Syb
          (5) − −∀yScy
          (6) ∀yScy
          (7) −Scb
          (8) Scb
          (9) Scb & −Scb
         (10) ∀x−∀ySxy

(c) 1   (1) ∀xTxd   A
          (2) ∀x∀y(Txy → Tyx)   A
          (3)   PA
          (4)   3 QE
          (5) −Tde
          (6)   2 ∀O
          (7)   6,5 MT
          (8)
          (9)   8,7 &I
          (10) ∀xTdx

Note: To practice relational proof construction without the need for prior symbolization, see the Chapter Eleven practice problems in the Proofs section of "PredLogic."

Instructions: Symbolize each argument on one horizontal line, using the suggested abbreviations. Construct a proof for each sequent.

2. [G]od did not {c}reate everything since nothing created God.

3. Prove that "Everybody {l}oves everybody" entails each of the following statements:

   *(a) [C]hris loves [B]eth.   (d) There is a person whom Beth and Chris
    (b) Chris loves himself.   both love.
    (c) Chris loves someone.   *(e) Beth loves someone who also loves her.
                                          (f) There is a person who loves everyone.

   (domain: people)

4. An attorney in a cigarette-related cancer case told the jury in his opening statement:

   R.J. Reynolds is a drug company, and I'm going to prove it to you. They sell a drug called nicotine. They sell it in cigarettes. They sold it to Jean Connor.[3]

   His argument:

   Any (c)ompany that {s}ells a (d)rug is a dr(u)g-company. R. J. [R]eynolds is a company that sells [n]icotine. Nicotine is a drug. So, R. J. Reynolds is a drug-company.

   (Sxy = x sells y, Dx = x is a drug, Ux = x is a drug-company)

5. Will Rogers said:

   I'm not a {m}ember of any (o)rganized party−[I]'m a Democrat.

---

   [3](AP) Ron Word, "Decision to smoke argued in tobacco case," *Miami Herald* (April 10, 1997), p. 5B.

Show that this entails:

The [D]emocratic Party is not an organized party.

(Mxy = x is a member of y, Ox = x is an organized party, i = Will Rogers, d = the Democratic Party)

*6. A poem by R. D. Laing[4] begins:

> *[I] don't {r}espect myself*
> *I can't respect anyone who respects me.*

Prove that the second line entails the first. (domain: people; Rxy = x respects y)

7. It is false that there is an integer that is greater than all integers simply because no integer is {g}reater than itself.

(domain: integers; Gxy = x is greater than y)

8. There is an event that {c}auses all events. So, every event is caused by some event.

(domain: events)

9. Plato offers this argument in the *Republic*.[5]

> If A is {m}aster of B, then B is {s}ervant of A. Therefore, because no one is servant of himself or herself, no one is master of himself or herself.

(domain: people)

*10. Sonya Holloway and Michael Cresse filed for divorce, but Michael died in a construction accident on the day the decree was signed. Sonya contended that he died before the decree was signed and asked to have the divorce nullified so that she could collect his workers compensation and life insurance benefits.[6] Her reasoning:

> Two people can obtain a {d}ivorce only if both are (a)live. [M]ichael was not alive. So, [S]onya and Michael did not obtain a divorce.

(domain: people; Dxy = x and y obtain a divorce, Ax = x is alive)

11. In the third panel of the comic strip on the next page Anthony offers this possible explanation for Candace's unfriendliness:

> Being {f}riends means {t}rusting. [C]andace doesn't trust anyone. Hence, Candace isn't friends with anyone.

(domain: people in this comic strip world; Fxy = x is friends with y, Txy = x trusts y)

[4]R. D. Laing, *Knots* (New York: Random House, 1970), p. 18.

[5]430e. *The Dialogues of Plato*, tr. by B. Jowett (2 vols.; New York: Random House, Inc., 1937), I, 694.

[6]"Widow or divorcee? Court to rule," *Miami News* (April 6, 1981), p. 4A.

© Lynn Johnston Productions, Inc./Dist. by United Feature Syndicate, Inc.

12. Everybody {l}oves everybody. It follows that everyone loves and is loved by everyone.

    (domain: people)

13. I advanced this argument in Chapter Three:

    ... We know that not all six statements can be true because the [c]onclusion of "Kodiak II" is the negation of the [f]irst premise of "Kodiak I."

    Add this unstated premise: "If one of these statements is the {n}egation of another, then the first is (t)rue iff the second is not." (domain: the six statements under discussion)

*14. Philosophers W. V. Quine and J. S. Ullian consider this simplistic analysis of *explanation*: "A sentence explains whatever it implies." They reject the proposal for the following reason:

    This would count every sentence as its own explanation, since, trivially, every sentence implies itself.[7]

    Their argument:

    Every sentence {i}mplies itself. It is false that every sentence is its own explanation. Hence, it is false that a sentence {e}xplains whatever it implies.

    (domain: sentences; $Ixy = x$ implies y, $Exy = x$ explains y)

15. In 1989 an officer of the Ku Klux Klan was ejected from the organization when it was discovered that he was Jewish. A newspaper story quoted a rabbi who surmised that the man must hate himself. The rabbi may have reasoned as follows:

    Every member of the (K)KK {h}ates every (J)ew. So, any Jewish member of the KKK hates himself.

---

[7] *The Web of Belief* (New York: Random House, 1970), p. 76.

16. A line from Bob Dylan's song, *Like a Rolling Stone,*[8] "When you got nothing, you got nothing to lose," suggests this argument:

    A thing can be {l}ost only if it is {p}ossessed. Therefore, if you got nothing, you got nothing to lose.

    (Lxy = x can lose y, Pxy = x possesses y)

17. A story in the University of Miami student newspaper about dormitory searches includes these paragraphs:

    All the Search and Seizures have been illegal, according to SBG Vice President Sami Burstyn. To be able to search a student's room, an application for authorization to search must be filled out and signed by a magistrate.

    None of the "Searches" which have taken place this semester have had a magistrate's signature, simply because the magistrates have not been selected.[9]

    Burstyn's argument:

    A (s)earch is (l)egitimate only if some (m)agistrate {a}pproves it. Since there are no magistrates, none of the searches are legitimate.

*18. In 1997 the Air Force published a book-length report intending to put to rest for good rumors about a supposed UFO crash in Roswell, New Mexico, in 1947. According to a newspaper article[10] a main explanation offered in the report for the alleged alien sightings was the Air Force's experiment in the 1950s that involved dropping crash-test dummies from high-altitude balloons. Folks are not buying the explanation for an obvious reason:

    If one event occurs {a}fter another it cannot {e}xplain it. All of the dummy (d)rops occurred after all of the alleged alien (s)ightings. Hence, no dummy drop can explain any of the alleged alien sightings.

    (domain: events; Exy = x can explain y)

19. This explanation in a children's book is formulated as an argument:

    All (s)ounds are {c}aused by something (m)oving back and forth very fast. When something moves back and forth very fast we say it (v)ibrates. So sounds are caused by vibration.[11]

    (Cxy = x causes y) The second premise is a definition.

---

[8]Copyright 1965; renewed 1993 Special Rider Music.

[9]Scott Bressler, "'Room Checks' Cover Up Illegal Searches," *Miami Hurricane* (September 21, 1971), p. 1.

[10](AP) "Air Force: No aliens, just dummies," *Asheville Citizen-Times* (June 25, 1997), p. A2.

[11]Illa Podendorf, *The True Book of Sounds We Hear* (Chicago: Children's Press, 1955), p. 8.

20. (CHALLENGE)

> Logical e{q}uivalence is mutual e{n}tailment. Every statement entails any logical (t)ruth. Therefore, all logical truths are logically equivalent.

(domain: statements; Qxy = x is logically equivalent to y, Nxy = x entails y) The first premise is a definition.

21. (CHALLENGE) The prose-poem *Desiderata*[12] includes this passage:

> *If you compare yourself with others, you may become vain and bitter; for always there will be greater and lesser persons than yourself.*

An argument is suggested:

> If one {c}ompares oneself with {g}reater people, one will become (b)itter. And if one compares oneself with lesser people, one will become (v)ain. If people compare themselves with others, they will compare themselves with some who are greater as well as some who are lesser. Consequently, if you compare yourself with others, you will become vain and bitter.

(domain: people; Cxy = x compares x with y)

22. (CHALLENGE) Plato has this to say in the *Gorgias* about the brigand with undisciplined appetites:

> *... Such a man could be dear neither to any other man nor to God, since he is incapable of fellowship, and where there is no fellowship, friendship cannot be.*[13]

Symbolize the argument using this dictionary. domain: persons; Ux = x is undisciplined, Hx = x is a human, Rxy = x can have friendship with y, g = God, Exy = x can have fellowship with y. Set the argument up with two premises.

---

[12]This piece has been widely reported to date from the American Colonial period but in fact was composed in 1927 by Max Ehrmann.

[13]507e. *The Collected Dialogues of Plato*, ed. by Edith Hamilton and Huntington Cairns (Princeton, N.J.: Princeton University Press, 1961), p. 290.

12

Relational CEXes and Trees

A newspaper letter-writer appeals to the U.S. Constitution in his defense of capital punishment:

> ... *"Nor shall any state deprive any person of life ... without due process of law." (14th Amendment.)*
>
> *Therefore, one may conclude correctly that, after applying due process, a state may deprive a person of his life.*[1]

The author of the letter appears to be employing this reasoning (call the argument "Capital Punishment"):

> A U.S. (s)tate {m}ay not deprive a person of {l}ife without providing due p(r)ocess. Therefore, a state may deprive a person of life if it provides due process.
>
> $\forall x \forall y[(Sx \ \& \ Lyx) \rightarrow (-Rxy \rightarrow -Mxy)]$
> $\vdash \forall x \forall y[(Sx \ \& \ Lyx) \rightarrow (Rxy \rightarrow Mxy)]$

(Lxy = x is y's act of carrying out a death penalty, Rxy = x provides due process in connection with y, Mxy = x may perform y) This reasoning is invalid. The premise asserts that due process is a necessary condition for the legitimacy of capital punishment, and the conclusion claims that it is a sufficient

---

[1] *Miami Herald* (August 4, 1993), p. 12A.

condition. We have not yet discussed techniques for establishing the invalidity of relational arguments such as this one. The two techniques explained previously for establishing the invalidity of property arguments may be extended to relational logic; that is the subject of this chapter. We will soon be able to demonstrate the invalidity of "Capital Punishment."

12.1 CEXes

Let's begin by considering a quite simple argument (call it "Causation I"):

> Every event has a cause. Hence, some event is the cause of all events.
>
> $\forall x \exists y Cyx \vdash \exists x \forall y Cxy$

(domain: events; Cxy = x causes y) This actual-world CEX will establish invalidity:

CEX dictionary:	domain: people; Cxy = x is a parent of y
CEX:	Everyone has (or had) a parent. (T)
	So, there is a person who is a parent of all people. (F)

And here is a second CEX that does the job:

CEX dictionary:	domain: integers; Cxy = x is greater than y
CEX:	For every integer there is a greater integer. (T)
	So, there is an integer that is greater than all integers. (F)

When creating relational CEXes you must distinguish between property and relational predicates. The new meanings assigned to property predicate letters must involve properties rather than relations, and the meanings assigned to relational predicate letters must involve relations and not properties. Each of the following would be a mistaken assignment:

> Ax = x is mother of y
> Bxy = x is female

Note that "is a mother" is a property predicate, while "is mother of" is a relational predicate. Most relational predicate letters we have considered represent two-place relations, but we will consider some relations involving three or more relata. Meanings assigned to relational predicate letters must observe this distinction. The following assignments would be wrong:

Cxy = x gave y to z
Dxyz = x is mother of y

These meaning assignments are legitimate:

Cxy = x gave a watch to y
Cxy = x gave y to John
Dxyz = x is mother of y and z

We can apply the technique of possible-world CEXes to relational arguments, and in particular we may employ the graphic CEXes devisable in the tutorial program *PredLogic*. For example, this CEX does the trick for "Causation I:"

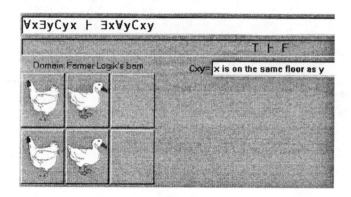

CEX: Each animal is on the same floor as some animal. (T)
So, there is some animal that is on the same floor as every animal. (F)

Note that we could simplify this CEX by deleting the ducks (or, alternatively, by expelling the chickens). The premise would remain true and the conclusion would still be false if we removed the ducks from the barn.

Now let's apply these CEX techniques to "Capital Punishment," which we symbolized:

∀x∀y[(Sx & Lyx) → (−Rxy → −Mxy)]
⊢ ∀x∀y[(Sx & Lyx) → (Rxy → Mxy)]

An actual-world CEX:

CEX dictionary: domain: people; Sx = x is an adult, Lxy = x is related to y, Rxy = x is a parent of y, Mxy = x is mother of y

CEX: An adult to whom an individual is related is not
                            that person's mother if he or she is not that per-
                            son's parent. (T)

                            So, an adult to whom an individual is related is
                            that person's mother if she or he is that person's
                            parent. (F)

For proof that the conclusion is false consider that Chelsea Clinton is related to
an adult (namely, Bill Clinton) who is her parent but is not her mother.

We can also create a CEX for "Capital Punishment" using *Farmer Logik's
barn*:

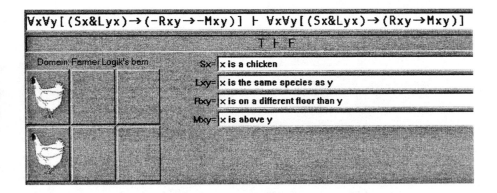

$\forall x \forall y [(Sx \& Lyx) \rightarrow (-Rxy \rightarrow -Mxy)] \vdash \forall x \forall y [(Sx \& Lyx) \rightarrow (Rxy \rightarrow Mxy)]$

T ⊢ F

Domain: Farmer Logik's barn

Sx= x is a chicken
Lxy= x is the same species as y
Rxy= x is on a different floor than y
Mxy= x is above y

CEX: For any chicken and any animal of the same species, if the
            chicken is not on a different floor than (that is, if it *is* on the
            same floor as) the animal, then it's not above the animal. (T)
            So, for any chicken and any animal of the same species, if the
            chicken is on a different floor than the animal, then it's above
            the animal. (F)

The lower chicken makes the conclusion false because, while it is on a different
floor than the higher chicken, it is not above it.

Consider this argument ("Causation II"):

> Every event *has* a cause. Thus, every event *is* a cause.
>
> $\forall x \exists y Cyx \vdash \forall x \exists y Cxy$

(domain: events; Cxy = x causes y) This actual-world CEX proves invalidity:

CEX dictionary: domain: positive integers; Cxy = x is greater
                        than y

CEX: For every positive integer there is a greater posi-
                   tive integer. (T)
                   So, every positive integer is greater than some pos-
                   itive integer. (F)

Of course the conclusion is false because one is greater than no positive integer.

Proving the invalidity of "Causation II" in *Farmer Logik's barn* proves to be somewhat of a challenge because almost all of the meanings available in the program for a two-place (dyadic) relational predicate either make the premise false or the conclusion true, and neither of these conditions will lead to a successful CEX. A couple of unusual meanings were included in the program for problems like this one.

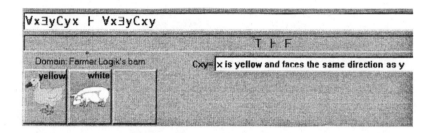

CEX: For each animal (in the barn) there is some yellow animal that faces the same direction. (T)
             So, each animal is yellow, and faces the same direction as some animal. (F)

The conclusion is false because the pig is not yellow.

This argument involves the triadic relation *giving:*

Everyone {g³}ave something to someone. Therefore, someone gave everything to someone.

$$\forall x[Px \rightarrow \exists y(Py \ \& \ \exists z Gxzy)] \vdash \exists x[Px \ \& \ \exists y(Py \ \& \ \forall z Gxzy)]$$

(Px = x is a person, Gxyz = x gives y to z) An actual-world CEX:

CEX dictionary: Px = x is a person, Gxyz = x has touched both y and z
CEX: Each person has touched something and some person. (T)
                        So, there is a person who has touched everything and some person. (F)

A possible-world CEX:

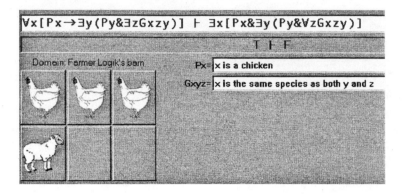

$\forall x[Px \rightarrow \exists y(Py\&\exists zGxzy)] \;\vdash\; \exists x[Px\&\exists y(Py\&\forall zGxzy)]$

T ⊢ F

Domain: Farmer Logik's barn

Px= x is a chicken

Gxyz= x is the same species as both y and z

CEX: Each chicken is the same species as some chicken and some animal. (T)
So, there is a chicken that is the same species as some chicken and each animal. (F)

The conclusion is false because there is no chicken that is the same species as the sheep.

Here is a fine point about quantification: two (or more) variables in a wff may refer to the same individual. So, you could boot two chickens out of the barn and the CEX above will still work. The premise of the CEX will remain true even though there is but one chicken left in the domain.

Finally, let's consider an argument whose symbolization involves a mixed wff.

> If all who accept bribes are (c)orrupt, then so are all who give them. It follows that in any case of bribery, if the acceptor is corrupt, then so is the briber.

> $\forall x(\exists yByx \rightarrow Cx) \rightarrow \forall x(\exists yBxy \rightarrow Cx) \;\vdash\; \forall x\forall y[Bxy \rightarrow (Cy \rightarrow Cx)]$

(domain: people; Bxy = x bribes y) An actual-world CEX:

CEX dictionary: domain: people; Bxy = x is older than y, Cx = x is a minor

CEX: If all who are younger than someone are minors, then all who are older than someone are minors. (T)
So, if one person is older than another, then if the second is a minor so is the first. (F)

It is easy to see why the conclusion is false; George W. Bush is not a minor and is older than any number of minors. But why is the premise true? Because its antecedent is false; remember that a conditional is false iff its antecedent is true and its consequent false. The antecedent is false because some people—in fact billions—who are younger than others are not minors.

While this CEX establishes invalidity conclusively, it may not be intuitively satisfying. If we expend some mental effort we should be able to devise a more satisfying CEX. Here is one:

CEX dictionary: domain: people; Bxy = x is a sibling of y, Cx = x is female

CEX: If all who have siblings are females, then all who are siblings are females. (T)
So, if one person is a sibling of another, then if the second is female so is the first. (F)

The conclusion is falsified by any brother–sister pair.

In general, the CEX method requires more ingenuity when applied to relational arguments than when used with property arguments. To some extent it will be necessary to operate on a trial-and-error basis. When one attempt at finding a suitable interpretation fails, you will need to modify it or scrap it and begin again.

EXERCISES

Instructions: Symbolize (where necessary) and establish invalidity by constructing (either actual-world or possible-world) CEXes. If you use "PredLogic," remember to add the English version of your CEX.

1. Prove that "Somebody {l}oves somebody" does not entail any of the following statements. Assign the same meaning to the predicate for all six problems.

   (a) [C]hris loves [B]eth.   (d) Each person loves someone (or other).

   *(b) Chris loves himself.   (e) There is a person who loves everyone.

   (c) Chris loves someone.   *(f) Everybody loves everybody.

   (domain: people)

2. (a) Since [D]enise {k}nows [H]ope, Hope knows Denise.

   (b) Whoever knows Hope knows [R]achel. It follows that anyone known by Hope is known by Rachel.

   (c) Whoever knows Hope knows Rachel. Hence, anyone who doesn't know Hope doesn't know Rachel.

   *(d) Denise knows Hope and Rachel. Thus, Hope knows Rachel.

   (domain: people)

3. The cavemen seem to reason:

> Snowflake [a] is not like snowflake [b]. This shows that no two
> snowflakes are alike.

(domain: snowflakes in this fictional realm; Lxy = x is like y)

By permission of Johnny Hart and Creators Syndicate, Inc.

4. One introduction-to-philosophy textbook advances this argument (not
   stated quite so explicitly, of course):

> Human (a)cts are not {c}aused by (m)otives. Thus, human acts are not
> caused by anything.

(Cxy = x causes y)

5. Anyone who {l}oves anyone loves herself because anyone who loves everyone
   loves herself.

(domain: people)

6. *(a) ∃x(Bax v Cax) ⊢ ∃x(Bax & Cax)
   (b) ∃x∃y[(Dx & Ey) & Fxy] ⊢ ∃x∃y[(Dx & Ey) & Fyx]
   (c) ∀x∀y(Gxy → Hxy) ⊢ ∀x∀y(−Gxy → −Hxy)
   (d) ∀x(Ix → ∃yKyx) ⊢ ∀x(Ix → ∃yKxy)
   *(e) ∀x∀y(Jxy → Jyx) ⊢ ∀xJxx

7. For any consistent formal (s)ystem of arithmetic there is some truth of (a)rith-
   metic that is not a {t}heorem in that system.[2] Therefore, there is some truth of
   arithmetic that is not a theorem of any consistent formal system of arithmetic.

(Sx = x is a consistent formal system of arithmetic, Ax = x is a truth of
arithmetic, Txy = x is a theorem of y)

8. If someone is a {b}rother of someone, then the first person is a {s}ibling of the
   second. [T]ed is brother of [C]armen. Hence, Carmen is brother of Ted,
   because if anyone is a sibling of anyone, then the second person is a sibling of
   the first.

(domain: people)

[2]Established by Kurt Gödel.

9. Philosopher Carl Hempel seems to advance this argument:[3]

> Any two evolutionary ethical systems that are (v)alidly derived from the theory of evolution will not {c}onflict. Every system of evolutionary ethics conflicts with some evolutionary ethics. It follows that no evolutionary ethical systems are validly derived from the theory of evolution.

(domain: evolutionary ethical systems; Vx = x is validly derived from the theory of evolution, Cxy = x conflicts with y)

*10. A draft of a master's thesis contained this passage:

> *Temporal priority is not essential to the idea of causation. For surely there are events which are temporally prior to other events without being considered as the cause of those events.*

(domain: events) The conclusion of this argument (the first sentence) may be restated "It is false that every event that {c}auses an event is {p}rior to it."

11. Philosopher Norman Malcolm writes:

> *Bodily sensations are located where they are felt to be. People do not feel sensations in their brains. (Brain tissue is actually insensitive.) Therefore, bodily sensations are not brain processes.*[4]

On one interpretation of this passage, Malcolm is arguing:

> If a (s)ensation is {f}elt to be at a given place, then it is {l}ocated at that place. No sensation is felt to be in a (b)rain. Therefore, sensations are not located in brains.

(Fxy = x is felt to be in place y, Lxy = x is located in place y)

12. (CHALLENGE)

> Every (v)alid wff in (n)ormal form is (d)erivable. Any wff either is in normal form or is {r}educible to some wff in normal form. A wff that is reducible to a derivable wff in normal form is itself derivable. Therefore, every valid wff is derivable.

(domain: wffs)

12.2   Truth Trees

This argument is valid:

> If a (p)erson is infected with {A}IDS by means of some substance, that substance contains (w)hite blood cells. No (s)weat contains white blood cells.[5] It follows that no one is infected with AIDS by means of sweat.

[3]See *Aspects of Scientific Explanation* (New York: The Free Press, 1965), pp. 86–87.
[4]*Problems of Mind* (New York: Harper & Row, Publishers, 1971), pp. 69–70.
[5]An exception to the second premise would occur if sweat commingled with a trace of blood.

∀x∀y[(Px & Ayx) → Wy], ∀x(Sx → −Wx) ⊢ ∀x∀y[(Px & Ayx) → −Sy]

(Axy = substance x infects y with AIDS) A truth tree will establish validity.

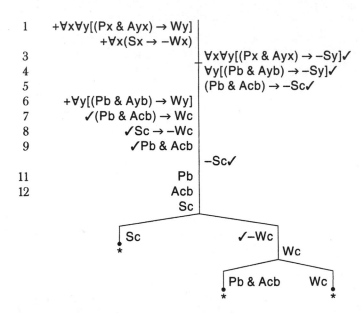

All tree branches close, so we have a demonstration of validity. In the ∀R move from the third line to the fourth (and the ∀L move from line 1 to 6) we use the revised definition of *instance* that was introduced in the last chapter; this definition accommodates quantifications having more than one quantifier. In the two ∀ steps (from line 3 to 4 and from 4 to 5) I arbitrarily selected *b* and *c* as constants; of course, both had to be new to the branch. Every subsequent instantiation was made with the goal of achieving branch closure. So, for example, on line 6 I chose *b* as my instantiating constant because I saw that it follows the predicate *P* on line 5. In the move from 6 to 7, I selected *c* because it follows the predicate *A* on 5. Just as with relational proofs, the most difficult aspect of relational truth trees is the wise selection of instantiating constants.

It is good general strategy to postpone branching as long as possible. With that in mind I decomposed the conjunction on line 9 before working with the conditionals on lines 7 and 8. However, after I had completed the tree I realized that there was no need to decompose line 9 at all. Note that the wffs on lines 11 and 12 (the ones derived from line 9) play no role in closing any branch. The tree above is correct although inelegant.

Let's adopt shortcuts for the tree rules that parallel the proof-rule shortcuts explained in the last chapter. Whenever a quantification on the left of a branch begins with two or more contiguous universal quantifiers, we may eliminate all those quantifiers in one step of ∀L. Similar shortcuts may be taken with the other three rules. These shortcuts may not be taken when the quantifiers involved are both universal and existential. Of course, when taking the ∃L and ∀R shortcuts each variable must be replaced by a different constant that is new to the branch. Applying shortcuts to the tree above would shorten it by two lines.

Next let's construct a tree for this invalid argument:

Someone does not {l}ove someone. Thus, someone does love someone.

∃x∃y−Lxy ⊢ ∃x∃yLxy

(domain: people)

```
                ✓∃x∃y−Lxy
        2                  |  ∃x∃yLxy+
        3           ✓−Lab  |
        4                  |  Lab
        5                  |  Laa
        6                  |  Lab
        7                  |  Lba
        8                  |  Lbb
                           o
```

("Lab" occurs on lines 4 and 6; 4 comes from line 3 and 6 from 2.) The tree is open, establishing the sequent's invalidity. Recall the Plus Principle from Chapter Eight:

> **If an open branch contains a quantification marked with a plus that has not yet been instantiated to some constant that occurs on that branch, then the quantification must be instantiated to that constant also before the branch may be marked open.**

That principle requires that the quantification on line 2 be instantiated four times over (which is done on lines 5 through 8). The requirement is theoretically desirable but impractical for relational trees. Observing it would produce some trees so large as to be entirely unfeasible. Consider an example.

∃x∃y∃zRxyz ⊢ ∃x∃y∃z−Rxyz

```
                ✓∃x∃y∃zRxyz
        2                    |  ∃x∃y∃z−Rxyz+
        3              Rabc  |
                             |  −Rabc✓
                       Rabc  |
                             o
```

If we adhered to the Plus Principle when constructing this tree, we would instantiate the wff on line 2 exactly 27 times because each of its variables would be instantiated to each of the three constants that appear on line 3 ($3 \times 3 \times 3 = 27$). But clearly, instantiating the first variable of the wff on line 2 to *b* or *c* will not lead to branch closure, so those moves would be a waste of effort and paper. The same applies to instantiating the second variable to *a* or *c* and the third to *a* or *b*. So, for reasons of practicality we now relax the Plus Principle:

> **(The Relaxed Plus Principle) If an open branch contains a quantification marked with a plus that has not yet been instantiated to some constant that occurs on that branch, then the quantification must be instantiated to that constant also *if doing so could lead to branch closure.***

But someone might realize that even the first instantiation of the wff on line 2 in the tree above cannot lead to branch closure and so, in the spirit of the Relaxed Plus Principle, mark the tree open after the third line in the tree. But that would overlook another requirement that applies to all truth trees: **A branch may not be marked open if it contains undispatched decomposable wffs**.

Replacing the Plus Principle with the Relaxed Plus Principle makes a fundamental change in the logical nature of the device of truth trees. Having adopted the Relaxed Plus Principle we can no longer say with absolute certainty that a sequent for which we have produced an open tree is invalid, because it is possible that we failed to see that an additional instantiation of some plus-marked wff would in fact have led to tree closure. This is a theoretical problem but not much of a practical problem because almost always we will be able to determine whether additional instantiations would be productive. Notice that this problem does not infect trees that close. A closed tree still demonstrates validity with absolute certainty.

I can illustrate the use of the Relaxed Plus Principle by constructing a tree for "Capital Punishment:"

When I instantiate line 1 on line 10, I choose a and b in that order to match the order of the constants on line 3. There are three other possible instantiations of line 1 involving the constants a and b, but it is evident that none of those instantiations could lead to branch closure, so, in accordance with the Relaxed Plus Principle, I ignore those ∀L moves.

The tree for this invalid argument presents a situation we have not yet faced:

> Every integer is exceeded by some integer. Hence, there is an integer that {e}xceeds all integers.

∀x∃yEyx ⊢ ∃x∀yExy

(domain: integers)

```
1     +∀x∃yEyx |
2              |_∃x∀yExy+
      ✓∃yEya
       Eba
5              | ∀yEby✓
6              | Ebc
7     ✓∃yEyc
       Edc
9              | ∀yEdy✓
10             | Ede
              ∞
```

When we instantiate line 5 on line 6, we have to select a constant new to the branch (c), but the arrival of c requires us to re-instantiate line 1 (done on line 7). But now we have to instantiate line 7 to a constant new to the branch (d), and that leads to a re-instantiation of line 2 (on line 9), which in turn leads to the introduction of a new constant (e) on line 10. You can see that this cycle of instantiation could in principle go on infinitely. We make the practical decision to terminate the branch, and we mark it with the infinity symbol ("∞") to indicate that the branch has fallen into an endless cycle of instantiations. For practical purposes marking a branch with "∞" establishes the invalidity of the sequent, although there is always the theoretical possibility that continued instantiations could lead to branch closure. When may we terminate a "looping" branch with "∞"? Here is an arbitrary ruling:

Do not close a looping branch until each plus-marked line involved in the cycling has been instantiated twice.

That is the policy followed in the tree above. This pattern of quantifiers typically results in looping: "∀∃" on the left side of a branch coupled with "∃∀" on the right side of the same branch.

You can see that there are two reasons why the truth-tree method is not an effective procedure for relational sequents (as it was for property sequents): (1) we relaxed the Plus Principle, and (2) some trees involve looping. Of course we could overcome the first problem by sticking with the original version of the Plus Principle. However, there is no way to overcome the second problem.

In the interest of efficiency I recommend the adoption of one more short-cut for relational trees: When you complete an open (or a looping) branch, you may stop work on the tree. Continuing the tree could never show tree closure. (I could have recommended this shortcut for property trees, but the savings in effort would have been negligible.)

EXERCISES

13. Complete the following truth trees.

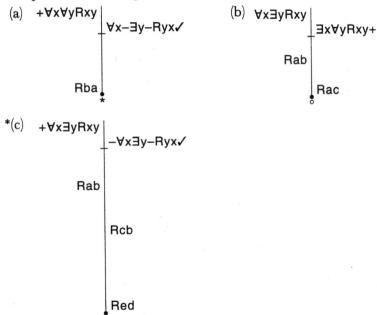

Instructions: Symbolize and test by the truth-tree method. Indicate whether the sequents are valid or invalid.

14. (a) An argument in *Propositional Logic*:

> ... *All contradictions (and therefore all (s)tandard contradictions) are logically {e}quivalent).*[6]

---

[6]Rev. 3rd ed. (Upper Saddle River, NJ: Prentice-Hall, Inc., 2000), pp. 63–64.

*(b) A related argument:

> All standard contradictions (and therefore all contradictions) are logically equivalent.

(domain: contradictory statements; Exy = x is logically equivalent to y, Sx = x is a standard contradiction)

15. Two attempts at representing the caveman's reasoning:

(a) [G]rog has a larger {c}ranium than the [s]peaker but is not more {i}ntelligent than the speaker. Thus, it is false that if one creature has a larger cranium than a second, the first is more intelligent than the second.

(b) [G]rog has a larger {c}ranium than the [s]peaker but is not more {i}ntelligent than the speaker. Thus, it is false that if one creature is more intelligent than a second, the first has a larger cranium than the second.

(domain: creatures in this fictional realm; Cxy = x has a larger cranium than y, Ixy = x is more intelligent than y) The best statement of the conclusion would be neither of the above, but rather "It is false that one creature is more intelligent than a second iff the first has a larger cranium than the second."

By permission of Johnny Hart and Creators Syndicate, Inc.

16. (a) Lyrics: "Everybody {l}oves a (w)inner, but nobody loves [m]e."[7] Does this entail "I am not a winner"?

*(b) The lyrics might have run "Everybody loves a winner, but I am not a winner." Does this entail "Nobody loves me"?

(domain: people)

17. Demonstrate the validity of these arguments from Chapter Eleven by constructing trees.

(a) 7; (b) 11; (c) 16; *(d) 15; (e) 17

---

[7]From the song *Maybe This Time*, lyrics by Fred Ebb.

18. Demonstrate the invalidity of these arguments from the previous section by constructing trees.

    (a) 10; (b) 4; *(c) 8; (d) 9; (e) 11

19. A Haywood County (North Carolina) commissioner was tried for attempting to bribe a sheriff's deputy. A newspaper reporter observed,

    > *If convicted of a felony charge Howell could no longer be a commissioner, since those holding elective offices must be able to vote for those offices, and convicted felons aren't allowed to vote.*[8]

    Treat the material following *since* as two premises (rather than one conjunctive premise). (Fx = x is a convicted felon, h = Howell, Oxy = x is permitted to hold office y, c = the office of Haywood County commissioner, Vxy = x is permitted to vote for office y)

20. *(a) There is a person who is hated by no one. So, no one {h}ates everyone.

    (b) No one hates everyone. So, there is a person who is hated by no one.

    (domain: people)

21. Philosopher David Hume writes:

    > *Since morals, therefore, have an influence on the actions . . . , it follows, that they cannot be deriv'd from reason; and that because reason alone, as we have already prov'd, can never have any such influence.*[9]

    Use this dictionary: m = morals, Ixy = x influences y, a = actions, Dxy = x can be derived from y, r = reason) Clearly there is an unstated premise that connects *influence* with *derivability*. Evaluate the two arguments that result from adding supplemental premises (a) and (b).

    (a) If one thing can be derived from a second, and the second influences a third, then the first influences the third.

    (b) If one thing can be derived from a second, and the first influences a third, then the second influences the third.

*22. Fredrik Pohl and C. M. Kornbluth often collaborated on science fiction stories. Pohl was also an editor who made publishing decisions. He comments:

    > *Nearly everything Cyril and I wrote together got published. After all, once I was finished revising it there was at least one editor who, by definition, was pleased with it. So if it didn't sell somewhere else the first time or two out, it always sold to me.*[10]

---

[8]Hannah Mitchell, "Haywood commissioner goes on trial for alleged bribery try," *Asheville Citizen-Times* (July 16, 1996), p. 1A.

[9]*A Treatise of Human Nature,* ed. by L. A. Selby-Bigge, Book III, section 1 (Oxford: The Clarendon Press, 1888, 1960), p. 457.

[10]Introduction by Pohl to Pohl and C. M. Kornbluth, *Before the Universe and Other Stories* (New York: Bantam Books, Inc., 1980), p. x.

Pohl's argument, made even more explicit:

> Everything[11] (c)o-authored by Pohl and Kornbluth was p(u)blished. Here are the reasons: All of the writings co-authored by Pohl and Kornbluth p{l}eased P[o]hl. All of the writings co-authored by Pohl and Kornbluth that pleased some (e)ditor were published. Pohl was an editor.

(Cx = x is a writing co-authored by Pohl and Kornbluth)

23. An aphorism by George Bernard Shaw:

> *The reasonable man adapts himself to the world; the unreasonable one persists in trying to adapt the world to himself. Therefore, all progress depends on the unreasonable man.*[12]

Shaw's argument is the valid one of these two:

(a) All (p)rogress {d}epends on people who (t)ry to adapt the world to themselves. All (u)nreasonable people try to adapt the world to themselves. Therefore, all progress depends on the unreasonable person.

(b) All progress depends on people who try to adapt the world to themselves. All people who try to adapt the world to themselves are unreasonable. Therefore, all progress depends on the unreasonable person.

(Tx = x is a person who tries to adapt the world to x, Ux − x is an unreasonable person)

24. Defense attorney Vincent Bugliosi writes:

> *Mr. Enoki [the prosecutor] argued that this shows Jennifer cannot be trusted to tell the truth now. In other words, once a liar, always a liar. The only problem with that type of reasoning is that I don't believe that any human being always tells the truth.*[13]

His inference appears to be:

> No (p)erson always tells the truth, but it is false that no people are to be trusted. Hence, it is false that every person who once told something that is not true is not to be trusted.

(Sxy = x says y, Ax = x is true, Bx = x is to be trusted)

---

[11] I employ "logician's license" and make this claim universal. (Pohl explains that there were two exceptions to the claim.) Note that by the time Pohl reaches the final sentence in the quotation he, himself, has switched to universal mode.

[12] "Reason," in "Maxims for Revolutionists," in *Man and Superman: A Comedy and a Philosophy* (New York: Brentano's, 1928), p. 238.

[13] *Outrage: The Five Reasons Why O. J. Simpson Got Away with Murder* (New York: W. W. Norton, 1996), p. 174.

25. (MAJOR CHALLENGE) Railroad labor law reasoning:[14]

> Anyone who is an agent of a union is an agent of each member of the union. Any grievance committee chair for a union is an agent of that union. A grievance committee chair for a union has a duty to prosecute (against the railroad) the claims made by anyone for whom he or she is agent. It follows that a grievance committee chair of a union has a duty to prosecute (against the railroad) the claims made by any union member.

(Axy = x is agent of y, Ux = x is a union, Mxy = x is member of y, Gxy = x is a grievance committee chair for organization y, Dxy = x has a duty to prosecute the claims against the railroad made by y)

[14]Marchitto v. Central R.R. Co. of New Jersey, 88 A.2d 851 (N.J. 1952).

13

Relational-Logic Refinements

I conclude the treatment of relational logic by discussing quantifier scope, quantifier order, and properties of relations, and by defining key logical terms such as *wff*.

13.1 Quantifier Scope

Here are four possible symbolizations for statement S1:

(S1) Whoever {k}ills any person is (w)icked.

(domain: people; Kxy = x kills y, Wx = x is wicked)

(F2) $\forall x \forall y(Kxy \rightarrow Wx)$
(F3) $\forall x(\forall yKxy \rightarrow Wx)$
(F4) $\forall x \exists y(Kxy \rightarrow Wx)$
(F5) $\forall x(\exists yKxy \rightarrow Wx)$

Two of these symbolizations are correct and two are not. Can you tell which are correct; can you explain what is wrong with the others? S2 through S5 are literal English readings of these four wffs:

(S2) For any two people, if the first kills the second, then the first is wicked.
(S3) Any person who kills everyone is wicked.

(S4) For any person there exists a person such that if the first kills the second, then the first is wicked.

(S5) Any person who kills someone *(anyone)* is wicked.

According to S2 and S5 (and F2 and F5) killing *a single* individual is a sufficient condition for wickedness (and that is the claim expressed by S1). S3 (and F3) expresses the very different claim that killing *everyone* is a sufficient condition for being wicked. Notice that the sole difference between F2 and F3 is the scope of the *y* quantifier. Recall that the scope of a quantifier consists of the quantifier plus the quantifier-scope groupers and everything located between those groupers. In F2 the scope of the *y* quantifier is "$\forall y(Kxy \rightarrow Wx)$," while in F3 it is merely "$\forall yKxy$." This CEX shows that F2 and F3 are not equivalent (by showing that F3 does not entail F2).

symbolization:	$\forall x(\forall yKxy \rightarrow Wx) \vdash \forall x\forall y(Kxy \rightarrow Wx)$
CEX dictionary:	domain: people; $Kxy = x$ hates y, $Wx = x$ is a misanthrope
CEX:	People who hate everyone are misanthropes. (T)
	So, people who hate anyone are misanthropes. (F)

F4 and F5 differ only in the scope of the *y* quantifier. F5 is another acceptable symbolization for S1. What about F4? Believe it or not, F4 is equivalent to F3 and so is not a correct symbolization of S1. You may find it hard to believe that F3 and F4 are equivalent, so I'll prove it with two trees.

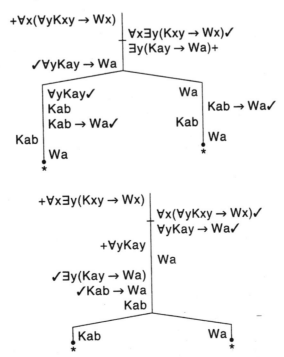

We know that F3 is a mistaken symbolization of S1, and these trees prove that F4 is also wrong. The moral of the preceding discussion is that quantifier scope is a critical element in determining the content of a wff. We won't master the finer parts of the art of symbolization without getting clearer about quantifier scope.

The two wffs in each cell of the table below are equivalent:

∀xFx & P	∀x(Fx & P)	P & ∀xFx	∀x(P & Fx)
∃xFx & P	∃x(Fx & P)	P & ∃xFx	∃x(P & Fx)
∀xFx v P	∀x(Fx v P)	P v ∀xFx	∀x(P v Fx)
∃xFx v P	∃x(Fx v P)	P v ∃xFx	∃x(P v Fx)

(*P* represents any wff that does not contain the variable *x*.) This shows that the scope of a quantifier can be expanded or contracted across an ampersand or a wedge without changing the content of the wff. It would be reasonable to expect that what holds for ampersands and wedges will hold also for arrows, and it does in some cases, but not in all. In this table the two wffs in each cell are equivalent.

∀xFx → P	∃x(Fx → P)	P → ∀xFx	∀x(P → Fx)
∃xFx → P	∀x(Fx → P)	P → ∃xFx	∃x(P → Fx)

So, when you expand the scope of a universal quantifier from the *antecedent* of a conditional to the entire wff, the quantifier must be replaced by an existential quantifier to retain equivalence. And when you expand the scope of an existential quantifier from the antecedent to the whole wff, the quantifier must be replaced by a universal quantifier to maintain equivalence. On the other hand, when you expand from a *consequent* the quantifier remains the same. How is this surprising asymmetry to be explained? Consider this series of steps:

∀xFx → P		P → ∀xFx
−∀xFx v P	equivalent to the above by the Arrow Rule	−P v ∀xFx
∃x−Fx v P	equivalent in virtue of the QE pattern[1]	
∃x(−Fx v P)	equivalent by the expansion of quantifier scope across a wedge	∀x(−P v Fx)
∃x(Fx → P)	equivalent in virtue of the Arrow Rule	∀x(P → Fx)

---

[1] In our proof system the QE Rule may not be applied to line fragments, but the equivalence of the second and third wffs (in the left column) could be established in a series of steps. Similarly, regarding the move to the last wff (in both columns), it would not be correct to apply the Arrow Rule inside the scope of a quantifier, but the result could be established by a series of moves.

You see that the QE pattern comes into play when the expansion begins with an antecedent but not when it starts from a consequent.

Now we can see why F2 and F5 are equivalent.

(F2) $\forall x \forall y (Kxy \rightarrow Wx)$ (F5) $\forall x (\exists y Kxy \rightarrow Wx)$
(F3) $\forall x (\forall y Kxy \rightarrow Wx)$

The expanded scope of the y quantifier in F2 is contracted to the antecedent in F5 and the two y quantifiers are different—one universal and the other existential. (A similar account applies to the equivalence of F3 and F4.) We can also see why F2 is not equivalent to F3, because both y quantifiers are universal.

Dialogue from an old mummy movie:

> *He who de{f}iles an Egyptian (t)omb, d(i)es.*

(Px = x is a person, Fxy = x defiles y, Tx = x is an Egyptian tomb, Ix = x dies) A claim is being made about *any*one who does this dastardly act, so the symbolization will begin with a universal quantifier:

$\forall x [(x$ is a person & x defiles some Egyptian tomb$) \rightarrow x$ dies$]$

We need another quantifier to refer to the tomb, but will it be universal or existential? That depends on the scope we give to the new quantifier. We have these three choices:

(F6) $\forall x \{[Px \ \& \ \exists y (Ty \ \& \ Fxy)] \rightarrow Ix\}$
(F7) $\forall x \{\exists y [Px \ \& \ (Ty \ \& \ Fxy)] \rightarrow Ix\}$
(F8) $\forall x \forall y \{[Px \ \& \ (Ty \ \& \ Fxy)] \rightarrow Ix\}$

In F6 the y quantifier has the smallest scope possible given that it must bind all occurrences of y. The existential quantifier is the right choice since (according to the claim being advanced) it takes only *one* defiled tomb to trigger death. In F7 the quantifier has been expanded across the ampersand and it remains existential. But in F8 the scope is expanded further, from the antecedent of the conditional to the entire conditional,[2] and that calls for a change to a universal quantifier.

In Chapter Ten I offered two symbolizations for the Alcoholics Anonymous principle "Only a drunk can help another drunk:"

$\forall x \forall y [(Dx \ \& \ Hyx) \rightarrow Dy]$
$\forall x [\exists y (Dy \ \& \ Hxy) \rightarrow Dx]$

---

[2]Strictly speaking "[Px & (Ty & Fxy)] → Ix" is not a conditional because the formula fragments preceding and following the arrow are not themselves wffs, but it will be convenient to write in this loose way.

This sequence of steps shows why these two wffs are equivalent.

∀x∀y[(Dx & Hyx) → Dy]	first symbolization
∀y∀x[(Dx & Hyx) → Dy]	reordering quantifiers
∀y[∃x(Dx & Hyx) → Dy]	reducing the scope of the x quantifier
∀x[∃y(Dy & Hxy) → Dx]	interchanging variables; second symbolization

Consider one more example:

(S9) Anyone who {l}oves everyone is a (s)aint.

(F9)   ∀x(∀yLxy → Sx)
(F10) ∀x∃y(Lxy → Sx)

F9 is the obvious symbolization. Surprising though it may be, F9 and F10 are equivalent. Should we then consider F10 an equally satisfactory symbolization of S9? I would say *no* on the grounds that F10 doesn't "track" S9 well; the existential quantifier does not correlate with the term *everyone*.

A quantification is said to be in *prenex normal form* when all of its quantifiers appear at the beginning and are not separated by dashes or groupers. So, F8 and F10 (above) are in prenex normal form but F6, F7, and F9 are not. For any predicate-logic wff there are equivalent wffs in prenex normal form. Here is a simple example:

(F11) ∀xFx & ∃yGy
(F12) ∀x∃y(Fx & Gy)

Another example, with intermediate steps supporting the claim of equivalence:

∀xHx → −∃xlx	starting point
∀xHx → ∀x−lx	QE pattern
∀xHx → ∀y−ly	variable replacement
∃x(Hx → ∀y−ly)	expanding the scope of the antecedent quantifier
∃x∀y(Hx → −ly)	expanding the scope of the consequent quantifier; ending point

Every variable in a wff falls within the scope of exactly one quantifier using that variable. That principle forced the step of variable replacement in the third line of the list above. When you bring a quantifier toward the front of a wff, you should locate it to the right of any quantifiers already at the front (as I did in the last step above). The reason for that will become evident in the next section.

EXERCISES

1. For each of the following sentences provide two equivalent symbolizations that track well but differ in quantifier scope.

    (a) (*Jesse McCrary*) "Injustice anywhere is injustice everywhere." (Ix = justice exists in area x)

    *(b) (*Tsar Nicholas II*) "I will never make peace so long as a single (e)nemy remains on (R)ussian soil." (P = I will make peace, Rx = x is in Russia)

    (c) (*Gerry Spence*) "If the [American] government can (p)ut any (c)riminal away on less than beyond a reasonable doubt, it can put us away as well." (domain: Americans; Px = the government can put x away on less than beyond a reasonable doubt, Cx)

    (d) (*President Bill Clinton, 1998 State of the Union address*) "{D}iscrimination against any (A)merican is (u)n-American." (Dxy = x is an instance of discrimination against y, Ax = x is an American, Ux = x is un-American)

    (e) (*NY Knick's president*) "If you [i.e., any (N)BA player] {t}hrow a punch, it's an automatic (s)uspension." (Txy = x throws punch y)

    *(f) (*folklore*) "Any {s}eventh son of a seventh son can (h)eal." (domain: people; Sxy = x is the seventh son of y)

2. Using either proofs or truth trees (or a combination), establish the equivalence of the wffs in each of these pairs.

    (F1) $\forall xFx \rightarrow P$ (F2) $\exists x(Fx \rightarrow P)$
    (F3) $\exists xFx \rightarrow P$ (F4) $\forall x(Fx \rightarrow P)$
    (F5) $P \rightarrow \forall xFx$ (F6) $\forall x(P \rightarrow Fx)$
    (F7) $P \rightarrow \exists xFx$ (F8) $\exists x(P \rightarrow Fx)$

    (a) F1 entails F2.   (e) F5 entails F6.
    *(b) F2 entails F1.   *(f) F6 entails F5.
    (c) F3 entails F4.   (g) F7 entails F8.
    (d) F4 entails F3.   (h) F8 entails F7.

3. Using either truth trees or CEXes, establish the non-equivalence of the wffs in each of these pairs.

    (a) $\forall xFx \rightarrow P$ $\forall x(Fx \rightarrow P)$
    *(b) $\exists xFx \rightarrow P$ $\exists x(Fx \rightarrow P)$

4. For each wff provide an equivalent wff in prenex normal form.

    (a) $\forall x(Fx \rightarrow \forall yGy)$

    *(b) $\forall x(\forall yFy \rightarrow Gx)$

    (c) $\forall xFx \rightarrow \forall xGx$

    (d) $\forall x[\exists y(Hy \& Iy) \rightarrow Jxy]$

    (e) $\forall x\{Kx \rightarrow [\forall yLy \rightarrow \forall z(Mz \rightarrow Nxz)]\}$

5. (CHALLENGE) For each of the following sentences provide two symbolizations—one that tracks well but is not in prenex normal form and another equivalent symbolization in prenex normal form.

   (a) (*Samuel Johnson*) "He who {p}raises everybody praises nobody." (domain: people)

   (b) (*Goldbach's conjecture*) Every (e)ven number is the {s³}um of two (p)rimes. (domain: numbers; Sxyz — x is the sum of y and z)

   (c) (*Rudyard Kipling*) "Those who {k}ill (s)nakes get killed by snakes."

   (d) (*President Bill Clinton, 1998 State of the Union address*) "A {c}risis anywhere can {a}ffect {e}conomics everywhere." (Cxy = x is a crisis in location y, Axy = x affects y, Exy = x is an economy in location y)

   (e) (*Platonic thesis*) If a (p)erson {h}as one (v)irtue she has them all.

   (f) ("*Believe it or Not*" by Ripley) "A (M)ekeo tribesman of New Guinea (w)ears a turtle shell disk on his forehead only if he—or an {a}ncestor—has (k)illed an enemy in battle." (domain: men; Axy = x is an ancestor of y, Kx = x has killed some enemy in battle)

6. (CHALLENGE) Provide a wff in prenex normal form that is equivalent to this wff: $-\forall xFx \leftrightarrow \forall xGx$

7. (CHALLENGE) F9 and F10 are demonstrably equivalent. Provide an argument (that does not employ logic symbols) to show that S9 and S10 are also equivalent.

   (S9) Anyone who {l}oves everyone is a (s)aint.   (F9) $\forall x(\forall yLxy \rightarrow Sx)$

   (S10) For any person there is a person such   (F10) $\forall x\exists y(Lxy \rightarrow Sx)$
   that if the first loves the second, the
   first is a saint.

13.2   Quantifier Order

In Chapter Twelve we examined the invalid argument, "Causation I:"

> Every event has a cause. So, some event is the cause of all events.
>
> $\forall x\exists yCyx \vdash \exists x\forall yCxy$

(domain: events; Cxy = x causes y) It is customary to select *x* as the initial quantifier variable in a wff, *y* as the second variable, and so on, but there is no logical requirement that this be done. To make a point I resymbolize "Causation I" beginning the symbolization of the conclusion with a *y* quantifier:

> $\forall x\exists yCyx \vdash \exists y\forall xCyx$

The premise and conclusion wffs are identical except for the order of the quantifiers. Because we realize that the sequent is invalid, we see that quantifier order can make a big difference in the content of a wff. However, it doesn't always make a difference. The formulas in each of these (horizontal) pairs are equivalent:

$$∀x∀yRxy \qquad ∀y∀xRxy$$
$$∃x∃ySxy \qquad ∃y∃xSxy$$

Contiguous universal quantifiers can be re-ordered without altering the content of a wff, and the same is true of contiguous existential quantifiers. There is even one case where a universal and an existential quantifier can trade places while retaining equivalence; that happens when the two variables of quantification do not follow the same relational predicate letter. An example:

$$∀x∃y(Fx \& Gy) \qquad ∃y∀x(Fx \& Gy)$$

The following progression shows the equivalence of these wffs:

∀x∃y(Fx & Gy)	
∀x(Fx & ∃yGy)	contracting the scope of the y quantifier
∀xFx & ∃yGy	contracting the scope of the x quantifier
∃y(∀xFx & Gy)	expanding the scope of the y quantifier
∃y∀x(Fx & Gy)	expanding the scope of the x quantifier

If one of the predicate letters were followed by both variables, then one of the contraction steps made above would have been impossible.

Let's focus on the case where changing the order does alter the content. Note that a switch in one direction preserves truth even though it does not preserve content. That is to say, if you move a universal quantifier out in front of an existential quantifier, the newly created wff will be entailed by the original although they will not be equivalent. If we turn "Causation I" on its head (that is, switch the premise and conclusion), we will have an example of this move.

Some event is the cause of all events. So, every event has a cause.

$$∃y∀xCyx ⊢ ∀x∃yCyx$$

I begin the symbolization of the premise with y to make the point about quantifier order. We can construct a tree to establish the validity of the argument.

```
    ✓∃y∀xCyx
                  ∀x∃yCyx✓
       +∀xCax
                  ∃yCyb+
         Cab
                  Cab
            *
```

The move that can lead from truth to falsity (the move exemplified by "Causation I") involves moving an existential quantifier in front of a universal quantifier. This move has come to be known as *illicit quantifier shift*. The philosopher–logician Peter Geach has shown that many philosophers have unwittingly committed this fallacy in their reasoning.[3] Here are two examples. The philosopher Thomas Aquinas seems to reason as follows in part of his third cosmological argument for the existence of God:

> For each (c)ontingent thing there is a time when it does not {e}xist. Hence, there is a time when no contingent thing exists.

$$\forall x(Cx \rightarrow \exists y - Exy) \vdash \exists x - \exists y(Cy \, \& \, Eyx)$$

(Exy = x exists[4] at time y) It may not be obvious that this argument commits the fallacy of illicit quantifier switch, but if we rewrite the sequent with equivalent wffs in prenex normal form (doing a variable swap along the way) it becomes evident.

$$\forall x \exists y(Cx \rightarrow -Exy) \vdash \exists y \forall x(Cx \rightarrow -Exy)$$

Bishop Berkeley appears to advance this argument for the existence of God based on his metaphysical theory:[5]

> Every se(n)se idea has some {c}ause. Everything that exists is either s(p)irit or (i)dea. Ideas do not cause anything. This shows that there is a spirit [God, naturally] who causes all sense ideas.

$$\forall x(Nx \rightarrow \exists yCyx), \; \forall x(Px \lor Ix)$$
$$\forall x(Ix \rightarrow \forall y - Cxy) \vdash \exists x[Px \, \& \, \forall y(Ny \rightarrow Cxy)]$$

The problem here is that what Berkeley is entitled to conclude from these three premises is S1 and not S2.

(S1) Every sense idea is caused by some spirit.	(F1) $\forall x[Nx \rightarrow \exists y(Py \, \& \, Cyx)]$
(S2) Some spirit causes all sense ideas.	(F2) $\exists x[Px \, \& \, \forall y(Ny \rightarrow Cxy)]$

Moving from S1 to S2 involves the quantifier-shift fallacy. When Berkeley's argument is stripped to the elements it reduces to "Causation I."

Our discussion of quantifier order shows the wisdom of this advice from the previous section: "When you bring a quantifier toward the front of a wff, you should locate it to the right of any quantifiers already at the front." Failing to observe this advice can lead to the quantifier-shift fallacy. As an example, suppose you want to rewrite F3 in prenex normal form, and you do it with F4, moving the *y* quantifier past the *x* quantifier to the front of the wff:

---

[3] *Logic Matters* (Berkeley and Los Angeles: University of California Press, 1972), pp. 1–13.

[4] Ordinarily we avoid using *exists* in a predicate; the task of asserting existence is assigned to the existential quantifier. In this instance, however, it appears to be unavoidable.

[5] *A Treatise Concerning the Principles of Human Knowledge* (Indianapolis: The Bobbs-Merrill Co., Inc., 1957), pp. 35–38. The second premise expresses his view that matter does not exist.

(S3) Whoever commits suicide {k}ills someone. (F3) $\forall x(Kxx \rightarrow \exists y Kxy)$

(F4) $\exists y \forall x(Kxx \rightarrow Kxy)$

(domain: people) In doing so you have committed the quantifier-shift fallacy and have altered the content of F3. F4 symbolizes a statement whose content is very different from S3:

(S4) There is a person who is killed by all who commit suicide.

The correct prenex transform of F3, of course, is F3'.

(F3') $\forall x \exists y(Kxx \rightarrow Kxy)$

Notice that whenever you change the order of quantifiers you also change their scope. The scope of the y quantifier in F4 is greater than the scope of the y quantifier in F3' That explains the difference in content between these two wffs. In F4 we are asserting that there is some one thing y that stands in a certain relation to all x's, while in F3' we are merely claiming that for each x there is some y that stands in that relation—for different x's it can be different y's. So, F3' makes a much weaker claim, and that is why it is illicit to pass from F3' to F4.

Humor sometimes depends on quantifier shifts. This "Fox Trot" comic provides an example:

Fox Trot   by Bill Amend

FOX TROT © Bill Amend. Reprinted with permission of UNIVERSAL PRESS SYNDICATE. All rights reserved.

Two ways to understand "Each of the words on the list is used in a sentence:"

Jason's teacher's interpretation: $\forall x[Wx \rightarrow \exists y(Sy \,\&\, Iyx)]$

Jason's interpretation: $\exists x[Sx \,\&\, \forall y(Wy \rightarrow Ixy)]$

($Wx = x$ is a word on the list, $Sx = x$ is a sentence, $Ixy = x$ includes y) The "Dilbert" strip in exercise 8 is another example.

EXERCISES

8. Symbolize, paying attention to quantifier scope and order.

   (a) There is an integer {g}reater than all integers. (domain: integers)

 *(b) For each integer there is a greater.

   (c) For each (p)erson there exists some person who is {s}oul mate for that person. (This is Dilbert's friend's intended claim; domain: Dilbert's world; Sxy = x is soul mate for y)

   (d) There is a person who is soul mate for all persons. (This is Dilbert's first misinterpretation).

   (e) For each person there exists something that is his or her soul mate. (This is Dilbert's second misinterpretation).

DILBERT reprinted by permission of United Feature Syndicate, Inc.

9. Translate each wff into a colloquial English sentence using this dictionary: Lxyz = person x loves person y at time z

   (a) $\forall x \exists y \exists z Lxyz$ (d) $\exists x \forall y \forall z Lxyz$

 *(b) $\exists y \forall x \exists z Lxyz$ (e) $\forall y \exists x \forall z Lxyz$

   (c) $\exists y \exists z \forall x Lxyz$ *(f) $\forall y \forall z \exists x Lxyz$

10. Wffs F1 and F2 are an exception to the general rule that interchanging universal and existential quantifiers changes the content of a wff. (The exception occurs because no predicate in these wffs involves both variables.) Establish mutual entailment by constructing proofs or truth trees.

      (F1) $\exists x \forall y (Fx \ \& \ Gy)$
      (F2) $\forall y \exists x (Fx \ \& \ Gy)$

   (a) F1 entails F2.

 *(b) F2 entails F1.

11. (CHALLENGE) Establish the invalidity of each of these arguments discussed in section 13.2 by constructing either a CEX or a truth tree.

   (a) $\forall x (Cx \rightarrow \exists y - Exy) \vdash \exists x - \exists y (Cy \ \& \ Eyx)$ (Saint Thomas's argument)

(b) $\forall x(Nx \rightarrow \exists yCyx)$, $\forall x(Px \lor Ix)$, $\forall x(Ix \rightarrow \forall y-Cxy)$
        $\vdash \exists x[Px \,\&\, \forall y(Ny \rightarrow Cxy)]$(Bishop Berkeley's argument)

13.3   Properties of Relations

Themistocles (c.528–c.462 B.C.) reportedly told his wife, Phthia, the following:

> *The Athenians govern the Greeks; I govern the Athenians; you, my wife, govern me;*
> *your son governs you.*[6]

His quip is an argument with this unstated conclusion: Your son governs Greece. We can symbolize his argument like this:

Gar, Gta, Gpt, Gsp ⊢ Gsr

(Gxy = x governs y, a = Athens, r = Greece, t = Themistocles, p = Phthia, s = Phthia's son) The sequent is invalid because it fails to specify an aspect of governing on which the reasoning depends, namely, that if *a* governs *b* and *b* governs *c*, then *a* governs *c*. That feature of governing can be expressed in symbols easily:

$\forall x\forall y\forall z[(Gxy \,\&\, Gyz) \rightarrow Gxz]$

When we add that wff to the premise set the sequent becomes valid, as this proof demonstrates.

(1)	Gar	A
(2)	Gta	A
(3)	Gpt	A
(4)	Gsp	A
(5)	$\forall x\forall y\forall z[(Gxy \,\&\, Gyz) \rightarrow Gxz]$	A
(6)	$(Gta \,\&\, Gar) \rightarrow Gtr$	5 $\forall$O
(7)	Gta & Gar	2,1 &I
(8)	Gtr	6,7 $\rightarrow$O
(9)	$(Gpt \,\&\, Gtr) \rightarrow Gpr$	5 $\forall$O
(10)	Gpt & Gtr	3,8 &I
(11)	Gpr	9,10 $\rightarrow$O
(12)	$(Gsp \,\&\, Gpr) \rightarrow Gsr$	5 $\forall$O
(13)	Gsp & Gpr	4,11 &I
(14)	Gsr	12,13 $\rightarrow$O

[6]Quoted in Plutarch, *Parallel Lives,* "Themistocles," section 18.

Logicians call this attribute of governing **transitivity.** As this example illustrates, relations have properties. Some of these properties are of particular interest to logicians; they are the subject of this section. We concentrate on properties of dyadic relations. We will consider ten properties of relations that fall into three families: *transitivity, symmetry,* and *reflexivity.*

Transitivity Family

Property	Symbolic Representation	Examples
transitivity	∀x∀y∀z[(Rxy & Ryz) → Rxz]	being greater than, being an ancestor of, moving faster than
intransitivity	∀x∀y∀z[(Rxy & Ryz) → −Rxz]	being mother of, being two inches taller than, being immediate successor of
non-transitivity	∃x∃y∃z[(Rxy & Ryz) & −Rxz] & ∃x∃y∃z[(Rxy & Ryz) & Rxz]	admiring, fearing, being ten feet from

An **intransitive** relation is one such that (for any *a, b,* and *c*) if *a* bears it to *b* and *b* bears it to *c*, then *a* does *not* bear it to *c*. For example, if Elizabeth is mother of Carmen and Carmen is mother of Amy, then Elizabeth will *not* be mother of Amy, but rather Amy's grandmother. A dyadic relation that is neither transitive nor intransitive is **non-transitive.** Consider *admiring* as an example. Ada admires Bob and Bob admires Carla, but Ada does not admire Carla; therefore *admiring* is not transitive. On the other hand, Ada admires Bob (as already noted) and both of them admire Doris, hence *admiring* is not intransitive either. Because it is neither transitive nor intransitive, we label it *non-transitive.*

Symmetry Family

Property	Symbolic Representation	Examples
symmetry	∀x∀y(Rxy → Ryx)	being cousin of, being next to, being a coauthor with
asymmetry	∀x∀y(Rxy → −Ryx)	weighing more than, being a daughter of, being north of
non-symmetry	∃x∃y(Rxy & −Ryx) & ∃x∃y(Rxy & Ryx)	loving, seeing, being brother of

If one individual is cousin of a second, then the second is cousin of the first; *being cousin of,* therefore, is a **symmetrical** relation. If one person weighs more than a second, then the second will not weigh more than the first; *weighing more than* is **asymmetrical.** A relation that is neither symmetrical nor asymmetrical is said to be **non-symmetrical.** The lyrics of many country songs dwell on the fact that *loving* is not a symmetrical relation, but happily it isn't asymmetrical either; so *loving* is non-symmetrical.

Reflexivity Family

Property	Symbolic Representation	Examples
total reflexivity	∀xRxx	being identical with
partial reflexivity	∀x[∃y(Rxy v Ryx) → Rxx]	entailing, being divisible by, being as tall as
irreflexivity	∀x−Rxx	being mother of, standing next to
non-reflexivity	∃x[∃y(Rxy v Ryx) & −Rxx] & ∃xRxx	killing, respecting, seeing

A relation that everything bears to itself is **totally reflexive**; *identity* is the main example. *Total* reflexivity is rare; *partial* reflexivity is more common. A relation is **partially reflexive** iff any individual that enters into the relation with anything at all bears the relation to itself. *Entailment* is a partially reflexive relation. Not everything entails itself (Boston does not entail itself), so *entailment* is not totally reflexive, but anything that entails or is entailed by other individuals (that is, anything that is a statement) entails itself. An **irreflexive** relation is one that no individual bears to itself. Since no woman is her own mother, *being mother of* is irreflexive. A relation that is neither (totally or partially) reflexive nor irreflexive is **non-reflexive.** Some who kill others do not kill themselves, so *killing* is neither totally nor partially reflexive; and some people commit suicide, so *killing* is not irreflexive.

Every dyadic relation has at least one (and usually *exactly* one) property from each of these families. You can give a logical characterization of a dyadic relation by describing where it falls in each family. *Being father of,* for example, is intransitive, asymmetrical, and irreflexive, while *hating* is non-transitive, non-symmetrical, and non-reflexive.

Various logical connections hold between these properties. For example, every totally reflexive relation is also partially reflexive, and so is every transitive, symmetrical relation. These results can be established by proof or truth tree. An exercise at the end of the section involves such logical facts.

When you encounter an argument whose validity hinges on a relation's possessing one (or more) of these properties, the relevant additional premise(s) should be supplied. Here's an example; I advanced this argument in Chapter Two:

Consider these four statements:

(SA) All priests are males.
(SB) No priests are non-males.

(SC) *No non-males are priests.*
(SD) *Only males are priests.*

Each of the first three statements in this list is logically equivalent to the statement directly beneath it. Therefore, SD is logically equivalent to SA.

Eab, Ebc, Ecd ⊢ Eda

This sequent will not be valid unless we add two supplementary premises:

∀x∀y∀z[(Exy & Eyz) → Exz]   (transitivity)
∀x∀y(Exy → Eyx)   (symmetry)

Sometimes you will "see" what is missing by thinking about the argument, sometimes you can figure it out by beginning a proof or tree and determining why completion is stymied, and sometimes you may have to fall back on trial and error. It should be clear that the properties of non-transitivity, non-symmetry, and non-reflexivity, being represented with multiple existential quantifiers, are so weak that adding premises concerning them to a premise set is not likely to render the argument valid.

In Chapter Twelve I offered this CEX:

target:	If all who accept bribes are corrupt, then so are all who give them. It follows that in any case of bribery, if the acceptor is corrupt, then so is the briber.
target dictionary:	domain: people; Bxy = x bribes y, Cx = x is corrupt
symbolization:	∀x(∃yByx → Cx) → ∀x(∃yBxy → Cx) ⊢ ∀x∀y[Bxy → (Cy → Cx)]
CEX dictionary:	domain: people; Bxy = x is sibling of y, Cx = x is female
CEX:	If all who have siblings are females, then all who are siblings are females. (T) So, if one person is sibling of another, then if the second is female so is the first. (F)

Someone might justly complain about this CEX as follows: *Bribing* is non-symmetrical while *being sibling of* is symmetrical. So, the two arguments are not logically comparable. A better CEX would involve a relation that has the same logical properties as *bribing*. One way to insure that the relation in the CEX meets this requirement is to use the relation in the target argument. That is the strategy behind this possible-world CEX:

CEX dictionary:	domain: Al and Beth; Bxy = x bribes y, Cx = x is corrupt
Facts about the possible world:	Each bribes the other, but only Beth is corrupt.
CEX:	If all who accept bribes (that is, Al and Beth) are corrupt, then so are all who give them (Al and Beth). (T) So, in any case of bribery, if the acceptor is corrupt, then so is the briber. (F)

The conclusion of the CEX is false because in some cases of bribery the acceptor (Beth) is corrupt although the briber (Al) is not.

EXERCISES

12. Establish these truths by proof or truth tree.
    (a) A totally reflexive relation is partially reflexive.
    *(b) An asymmetrical relation is irreflexive.
    (c) An intransitive relation is irreflexive.
    (d) A transitive and irreflexive relation is asymmetrical.
    (e) A transitive and asymmetrical relation is irreflexive.
    *(f) A transitive and totally reflexive relation is not asymmetrical.
    (g) A transitive and symmetrical relation is partially reflexive.

    Problem (a) may be set up like this: $\forall x Rxx \vdash \forall x[\exists y(Rxy \lor Ryx) \rightarrow Rxx]$

13. Establish the falsity of these claims by CEX.
    (a) A transitive relation is symmetrical.
    *(b) A symmetrical relation is transitive.
    (c) A transitive relation is partially reflexive.
    (d) A symmetrical relation is partially reflexive.
    (e) A partially reflexive relation is totally reflexive.
    *(f) An irreflexive relation is asymmetrical.
    (g) An irreflexive relation is intransitive.
    (h) A transitive and symmetrical relation is totally reflexive.

14. Logicians Karel Lambert and Bas C. van Fraassen[7] claim that *being sibling of* is a transitive relation. Show that they are mistaken.

---

[7] *Derivation and Counterexample: An Introduction to Philosophical Logic* (Encino, California: Dickenson Publishing Company, Inc., 1972), p. 107.

15. I characterized partial reflexivity with F1; F2 is an alternate formulation. Prove their equivalence by constructing proofs or truth trees.

   (F1) ∀x[∃y(Rxy v Ryx) → Rxx]
   (F2) ∀x∀y[Rxy → (Rxx & Ryy)]

   (a) F1 entails F2.
   (b) F2 entails F1.

*16. Advertising slogan:

   Häagen-Dazs® ...
   It's better than anything.™

A refutation of the slogan:

   It is false that [H]äagen-Dazs ice cream is {b}etter than anything since ...

Supply the missing premise that characterizes the relevant logical property of the relation *being better than*, then establish the validity of the sequent by proof or truth tree.

Instructions for exercises 17 through 21: (a) Symbolize and establish the invalidity of the sequent by CEX or truth tree. (b) Add the supplementary premise(s) ascribing logical properties to relations that transforms the sequent into a valid one, and establish the validity of the augmented sequent by proof or truth tree.

17. A passage from Chapter Ten:

   Consider a second argument ("Sheila"):
   Everyone loves Sheila.
   So, Sheila loves someone.

   ... *"Sheila" is valid because the premise entails "Sheila loves Sheila," and that statement in turn entails the conclusion.*

The argument you are to evaluate is not "Sheila" itself, but the argument about "Sheila" expressed in the last sentence of the quotation. (domain: statements; Exy = x entails y, a = the premise of "Sheila," b = the statement *Sheila loves Sheila*, c = the conclusion of "Sheila") You can symbolize the statement *"Sheila" is valid* as "Eac."

18. A magazine ad proclaims "Lowenbräu costs more than beer." The following argument aims to refute the slogan.

   [L]owenbräu is a (b)eer. Therefore, it is false that Lowenbräu costs {m}ore than (all) beer.

19. This argument presents a theological puzzle for Christians who wish to reject its conclusion.[8]

___
[8]The Catholic doctrine of the immaculate conception of Mary offers one solution to the puzzle.

Every {d}escendant of [A]dam possesses original (s)in. [M]ary is a descendant of Adam. [J]esus is a descendant of Mary. It follows that Jesus possessed original sin.

(domain: people)

*20. Term [*a*] is not {s}ynonymous with term [*b*]. Hence, it is not the case that term [*c*] is synonymous with both *a* and *b*.

21. The bureaucratic run-around depicted in the following cartoon presents Blondie with an impossible task.

Approval by [A]rchitectural Review is preceded by approval by Occupational [L]icensing and Permits. The latter approval is preceded by approval by C[o]unty Health. The latter approval is preceded by approval by C[i]ty Health. The latter approval is preceded by approval by Zo[n]ing and Planning. The latter approval is preceded by approval by Architectural Review. So, approval by Architectural Review is preceded by approval by Architectural Review.

(domain: government offices in Blondie's community; Pxy = approval by office x precedes approval by office y, a = Architectural Review, l = Licensing and Permits, o = County Health, i = City Health, n = Zoning and Planning)

22. (CHALLENGE) Logician E. J. Lemmon[9] claims that *being parent of* is an intransitive relation. What Greek tragedy shows the claim to be mistaken?[10]

23. (CHALLENGE) Cite a relation that is both transitive and intransitive, both symmetrical and asymmetrical, and both partially reflexive and irreflexive.

13.4   Definitions

Throughout the book I have used certain concepts such as *formula of predicate logic* that have not received explicit definitions. In this section I will provide those definitions. Considering matters from the standpoint of logic alone, it would have been better to define these terms near the beginning of the book, but considering also pedagogy I think it was right to postpone the project until now. This section is "dryer" than the rest of the book, and some readers may prefer to skip over it.

I will start with definitions for the building blocks of formulas and gradually work up to the term *wff* (and after that, *sequent* and *quantifier scope*). As you know by now, wffs are a species of formula, namely, those formulas that are constructed according to the rules of logical grammar. The rules of formula construction are contained in the definition of *wff*. (The symbol "$=_{df}$" is short for *equals by definition*.

capital	$=_{df}$	an upper-case letter of the English alphabet (with or without one or more prime marks)
variable	$=_{df}$	a lower-case double-u, ex, wye, or zee (with or without one or more prime marks)
constant	$=_{df}$	a lower-case letter of the English alphabet other than a variable (with or without one or more prime marks)

---

[9] *Beginning Logic* (Indianapolis: Hackett Publishing Company, 1978), p. 183.

[10] My student, Ray Bielec, taught me this.

flipped-*E*	$=_{df}$	the mark "∃"
flipped-*A*	$=_{df}$	the mark "∀"
connective	$=_{df}$	an arrow, ampersand, double arrow, wedge, or dash
grouper	$=_{df}$	a parenthesis, bracket, or brace
symbol	$=_{df}$	a capital, variable, constant, flipped-*E*, flipped-*A*, connective, or grouper
formula	$=_{df}$	a symbol or a horizontal finite string of symbols

Each of the following counts as a formula:

> B
> ∀xFx
> ∃&x
> &cK

Only the first two of these formulas are well formed.

To pave the way for the definition of *wff*, several more terms must be defined.

simple statement	$=_{df}$	a capital or a capital followed by one or more constants
left-hand grouper	$=_{df}$	either the mark "(" or "[" or "{"
matching right-hand grouper	$=_{df}$	the mirror image of a left-hand grouper
dyadic connective	$=_{df}$	connective other than the dash
existential quantifier	$=_{df}$	a flipped-*E* followed by a variable
universal quantifier	$=_{df}$	a flipped-*A* followed by a variable
quantifier	$=_{df}$	an existential or universal quantifier

Now we can provide this recursive definition of *wff*:[11]

wff $=_{df}$ (i)   **a simple statement, or**

(ii) **a dash followed by a wff, or**

(iii) **a left-hand grouper followed by a wff followed by a dyadic connective followed by another wff followed by a matching right-hand grouper, or**

(iv) **a formula that can be generated from a wff by pre-fixing a quantifier (whose variable does not occur**

---

[11]In constructing this definition I have depended on the account given in E. J. Lemmon, *Beginning Logic*, pp. 138–42. My definition of *quantifier scope* is derived from the same source (pp. 143–45).

in the wff) and replacing at least one occurrence of
a constant by the variable.

(v)   No formula is a wff unless its being so follows from
clauses one through four.

By applying this definition we can decide for any given formula whether it is
well formed. I will give several examples, beginning with F1.

(F1) P

F1 is a simple statement and so by clause (i) of the definition of *wff*, it is a wff. F1
is a wff of propositional logic; in fact, every wff of propositional logic will also
be a wff of predicate logic. That is to be expected because predicate logic is an
extension of propositional logic.

(F2) & Q

F2 is not covered by any of the clauses of the definition; therefore, it is not a wff.
       Clause (iv) of the definition covers quantifications. Let's see how it applies
to F3.

(F3) $\forall x(Ax \rightarrow Bx)$
(F4) $(Ac \rightarrow Bc)$

By clauses (i) and (iii), F4 counts as a wff. F3 can be generated from F4 in the
way described by clause (iv); hence, F3 is a wff. F5 is a more complex example.

(F5) $\exists x - \exists y Rxy$
(F6) Rab
(F7) $\exists y Ray$
(F8) $-\exists y Ray$

F6 is a wff according to clause (i). As F7 can be generated from F6 following
the directions contained in clause (iv), F7 is also a wff. Then by clause (ii), F8
is a wff. Finally, since F5 can be generated from F8, F5 is a wff by virtue of
clause (iv).
       The definition of *wff* has these consequences:

(1)   Every quantifier in a wff binds some variable (in addition to
the occurrence of the variable within the quantifier).
(2)   Every variable in a wff is bound by some quantifier.
(3)   No variable in a wff is bound by two quantifiers.

(A quantifier *binds* a variable iff they involve the same letter and the variable lies
within the scope of the quantifier.) Because of consequence one, F9 is not a wff.

(F9) $\forall x Ca$

Let's see how the definition of *wff* excludes F9. None of the first three clauses covers the formula. Nor does the fourth clause apply, for that clause specifies that the variable in the quantifier must also appear later in the formula. F9, then, is not a wff. F10 violates consequence two.

(F10) ∀xRxy

If F10 qualifies as a wff, it must do so in virtue of clause (iv). F10 can be generated (in the way described in that clause) only from a formula such as F11.

(F11) Ray

But F11, itself, is not a wff. Therefore, F10 fails to be a wff. F12 violates consequence three.

(F12) ∃x∀xCx

If any clause applies to F12, it is (iv). F12 can only be generated from a formula such as F9. But F9 (as we saw above) is no wff; thus F12 also is not a wff.

With a few minor exceptions pertaining to groupers, the formation principles laid down in the definition of *wff* correspond to our practices of wff construction throughout the book. That is, the formulas we have recognized as wffs all along satisfy this definition, and the formulas we have viewed as improperly constructed fail to satisfy the definition. It is a remarkable fact that such a concise definition can serve to subdivide satisfactorily the infinitely large class of formulas into the two (infinite) subclasses of wffs and non-wffs.

We may define a *sequent* of predicate logic like this:

turnstile $=_{df}$ the mark "⊢"

sequent $=_{df}$ a wff, or a string of wffs separated by commas, followed by a turnstile followed by a wff[12]

Previously we explained the scope of a quantifier as consisting of the quantifier plus the quantifier-scope groupers and everything located between those groupers. That is an incomplete account because some wffs lack quantifier-scope groupers, for example:

∀x∃yRxy

∃x−(Fx & Gx)   (has dash-scope groupers but no quantifier-scope groupers)

---

[12]We can amend this definition to allow for premiseless sequents if we wish: A sequent is either (a) a wff, or a string of wffs separated by commas, followed by a turnstile followed by a wff; or (b) a turnstile followed by a wff.

The notion of *quantifier scope* is critical because it is presupposed by the statement of the proof and tree quantifier rules. Those rules will be no more precise than that concept. The rules employ the concept of *quantification,* which in turn depends on the notion of quantifier scope.

Before producing a definition of *quantifier scope,* we must define *propositional function:*

> **A propositional function is a formula that results when zero or more (contiguous) quantifiers are deleted from the front of a formula that is a wff under clause (iv) of the definition of *wff.***

Some propositional functions are wffs, others are not. Examples:

∀x∃yRxy   (wff)

∃yRxy   (non-wff)

Rxy   (non-wff)

The definition of *quantifier scope:*

> **The scope of a quantifier in a wff is the shortest propositional function in which it occurs (provided that the next symbol, if any, in the wff is neither a variable nor a constant).**[13]

I apply this definition to F13.

(F13) ∃x(∀yRxy → Fx)

The shortest propositional function in which the universal quantifier occurs is F14. Accordingly, F14 is the scope of that quantifier.

(F14) ∀yRxy

We know that F14 is a propositional function because it results from deleting the initial quantifier of (for instance) F15, which is a wff by clause (iv) of the definition of *wff.*

(F15) ∀x∀yRxy

The shortest propositional function in which the existential quantifier of F13 occurs is F13 itself. F13, then, is the scope of that quantifier. The scope of the existential quantifier in F13 cannot be, for example, F16 because F16 is not a propositional function.

---

[13]The parenthetical clause is included so that (for example) the scope of the second quantifier in "∀x∀yRyx" will be "∀yRyx" and not just "∀yRy."

(F16) $\exists x(\forall y Rxy$

F16 is not a propositional function because of its solo parenthesis.

There is a lot more to predicate logic than has been covered in this volume. Typically the next steps in the development of this part of logic are the addition of symbols that represent identity, functions, definite descriptions, and second-order quantification (but not necessarily in that order). A logic that includes such symbols has the resources to provide a deeper analysis of arguments containing sentences like:

Muhammed Ali **is** Cassius Clay. (identity)

Beth's mother is an anarchist. (function)

The richest woman in Arkansas hates pasta. (definite description)

George W. Bush and Julia Roberts share **some quality**. (second-order quantification)

Many books treat these matters. I recommend one (by Bostock) in the postscript at the end of the next chapter.

14

Natural Arguments

14.1   Introduction

In the preceding chapters I have tried to show through examples that arguments occur in all media involving language–in books and newspapers, lectures and casual conversations, movies and television broadcasts, and so on. I call such arguments *natural arguments* and contrast them with the artificial arguments that populate the exercise sets of many logic textbooks. In the present chapter I discuss the procedures involved in assessing natural arguments. I hope that your ability to assess natural predicate arguments has been strengthened by your study of earlier chapters and that it will be further enhanced by your study of this chapter. The 29 natural-argument passages at the end of the chapter will help you gauge your proficiency in this area.

The first step in the process of assessing a natural argument is to **identify** it as an argument. I assume that by this stage in your study of logic you have developed the knack of spotting arguments. For a discussion of argument identification, see section 14.1 of the companion volume, *Introduction to Logic: Propositional Logic*.

When an argument has been located, the second step in its analysis can be taken: **formalization.** Natural arguments are not usually cast in "standard form"–they may contain extraneous material and very often essential elements are left unstated. By *formalization* I mean the process of restating the argument in a purified or regularized form, a form in which all essential parts are made explicit, all nonessentials are eliminated, and common elements that link statements are given the same wording. After an argument has been formalized, the next step is to **determine the branch of logic** to be used in its assessment. Most natural arguments treatable in deductive logic may be assessed in one or both of these branches of logic: propositional logic and predicate logic. Once the branch has been chosen, the formalization may be **symbolized.** If the argument will be treated in predicate logic, an appropriate domain must be selected and letters chosen to abbreviate predicates and singular terms. If propositional logic is employed, then, of course no domain is involved, but capital letters will be selected to abbreviate simple statements.

Once a natural argument has been symbolized, we can move on to the **evaluation of form.** If the argument is being assessed in predicate logic, two of the three techniques explained in this book will be appropriate: proofs, CEXes, and truth trees. If the argument is treated in propositional logic, two or more of these methods covered in the companion volume will apply: proofs, truth tables, and truth trees.

If the argument under study should prove to be valid, it does *not* follow that the argument establishes the truth of its conclusion. A valid argument proves its conclusion only if all its premises are true. I label the task of judging the truth of the premises of an argument **evaluating its content**. This is a crucial step in the assessment of an argument, but it has been ignored in this text for a simple reason. Because an argument can have any subject matter whatever, no one textbook or single college course could prepare you for the task of evaluating content. Furthermore, unless the subject matter of the argument under assessment is logic, a logician will probably not be the best person to judge its content or to teach others how to judge its content. For example, the content of an argument about the spawning habits of salmon can be assessed intelligently by an icthyologist or (perhaps) by a fisherman, but not by a logician (unless the logician happens also to be an icthyologist or fisherman). Your ability to assess correctly the *form* of arguments should be improved by your study of formal logic. Your capacity to judge accurately the *content* of arguments should be increased by your entire education (both in and out of schools).

I have analyzed the process of assessing natural arguments into six steps:

1. **identification**
2. **formalization**
3. **determination of branch of logic**
4. **symbolization**
5. **evaluation of form**
6. **evaluation of content**

The assessment of an argument will not always proceed exactly on this schedule. Sometimes when one is working at a later stage, it will become obvious that the formalization of the argument needs to be altered, or that the wrong branch of logic was selected, or that the argument was improperly symbolized. Some of these back-and-forth processes are illustrated in section 14.2.

Many natural arguments were presented by direct quotation in the text and exercise sets of preceding chapters. Usually I formalized such arguments for you, and in all cases I selected the domain and picked the abbreviating letters. In many cases I also chose the logical technique to be used in evaluating the form of the argument. The point is that you have had little practice in making decisions of these kinds. I devote the remainder of the chapter to a discussion of such decisions. My plan will be to provide a detailed assessment of four natural arguments, explaining my choices and decisions as I make them. I hope that you will then be in a position to make similar choices intelligently as you work through the natural arguments collected at the end of the chapter.

14.2 Examples

Example One "The Chameleon:" Upon spotting a chameleon on our patio wall, my son Mark (four years old at the time) remarked:

He's a live one, isn't he?—'cause he moves!

My first attempt at formalizing this argument yields:

> The chameleon on the wall moves.
> So, it is alive.

It is clear that an important element is missing from the argument as so far set forth. Most natural arguments are *enthymematic,* that is, have missing or unstated elements. The missing part or parts may be premises or the conclusion, or both. It is obvious that unstated elements must be made explicit before the analysis of an argument can proceed further. What is missing from my formalization of "The Chameleon" is a premise that asserts a connection between (chameleon) movement and life. Here are two distinct formulations of that premise:

> If the chameleon on the wall moves, then it is alive.
> All moving chameleons are alive.

It is impossible at this date to determine which of these statements (if either) Mark had in mind. Which should be added to the argument? In some cases where there are two distinct formulations of some suppressed element, there are good reasons for preferring one. In this instance, however, the two versions of the missing premise seem equally acceptable. Let's examine both formalizations of the argument that result from the inclusion of the two versions of this premise.

When we incorporate the conditional premise this version of the argument results:

> The chameleon on the wall moves.
> If it moves, then it is alive.
> So, it is alive.

This argument belongs to propositional logic. Two facts that point in this direction: (1) the argument contains no *general* statements, and (2) it does contain a *compound* statement (specifically, a conditional). Either of these facts by itself would suggest propositional-logic treatment; the two combined provide strong evidence.

Because of the simplicity of the argument's form (*modus ponens*), we can tell at a glance that it is valid. One might be inclined in this instance to skip the fourth step: symbolization. However, for purposes of illustration, let's take that step. We must devise a dictionary—that is, select capitals and indicate the simple statements they abbreviate.

> M = The chameleon on the wall moves
> A = The chameleon on the wall is alive

The argument is readily symbolized:

> M, M → A ⊢ A

The validity of this sequent may be demonstrated by various techniques.

If we incorporate into the argument the other version of the missing premise, we get this formalization:

> The chameleon on the wall moves.
> All moving chameleons are alive.
> So, the chameleon on the wall is alive.

This argument requires treatment in predicate logic. Two facts about the argument suggest this: (1) there is at least one general statement (the second premise), and (2) there are no compound statements.

The next stage in our analysis is symbolization, and at this point we must select a domain. As each statement in the argument treats only chameleons, it is permissible to employ *chameleons* as the domain. A dictionary is required. The formalization contains one singular term (*the chameleon on the wall*) and three predicates, but one of the predicates (*is a chameleon*) is not assigned an abbreviation because it corresponds to the domain adopted. I choose this dictionary:

> c = the chameleon on the wall
> Mx = x moves
> Ax = x is alive

The argument is symbolized:

> Mc, ∀x(Mx → Ax) ⊢ Ac

Of course, this sequent is valid.

We may employ the standard domain when analyzing "The Chameleon." With that domain selected we might initially reach this symbolization:

The [c]hameleon on the wall moves.	Mc
All (m)oving c(h)ameleons are (a)live.	∀x[(Mx & Hx) → Ax]
So, the chameleon on the wall is alive.	⊢ Ac

However, this sequent is invalid, as you can easily establish. What is missing from the symbolization is a wff asserting that individual c is a chameleon. This wff may be added as an extra premise or it may be conjoined to the first symbolized premise. The latter choice yields this symbolization:

Mc & Hc, ∀x[(Mx & Hx) → Ax] ⊢ Ac

Translating the symbolized first premise into English we reach:

The chameleon on the wall is a moving chameleon.

The redundancy may be removed by allowing the constant c to abbreviate "the *animal* on the wall" (rather than "the *chameleon* on the wall"). This involves modifying the formalization of the argument to:

The animal on the wall is a moving chameleon.
All moving chameleons are alive.
So, the animal on the wall is alive.

Symbolizing the argument has led to an alteration of the English formalization; this is not uncommon.

Example Two "Liza Minnelli:"   Another example is provided by this portion of a gossip column:

Q: Desi Arnaz, Jr., fathered a child with Patty Duke. Didn't he also father a child with Liza Minnelli?
—Mrs. E. B., Elmont, N.Y.

A: Impossible. Liza (with a "z") has never been a mother.[1]

When irrelevant matters (such as the business about Patty Duke) are dropped, this tentative formalization of the argument emerges:

[1]Marilyn and Hy Gardner, *"Glad You Asked That"* (Field Newspaper Syndicate), *Miami News* (July 24, 1973), p. 8B.

Liza Minnelli is not a mother.
Thus, Desi Arnaz, Jr., did not father a child with Liza.

This can be transformed into a valid propositional argument by introducing a conditional premise:

If Desi fathered a child with Liza, then Liza is a mother.

The resulting formalization exhibits the *modus tollens* pattern. While the argument may be handled in this manner, I think it is preferable to treat it as a predicate argument. When we view it as a predicate argument, we need not add any suppressed premises. As a general principle, if the validity of an argument is preserved in one treatment without the addition of extra premises while under a second treatment additional premises are required, the first treatment does a better job of revealing the logical structure of the argument.

A domain of *people* will be appropriate for the predicate-logic symbolization of this argument. There remains a question about which symbols to select and specifically whether the predicate letters should be regarded as abbreviating one-, two-, or three-place predicates. This is a question about the *depth* to which the analysis of the argument should be carried. Here are three symbolizations that involve analyses carried to different levels:

	Symbolization	Dictionary
Property analysis:	$-\exists x Lx \vdash -\exists x(Dx \& Lx)$	Lx = Liza is mother of x, Dx = Desi is father of x
Dyadic relational analysis:	$-\exists x Mlx \vdash -\exists x(Fdx \& Mlx)$	Mxy = x is mother of y, Fxy = x is father of y, l = Liza, d = Desi
Triadic relational analysis:	$-\exists x \exists y Fxyl \vdash -\exists x Fdxl$	$Fxyz$ = x fathers y with z, l = Liza, d = Desi

These three sequents are valid. I regard all three as acceptable symbolizations. Simplicity seems the only relevant respect in which they can be contrasted. On this ground I prefer the first symbolization. The "Liza" argument is unusual in that it can be symbolized on so many different levels.

Example Three "The Shanty:" An excerpt from Laura Ingalls Wilder's autobiographical book, *The Long Winter:*

"We've got to wait for the train," Pa said. ***"We can't move to the claim till it comes."***

> *Tightly as he had nailed and battened the tar-paper to the shanty, blizzard winds had torn it loose and whipped it to shreds, letting in the snow at sides and roof. And now the spring rains were beating in through the cracks.* **The shanty must be repaired before anyone could live in it and Pa could not repair it until the train came,** *for there was no tar-paper at the lumberyard.*[2]

This passage contains an argument whose conclusion is the claim that the (Ingalls) family cannot move into the claim shanty until the train arrives. The purpose of the argument is not to prove the conclusion but to *explain* it; the argument is an explanation. Concentrating on the parts of the passage that are in boldface, I produce this preliminary formalization:

> The shanty will be repaired before the Ingallses move into it.
> The shanty will not be repaired until the train comes.
> So, the Ingallses won't move into the shanty until the train comes.

Other formalizations of the argument are possible; here is a more complex version:

> The shanty will be repaired before the Ingallses move into it.
> The shanty will not be repaired until Pa buys tar-paper.
> Pa will not buy tar-paper until there is tar-paper at the lumberyard.
> There will be no tar-paper at the lumberyard until the train comes.
> So, the Ingallses won't move into the shanty until the train comes.

Both of these formalizations are legitimate interpretations of the argument presented in the passage, and there are still other acceptable interpretations. (It does *not* follow, of course, that just *any* interpretation is adequate.) Let's focus on the more concise formulation.

Noting the terms *before* and *until* in the formalization, I decide that the argument involves the relation of *occurring before* (temporal priority) and therefore that the appropriate domain will be *moments of time*. Having chosen this domain, I attempt to phrase each predicate in terms of moments of time. I developed this dictionary:

> Rx = the shanty is repaired at time x
> Bxy = time x is before time y
> Mx = the Ingallses move into the shanty at time x
> Tx = the train comes at time x

Wff F2 was my first attempted symbolization of premise one (S1).

> (S1) The shanty will be repaired before the Ingallses move into it.
> (F2) $\forall x \forall y[(Rx \ \& \ My) \rightarrow Bxy]$

---

[2](New York: Harper & Row, Publishers, 1940, 1953), p. 314. Boldface added.

For some time I believed that F2 was the correct symbolization; then I discovered that F2 is logically equivalent to F3, which symbolizes S3.

(F3) ∀x−Rx v ∀x∀y[(Rx & My) → Bxy]

(S3) Either the shanty is never repaired or else it is repaired before the Ingallses move into it.

It is obvious that S1 and S3 have different content;[3] hence F2 is not an acceptable symbolization of S1. The real difficulty with F2 is that it lacks the existential implications of S1. Even when coupled with the assertion that there was a time when the family moved into the shanty, F2 does not imply that there was a time when the shanty was repaired. This problem is overcome by F1, which is a correct symbolization of S1. R1 provides a literal reading of F1.

(F1) ∀x[Mx → ∃y(Ry & Byx)]

(R1) Any time when the Ingallses move into the shanty is preceded by some moment when the shanty is repaired.

How did I discover the inadequacy of F2? By attempting to construct a proof for my symbolization (which included F2). After some initial failures to complete the proof, I realized that a premise was required that asserted that there was a time when the shanty was repaired. At first I planned to add such a premise to my formalization of the argument, but more thought convinced me that the root of the problem was my symbolization of S1. When S1 was properly symbolized, the extra existential premise proved unneeded and was discarded. This experience of learning something about the proper symbolization of an argument while attempting to construct a proof (or tree) is a common one.

Eventually I reached this symbolization for "The Shanty:"

> The shanty will be repaired before the Ingallses move into it.
> The shanty will not be repaired until the train comes.
> So, the Ingallses won't move into the shanty until the train comes.

∀x[Mx → ∃y(Ry & Byx)], ∀x[Rx → ∃y(Ty & −Bxy)]
⊢ ∀x[Mx → ∃y(Ty & −Bxy)]

I was quite confident of the correctness of this symbolization, but the proof continued to elude me. I realized that one or more auxiliary premises stipulating logical features of the relation *occurring before* were required to complete the argument. My first guess was that the argument involved the transitivity of this relation, and this guess proved correct. When I added a premise asserting transitivity, I was able to finish the proof. Had I remained unsuccessful, I next would have added a premise asserting the asymmetry of the relation. Missing auxiliary premises are often discovered when initial proof or tree attempts fail.

---

[3]To grasp the difference in content, note that the following statement is consistent with S3 but inconsistent with S1: "Although the shanty was never repaired, the Ingallses did move into it."

One is especially motivated to search for auxiliary premises when (as in the present case) one is convinced of the validity of an argument but nevertheless cannot complete the proof or close the tree.

When you use formal logic to assess arguments, your understanding of their logical structure is often enhanced. "The Shanty" is an example. When I first encountered that argument, I judged it to be valid, but there was much about the argument that I did not grasp. For example, I had a hunch that the argument presupposed the transitivity of the relation *occurring before*, but I was not confident about the matter. I had no idea whether the argument presupposed the asymmetry of that relation. By the time I finished applying the methods of symbolic logic to the argument, I was clear about each of these points. In these and other ways my understanding of the structure of the argument had been aided by the technology of symbolic logic.

Example Four "Geometry:" The speaker at a philosophy lecture remarked, "No primitive man can do geometry." A friend (call him *Al*) sitting by me whispered, "Hell, *I* can't do geometry! Does that make me primitive?" It was clear from his tone of voice that Al thought he had refuted the speaker. I understood Al to be advancing an argument whose (unstated) conclusion is the negation of the speaker's comment. I formalize and symbolize the argument this way:

> [A]l can't do (g)eometry.
> Al is not (p)rimitive.
> Hence, it is false that no primitive person can do geometry.
>
> $-Ga, -Pa \vdash -\forall x(Px \rightarrow -Gx)$

(domain: people) It is easy to show that this formalization is invalid.

But here is an important question: in proving the invalidity of my formalization have I also shown that *Al* was making a logical mistake—that *his* argument (as distinct from *my* formalization of it) is invalid? Perhaps (it could be suggested) Al was employing some unstated premise(s) that, in combination with his stated premises, entails the conclusion. Notice that any invalid argument can be transformed into a valid one by the addition of suitably strong auxiliary premises. This thought raises another question: what criteria govern the (legitimate) addition of premises to an argument under investigation? If there are no such criteria, then any (apparently) invalid argument may be changed into a valid one. This would support the absurd thesis that no one ever advances an invalid argument.

I propose that we adopt these criteria:

An unstated premise may be added to an argument iff

1. **it is logically true or true by definition, or**
2. **it is recognized to be true by everyone, or**
3. **it would be accepted as true by the arguer.**

I suggest that it is legitimate to include in an argument a relevant premise that satisfies any one of these criteria and incorrect to add a premise that satisfies none of them. It is particularly important that relevant auxiliary premises be added to arguments we judge to be invalid, for otherwise our judgment of invalidity *may* result from a failure to include a premise that the arguer was assuming but not stating. The total argument may be valid although the exposed portion is not.

Some arguments will remain invalid even after every relevant additional premise satisfying one of my proposed criteria has been included. When this is the case the argument should be judged invalid. Returning to "Geometry," a little thought should convince you that no auxiliary premises satisfying any of the criteria listed above will transform it into a valid inference. Al can justly be accused of logical sin. The speaker had claimed that primitiveness is a sufficient condition of geometrical ignorance. Al's whispered comments refute a quite different claim, that geometrical ignorance is a sufficient condition of primitiveness. His transgression was to confuse these claims. A better grounding in logic might have enabled Al to avoid the mistake.

In assessing the natural arguments at the end of the chapter, I found it necessary to add suppressed elements (premises and/or the conclusion) in about half the cases. Your treatments, of course, may differ legitimately from mine.

14.3 Postscript

It is quite likely that one year from the day you close this book for the final time, you will have forgotten the restrictions on the $\exists$O Rule and will be unable to symbolize complex relational sentences. In spite of this, I believe that your study will have been worthwhile if it heightens your awareness of the natural arguments you encounter and increases the likelihood that you will question the form and content of such arguments, back up your assertions with arguments, and expect others to support their questionable claims with reasons.

If I have been fortunate enough to whet your appetite for further logic study, you might read some of the books listed below. Bostock's text provides a more advanced treatment of (propositional and) predicate logic. Hunter's book investigates in more detail the kinds of issues addressed by William Lycan in Appendix Two. The book by the Kneales is a comprehensive history of deductive logic. Quine addresses philosophical issues that arise in the study of logic. Iseminger has collected 21 essays on such issues.

David Bostock, *Intermediate Logic.* Oxford: Clarendon Press, 1997.

Geoffrey Hunter, *Metalogic: An Introduction to the Metatheory of Standard First Order Logic.* Berkeley and Los Angeles: University of California Press, 1996.

Gary Iseminger, ed., *Logic and Philosophy: Selected Readings.* New York: Appleton-Century-Crofts, 1980.

William and Martha Kneale, *The Development of Logic.* Oxford: The Clarendon Press, 1985.

Willard V. Quine, *The Philosophy of Logic.* Cambridge, Mass.: Harvard University Press, 1986.

EXERCISES

Instructions for exercises 1 through 29: Each passage contains an argument. (1) Formalize the argument, taking care to supply any suppressed elements. (2) Decide whether the argument should be treated in predicate logic or propositional logic. (Only a few are best treated as propositional.) (3) Select a domain (for predicate arguments), choose abbreviating symbols, and then symbolize the argument. (4) Demonstrate validity or invalidity using some appropriate method (proof, CEX, truth tree, or truth table).

*1. "They say that if your child doesn't crawl before he walks, he won't be a good reader. Well, Bryan crawled before he walked, and he can't read worth a hoot; so that shoots down that theory."

–Conversation with a mother, June 15, 1996.

*2.

A FED GATOR IS ...
A DEAD GATOR!

... Too many people regard the feeding of alligators as a helpful, harmless, well-intentioned gesture.

NOT SO!!!

Providing food for alligators causes them to lose their fear of people and become bold, aggressive, and possibly dangerous. When an alligator begins following canoes and approaching swimmers

IT WILL BE DESTROYED!!

If you enjoy seeing alligators

DO NOT FEED THEM.

You will be helping to prevent a possible human tragedy or a certain tragedy for the alligator. ...

–Sign at Blue Spring State Park (Florida).

*3. "Since I was a law student at Harvard, I have been against the death penalty. ... It's a system that has to be perfect. You cannot execute one innocent person. No system is perfect."

–Ralph Nader, *Meet the Press,* June 25, 2000.

4.

*5. "Now if one substance can exist apart from another the two are really distinct (Def. X). But the mind and the body are substances (Defs. V, VI and VII) which can exist apart from each other (as has just been proved). Therefore there is a real distinction between the mind and the body."

–Rene Descartes, "Objections and Replies" to *Meditations on First Philosophy,* in *Descartes: Selected Philosophical Writings,* tr. by John Cottingham, Robert Stoothoff, and Dugald Murdoch (Cambridge: Cambridge University Press, 1988), p. 159.

6. " 'Stop!' exclaimed the young man. 'Look! Do you see how the door resists when you pull it?'

" 'Well?'

" 'That means it's bolted, not locked! Can you hear the bar rattling?'

" 'Well?'

" 'Don't you understand? That means one of them is at home. If everybody were out, they would have locked the door from outside, not bolted it from inside. But now—do you hear the bolt rattle? But to bolt the door from inside, somebody must be at home.' "

—Feodor Dostoevsky, *Crime and Punishment*, Part One, Chapter VII,
3rd ed., tr. by Jessie Coulson, ed. by George Gibran
(New York: W. W. Norton & Company, 1989), p. 71.

7. "After the ladies were gone, we talked of the Highlanders' not having sheets; and so on we went to the advantage of wearing linen. Mr. Johnson said, 'All animal substances are less cleanly than vegetable. Wool, of which flannel is made, is an animal substance; flannel therefore is not so cleanly as linen.' "

—James Boswell, *The Life of Samuel Johnson* in *The Portable Johnson & Boswell*
(New York: The Viking Press, Inc., 1947), p. 401.

8. "STOIC: *... I can turn you into a stone right now if I like.*

"BUYER: *A stone? My dear chap, you aren't Perseus.*

"STOIC: *Just you listen. Is a stone a substance?*

"BUYER: *Yes.*

"STOIC: *Isn't an animate being a substance?*

"BUYER: *Yes.*

"STOIC: *And you're an animate being?*

"BUYER: *I suppose so.*

"STOIC: *Then you're a substance, so you're a stone.* "

—Lucian, *The Sale of Philosophers* in *Selected Works*
(Indianapolis: The Bobbs-Merrill Company, Inc., 1965), pp. 107–108.

*9. "Without water we can't have pigs; and pigs bring us income."

—Drought-stricken farmer Troy Alexander
interviewed on *NBC Nightly News* broadcast of May 16, 2000.

10. "Let's consider the first premise of the argument, that whatever has a beginning to its existence must have a cause. What reason is there to believe this causal principle is true? It's not self-evident; something is self-evident if and only if everyone who understands it automatically believes it. But many people, including leading theists such as Richard Swinburne, understand the principle very well but think it is false."

—Quentin Smith, "Big Bang Cosmology and Atheism,"
Free Inquiry, Spring 1998, p. 35.

11. "The set of real numbers greater than 0 but less than or equal to 1 is a subset of the set of real numbers. We have just shown that it is uncountable. By [previously established result] 13.1 any subset of a countable set is countable. So the set of (all) real numbers is uncountable. Q.E.D."

—Geoffrey Hunter,
Metalogic: An Introduction to the Metatheory of Standard First Order Logic
(Berkeley and Los Angeles: University of California Press, 1971), p. 32.

12. " ... It is advantageous to remember from the above that the sufficient, though not necessary, condition of inherent value is that the individual be a subject-of-a-life. A subject-of-a-life has beliefs, desires, a memory, a

sense of the future, etc. Hence, to possess inherent value an individual must have a memory, a sense of the future, etc."

—Senior honors thesis in philosophy, December, 1995.

*13. "A cause must be temporally prior to its effect. No cause follows its effect. If each cause were contemporary with its effect, then all events would be simultaneous. But this is patently absurd. So, a cause must be temporally prior to its effect."

—Philosophy master's thesis, rough draft.

14. " ... Laurie Leshen ... studied ancient meteorites that have fallen to Earth from Mars. In billion-year-old Mars rocks, she found that the ratio of hydrogen to its heavy cousin, deuterium, matched that measured in the Martian atmosphere today.

"'If all the water had frozen, that ratio would have changed radically,' said Donahue [another scientist], so the researchers concluded that water still bubbles to the surface, bringing new water vapor to the thin atmosphere."

—Faye Flam (Knight Ridder News Service),
"Liquid water might be on Mars, bolstering hopes of finding life,"
Miami Herald (June 22, 2000), pp. 1A & 2A.

15. "The best argument against considering the unusual features of the avian respiratory system [air sacs and pneumatized bones] as being necessary for flight is provided by bats. They have typical mammalian lungs and do not have air sacs or pneumatized bones, and yet they are excellent fliers."

—Knut Schmidt-Nielsen, "How Birds Breathe,"
Scientific American, December, 1971, p. 74.

16. "SAMANTHA: *You get on that plane, you will never, never, ever see me again.*
   "JERRY: *If I don't go, I'm dead!"*

—*The Mexican*
(with Julia Roberts as Samantha Barzel and Brad Pitt as Jerry Welbach).
© 2001 by DreamWorks LLC & Warner Brothers.

17. "One day when dining at old Mr. Langton's, where Miss Roberts, his niece, was one of the company, Johnson, with his usual complacent attention to the fair sex, took her by the hand and said, 'My dear, I hope you are a Jacobite.' Old Mr. Langton, who, though a high and steady Tory, was attached to the present Royal Family, seemed offended, and asked Johnson, with great warmth [i.e., heat], what he could mean by putting such a question to his niece! 'Why, Sir, (said Johnson) I meant no offence to your niece, I meant her a great compliment. A Jacobite, Sir, believes in the divine right of Kings. He that believes in the divine right of Kings believes in a Divinity. A Jacobite believes in the divine right of Bishops. He that believes in the divine right of Bishops believes in the divine authority of the Christian religion. Therefore Sir, a Jacobite is neither an Atheist nor a Deist.' "

—James Boswell, *The Life of Samuel Johnson* in *The Portable Johnson & Boswell*
(New York: The Viking Press, Inc., 1947), p. 107.

18.

19. "Determinism is the view that all events are caused. 'All events are caused' becomes basically the notion that any event is so connected with some preceding event that unless the earlier event had occurred, the later event would not have occurred. Hence, given any event *A*, it is so connected with a later event *B*, that given *A*, *B must* occur."

–Philosophy term paper.

20. "There is, therefore, a power of gravity tending to all the planets. ... And since all attraction (by Law III) is mutual, Jupiter will therefore gravitate towards all his own satellites. ... "

–Isaac Newton, *Mathematical Principles of Natural Philosophy*,
Book III, Proposition V, Corollary I
(Berkeley: University of California Press, 1960), p. 410.

21. " ... If essence requires necessity, and what is necessary is certain, and what is certain is self-evident, and self-evidence requires self-interpreting meanings, then the denial of essence is the denial of ... self-interpreting meanings. ... "

–Samuel C. Wheeler III, *Deconstruction as Analytic Philosophy*
(Stanford, California: Stanford University Press, 2000), p. 183.

22. "Every proposition is either true or false, and no proposition is both true and false. (Hence if something is neither true nor false, or is ... both true and false, it is not to count as a proposition in the present context.)"

–G. E. Hughes and M. J. Cresswell, *An Introduction to Modal Logic*
(London: Methuen and Co., Ltd., 1968), p. 5.

23.

© Joe Rimkus, Jr. *The Miami Herald* (April 24, 1995), p. 8A.

"I saw the April 15 *Herald* photo of two women of different colors conversing with their hands. Both are deaf. I noticed their smiles. I realized that regardless of religion, color, or ethnicity, deaf people become brothers and sisters because of their common condition.

"And then I found myself wishing that the whole world were deaf."

—Martin Bass, "Listen to the signs of equality" (letter to the editor),
Miami Herald (April 24, 1995), p. 8A.

24. "Tortoiseshell and calico cats have multicolored coats. A tortoiseshell cat is basically black, with patches of red and cream. A calico cat is a white cat, with patches of red and black, and white underparts. Both types are nearly always females. Scientists have figured out a reason for this. ...

"There are two kinds of sex chromosomes, X chromosomes and Y chromosomes. A female cat has two X chromosomes and no Y chromosomes, while a male cat has one of each. ...

"The red and black color genes are found on the X chromosome. If a kitten receives a red fur gene from one parent and a black gene from the other, it will be calico or tortoiseshell. But to have both colors, it must have two X chromosomes—and a male cat has only one."

—Alvin and Virginia Silverstein, *Cats: All About Them*
(New York: Lothrop, Lee & Shepard Co., 1978), pp. 63–64.

25. (CHALLENGE) "A set A is a *subset* of a set B iff there is no member of A that is not a member of B. The empty set, Ø, is a subset of every set, since for any set C there is no member of Ø that is not a member of C, simply because there is no member of Ø."

—Geoffrey Hunter, *Metalogic:*
An Introduction to the Metatheory of Standard First Order Logic
(Berkeley and Los Angeles: University of California Press, 1971), p. 21.

26. (CHALLENGE) "According to Behaviorist doctrine, mental events are behavioral events. ... So mental events are always effects of whatever causes human behavior. ... "

—Keith Campbell, *Body and Mind*
(Garden City, N.Y.: Doubleday & Company, Inc., 1970), p. 65.

27. (CHALLENGE) "(8.21) *Special Consequence Condition.* If an observation report confirms a hypothesis *H*, then it also confirms every consequence of *H*.

"(8.22) *Equivalence Condition.* If an observation report confirms a hypothesis *H*, then it also confirms every hypothesis which is logically equivalent with *H*.

"This follows from (8.21) in view of the fact that equivalent hypotheses are mutual consequences of each other."

—Carl G. Hempel, "Studies in the Logic of Confirmation (II),"
Mind, April, 1945, p. 103.

28. (CHALLENGE)

"AUGUSTINE: *If, now, we could find something which you could unhesitatingly recognize not only as existing but also as superior to our reason, would you have any hesitation in calling it, whatever it may be, God?*

"EVODIUS: *Well, ... I do not wish to say simply that God is that to which my*
                reason is inferior, but that above which there is no superior.

"AUG.:   *Clearly so.*

...

"AUG.:   *I promised, if you remember, to show you something superior to the*
                human mind and reason. There it is, truth itself.

...

"AUG.:   *You admitted for your part that if I could show you something su-*
                perior to our minds you would confess that it was God, provided
                nothing existed that was higher still. I accepted your admission
                and said it would be sufficient if I demonstrated that. If there is
                anything more excellent than wisdom [i.e., truth], doubtless it,
                rather, is God. But if there is nothing more excellent, then truth it-
                self is God. Whether there is or is not such a higher thing, you can-
                not deny that God exists, and this was the question set for our
                discussion."

—Augustine, "On Free Will," Book II, Chs. 6, 13 & 15 in
Augustine: Earlier Writings, trans. by John H. S. Burleigh
(Philadelphia: The Westminster Press, 1953), pp. 144, 157 & 159.

29. (CHALLENGE) " ... [The astronomer] Apelles says that the spots seen
in the sun are much blacker than any of those ever observed in the moon.
This I believe to be absolutely false; I hold, on the contrary, that the
sunspots are at least as bright as the brightest part of the moon, and my
reasoning is as follows. When Venus appears as evening star it is very
splendid; yet it is not seen until many degrees distant from the sun, particularly if both are well above the horizon. This is because the regions of
the sky around the sun are no less bright than Venus itself. From this we
may deduce that if we could place the full moon directly beside the sun, it
would remain quite invisible, being situated in a field no less bright than
itself. Now consider the fact that when we look at the brilliant solar disk
through the telescope, it appears much brighter than the field which sur-
rounds it; and then let us compare the blackness of the sunspots both with
the sun's own light and with the darkness of the adjacent surroundings.
From the two comparisons we shall find that the sunspots are no darker
than the field surrounding the sun. Now if this is so, and if the moon itself
would remain imperceptible in the brightness of those same surroundings, then we are forced to the conclusion that the sunspots are not a bit
less bright than the shining parts of the moon—even though, situated as
they are in the very brilliant field of the sun's disk, they look cloudy and
black to us. And if they yield nothing in brightness to the lightest parts of
the moon, what will they be in comparison with the moon's darkest
spots?"

—Galileo Galilei, "First Letter to Mark Welser concerning the Solar Spots,
May 4, 1612" in *Discoveries and Opinions of Galileo,* trans. by Stillman Drake
(Garden City, N.Y.: Doubleday & Company, Inc., 1957), pp. 92–93.

30. (CHALLENGE) Locate in newspapers, magazines, books (other than logic texts), films, television broadcasts, or radio broadcasts five natural arguments that fall within the scope of predicate logic. For each argument provide (1) an accurate quotation of the argument in its original form;[4] (2) a reference to the source (indicating title, date, and page number); (3) your formalization of the argument (with needed suppressed elements supplied); (4) a symbolization of your formalization (including a domain and a dictionary that indicates for each letter the predicate or singular term it abbreviates); and (5) an assessment of the argument that employs some technique explained in this book.

---

[4]Consider clipping or photocopying long passages.

APPENDIX 1

Propositional Logic: A Brief Review

Propositional logic treats the five connective expressions *not, and, or, if ... then,* and *if and only if (iff)*. The symbolic abbreviations of these connectives that are employed in this book are listed in the table below.

Propositional Connectives

English Connective	Symbol	Symbol Name
not	−	dash
and	&	ampersand
or	∨	wedge
if ... then	→	arrow
if and only if	↔	double arrow

Simple statements (statements having no parts that are themselves statements) are abbreviated by capital letters. When a well-formed formula (wff) contains several connectives, their *scopes* are shown by groupers: parentheses, brackets, and braces. In the wff below, for example, the scope of the ampersand is limited by the parentheses and the scope of the arrow by the brackets; the entire wff falls within the scope of the dash.

$$-[A \rightarrow (B \& C)]$$

Formal Proofs

A formal proof (or simply "proof") of the validity of a sequent[1] is a list of wffs with the premises of the sequent occurring at the top and the conclusion at the bottom. Each wff in the list is either an assumption or is deduced from wffs above it by a stated rule of inference. Finally, every assumption on which the conclusion wff depends is a premise. Completing the proof establishes the validity of the sequent.

---

[1]A sequent is a wff, or a string of wffs separated by commas, followed by a turnstile (⊢), followed by a wff. Sequents abbreviate arguments expressed in a natural language such as English.

There are many sets of inference rules for propositional-logic proofs. The set employed in this volume consists of eighteen rules. Ten of these rules are regarded as "primitive." There are two primitive rules for each connective: a rule that sanctions a move *to* a wff containing that connective (an "In" rule) and one that sanctions a move *from* a wff containing that connective (an "Out" rule). These ten rules are listed in the chart on page 278. The primitive rules constitute a *complete* set; that is, a proof that employs only these ten rules can be constructed for any valid propositional sequent. The remaining eight rules in our set of propositional inference rules are known as "derived" rules. They are derived in the sense that they can be validated by appeal to the primitive rules. The derived rules are also listed on page 278. Each of the eighteen rules will be applied to *whole* lines but not to *parts* of lines.

Formal proofs in our formulation of propositional logic may be divided into two groups. In the first group are proofs that do not use any of the following three inference rules: Arrow In, Dash In, and Dash Out. The format for these proofs consists of three columns: (1) line number, (2) formula, and (3) justification. I illustrate with a proof for this sequent:

$$-D \lor E, \ -D \to -E \vdash D \leftrightarrow E$$

The proof:

(1)	$-D \lor E$	A
(2)	$-D \to -E$	A
(3)	$D \to E$	1 AR
(4)	$E \to D$	2 CN
(5)	$D \leftrightarrow E$	3,4 $\leftrightarrow$I

The *A* entries in the justification column identify lines 1 and 2 as premises of the sequent. The justification on line 3 is an abbreviation of "Derived from line 1 by the Arrow Rule."

Proofs in the second group employ the Arrow In, Dash In, or Dash Out rules (in addition to other rules). Two kinds of assumptions occur in such proofs: *original* and *provisional* assumptions. The premises of the sequent whose validity is being proven are the original assumptions. Additional assumptions are made to facilitate construction of the proof and then are *discharged* before the proof is completed; these are provisional assumptions. Assumptions are discharged by the use of the three rules listed at the beginning of the paragraph. Proofs in this second group include a fourth column, the assumption-dependence column, located to the left of the line-number column. This column shows for each wff in the proof which assumption(s) it depends upon. One purpose of the assumption-dependence column is to help indicate when a proof is complete. A proof is incomplete if the last line depends on any provisional assumptions.

For each of our eighteen inference rules we adopt a principle for determining the assumption dependence of any line introduced by that rule. These principles are stated in the following chart.

Assumption-Dependence Principles

→I	$A \rightarrow B$ depends on whatever assumptions B depends on (less the assumption A).
−I	$-A$ depends on whatever assumptions B & $-B$ depends on (less the assumption A).
−O	A depends on whatever assumptions B & $-B$ depends on (less the assumption $-A$).
the other 15 rules	The wff derived depends on all of the assumptions on which the premise(s) of the step depend(s).

An assumption (original or provisional) depends upon itself.

I illustrate the format for proofs in the second group by constructing two proofs.

$$F \rightarrow G \vdash (F \& H) \rightarrow G$$

1	(1)	$F \rightarrow G$	A
2	(2)	$F \& H$	PA
2	(3)	F	2 &O
1,2	(4)	G	1,3 →O
1	(5)	$(F \& H) \rightarrow G$	2-4 →I

The wff on line 2 is a provisional assumption (PA) made to facilitate the Arrow In step on line 5. The justification entry on line 5 is short for "Derived by the Arrow In Rule from the derivation of line 4 from the assumption on line 2." (The use of a hyphen rather than a comma in the justification entries for steps of Arrow In, Dash In, and Dash Out is intended to distinguish these rules symbolically from the other fifteen inference rules.) Notice that lines 2 through 4 depend upon the provisional assumption but line 5 does not. Line 5 depends on whatever assumptions line 4 depends on (1 and 2) less assumption 2; hence it depends on 1 alone. Only numbers of assumption lines can appear in the assumption-dependence column.

The Dash Out Rule is used extensively in this volume. This proof illustrates its employment:

$$-I \rightarrow I \vdash I$$

1	(1)	$-I \rightarrow I$	A
2	(2)	$-I$	PA

1,2	(3)	I	1,2 →O
1,2	(4)	I & −I	3,2 &I
1	(5)	I	2-4 −O

The justification entry on line 5 is an abbreviation of "Derived by the Dash Out Rule from the derivation of the standard contradiction[2] on line 4 from the assumption on line 2." Although the conclusion of the sequent is reached on line 3, the proof cannot be concluded at that point because line 3 depends on the provisional assumption.

Truth Trees

Propositional sequents may also be evaluated by the truth-tree technique. A truth tree is a logic diagram that looks like a stick-figure tree turned upside down.

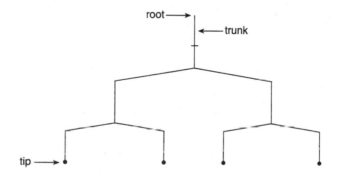

Every line connecting the root of the tree with a tip is called a *branch*. Wffs are written beside the vertical (and not the diagonal) segments of branches. Placing a wff on the left side of a branch represents it as true, while putting it on the right side represents it as false. The idea behind truth trees is to unpack the contents of wffs by decomposing them into smaller wffs. Propositional trees employ ten decomposition rules, two for each connective. These ten rules are listed on page 280.

To test a sequent for validity we write its premises on the left side of the trunk and the conclusion on the right. We draw a short horizontal line across the trunk just below the conclusion wff. Here is a tree for the sequent:

−(P v Q) ⊢ −(P & Q)

---

[2] A standard contradiction is a conjunction whose right conjunct is the negation of the left conjunct.

```
1   ✓−(P v Q)
2                −(P & Q)✓
3                P v Q✓
4                P
5                Q
6      ✓P & Q
7        P
8        Q
              *
```

(The line numbers are not part of the tree.) The main connective in a given wff determines which tree rule may be used. Thus, we apply the Dash Left (−L) Rule to line 1 (resulting in line 3) because the dash is the symbol of greatest scope in the wff on line 1. A checkmark is placed beside the wff on line 1 to show that it has been decomposed. The vR Rule, when applied to line 3, yields lines 4 and 5. Line 6 results from the application of −R to line 2, and that line in turn yields lines 7 and 8 by &L. When we inspect the tree we see that the wff *P* occurs on both the right and left sides of the branch. (The same is true for the wff *Q,* but let's focus on the *P.*) The wff *P* is being represented as both false and true, and of course that is logically impossible. We mark this impossibility by placing a star at the tip of the branch, and we say that the branch is *closed.* If every branch on a tree is closed, then the tree is closed. (This tree has just one branch; because it is closed the tree is closed.) If any branch of a tree is open, then the tree is open. If a tree for a sequent closes, this is proof that the sequent is valid; tree openness is proof of invalidity. Propositional truth trees are an effective logical test; they always yield a verdict (of *valid* or *invalid*) in a finite number of steps.

Let's construct a tree for this invalid sequent:

$$-(P \& Q) \vdash -(P \lor Q)$$

```
1          ✓−(P & Q)
2                      −(P v Q)✓
3                      P & Q✓
4          ✓P v Q
5       P                  Q
6   P      Q          P       Q
    *                         *
```

Line 1 yields line 3 by the −L Rule, and 2 yields 4 by −R. When the &R Rule is applied to line 3, the tree branches, and when vL is applied to the wff on line 4, the two branches each branch again. When a wff occurring above a split is decomposed below the split, that move must be made on every branch on which the wff appears. It is smart to postpone branching as long as possible;

doing this will result in more economical trees. The first branch (the left-most branch) of the above tree closes because P occurs on both the right and the left sides of the branch, the second and third branches remain open because no wff appears on both sides of either branch, and the fourth branch closes because Q is written on both the right and left sides of the branch. Because there are open branches, the tree itself is open, proving that the sequent is invalid.

Question: When is a truth tree complete? Answer: When every compound wff has been decomposed or every branch of the tree has closed. Second question: Is it ever safe to stop construction before a tree is complete? Answer: If all the compound wffs on one branch have been decomposed and that branch remains open, construction can cease. Because that branch is open, the tree will be open.

For a full presentation of the material treated briskly in this appendix, see Chapters One through Nine and Eleven of my *Introduction to Logic: Propositional Logic*, revised third edition.

APPENDIX 2

Metatheory: Soundness, Completeness, and Undecidability of the System 2L

William G. Lycan

In Appendix 1 of Professor Pospesel's *Introduction to Logic: Propositional Logic* (*PLA*1 for short), we jumped up an extra level of abstraction and considered his system of formal proof itself and as such. That is, rather than continuing to *use* the system to prove this sequent or that one, we looked at the system as a whole, named it "**PL**," and, in a more abstract language, proved things *about* it. This sort of activity is called "metatheory." Now we shall do the same for the system of predicate logic developed in this book, which I shall call "**QL**," for *quantifier logic*. Of course **QL** is based on and includes **PL**.

QL comprises: (i) The formation rules (provided in Section 13.4) that define what officially counts as a well-formed formula (wff) of the system; (ii) the primitive and derived rules of inference for the underlying propositional logic, summarized in Appendix 1; and (iii) the specifically quantificational rules ∀O, ∃O and QE.

In *PLA*1 we distinguished three separate concepts of validity: *intuitive* validity, *provability* in **PL** itself, and *truth-table* validity. Truth-table validity (or "tautologousness") was used as a gold standard against which provability in **PL** was tested. Specifically, we had to make sure that every sequent provable by **PL**'s rules was truth-table valid and that every truth-table valid sequent was provable. The former property was called *soundness*, the latter *completeness*. (Completeness is sometimes glossed as "getting what you want," while soundness is "wanting what you get.") We want the same sort of assurance regarding **QL**.

But truth tables apply only to propositional wffs and connectives, since the semantic values "true" and "false" are properties of whole wffs, not parts of them, such as individual constants, predicates, and quantifiers. For **QL**, then, we'll need a more fine-grained analogue of truth tables. Analogous how? Truth tables were a way of directly picturing *all the possibilities there are*–that is, all the various possible ways the world might be with regard to whatever wffs are in question. We want a similarly suitable way of doing that for wffs of **QL**. That way will be based on the notion of an *interpretation*.

In applying the method of counterexamples introduced in Chapter Seven, we provided new dictionaries for wffs, assigning new meanings to their predicates and new referents for their individual constants. Any assignment of meanings to predicates and referents for constants is what I shall now call an "interpretation."

To show that a **QL** sequent is invalid, we saw, one need only find a counterexample to it–that is, provide an interpretation of the sequent's constants and predicates that makes the sequent have true premises but a false conclusion–just as to show invalidity in **PL**, one finds a row of the sequent's truth table that makes the premises true but the conclusion false. A valid sequent in **QL** was officially defined (footnote 4 to Chapter One) as one such that every argument it can represent is a valid argument; translating this in terms of interpretations, we may say that a **QL** sequent is valid iff we cannot possibly devise an interpretation that makes the sequent's premises true and its conclusion false.

So we already have the notion of a wff being true on one interpretation but false under another. For example, Da & ∃xLxa is true on the interpretation:

Domain: integers

Dx = x is odd
Lxy = x is a prime number less than y
    a = 9

But that same wff is false on the interpretation:

Domain: people

Dx = x is Dean of Arts and Sciences
Lxy = x loves y
    a = Madonna

(because Madonna is not Dean of Arts and Sciences).

When we produce an interpretation of a wff, we assign members of the domain to its individual constants and predicates, as their *extensions*. (Here I expand the notion of an extension explained in Section 9.3 from parts of statements to parts of wffs.) The extension of a constant is just the constant's assigned referent, the individual item that constant denotes according to the interpretation. The extension of a property predicate is just the set of things to which the predicate applies; so the relevant extensions in Professor Pospesel's reinterpretation of the "Plato" argument on p. 84 are the set of all Episcopalians, the set of all Protestants, and Jesse Jackson. (It is more complicated to describe the extension of a relational predicate. I'll omit that here; the omission will not affect the proofs to follow.) When an individual member of the domain is in the extension of a particular property predicate, we'll say that the predicate is *true of* that member (on the interpretation in question).

We'll need to expand this notion of "truth of" slightly to apply to some formulas that are important even though they are not wffs. They are a subclass of the ones called *propositional functions* at the end of Chapter Thirteen, specifically, the propositional functions that result from stripping a universal or existential quantification of its main quantifier, leaving the quantifier's associated variable *free*, no longer bound by the quantifier. I shall call those particular propositional functions "open sentences." Lxa is an open sentence, since it could have resulted by stripping either from ∀xLxa or from ∃xLxa. More open sentences are: Hy → (Jya & Ky); Tx v ∃yMy; (Sx & Ux) → (Bx v Cx).

Open sentences have extensions just as property predicates do. For example, the extension of Lxa on the Madonna interpretation is the set of items that love Madonna; the extension of Dy on the integer interpretation is the set of odd numbers. An open sentence can now be said to be *true of* an individual member of the domain just in case the individual is a member of the open sentence's extension (on the interpretation in question).

For the purpose of doing truth tables in propositional logic, each propositional connective was given a truth-table definition. Those semantic definitions were appealed to constantly in the proofs of soundness and completeness for **PL**. For our **QL** metatheory, we must give our two quantifiers comparable semantic definitions as well. The definitions will not surprise you:

> **A universal quantification ∀ν𝒜ν is true on an interpretation I iff on I the open sentence 𝒜ν is true of every individual in the domain.**
>
> **An existential quantification ∃ν𝒜ν is true on I iff on I the open sentence 𝒜ν is true of at least one individual in the domain.**

These definitions can be used to compute truth values for longer wffs on the basis of truth values for shorter ones, just as we did in purely propositional logic. For example: Take the conditional wff (Da & ∀xLax) → ∀yAya, on the "Madonna" interpretation above plus the added dictionary entry, *Axy = x admires y*. Da is true iff Madonna is Dean of Arts and Sciences. By the new semantic definition, ∀xLax is true iff Lax is true of every individual in the domain, that is, iff all wffs of the form "Lan" (n being an individual constant) are true, which is to say, iff for every member of the domain, Madonna loves that person (including herself, of course). So our conditional's antecedent is true iff Madonna is Dean of Arts and Sciences and she loves everyone. Its consequent ∀yAya is true iff Aya is true of every individual in the domain, that is, iff all wffs of the form "Ana" are true, which is to say, iff for every member of the domain (including herself, of course), that person admires Madonna. So the whole conditional is true on the condition that if Madonna is Dean of Arts and Sciences and she loves everyone, then everyone admires her.

Further terminology, I'm afraid: Let us say that a *model* for a single wff is any assignment of extensions to the wff (that is, any interpretation of it) that makes it come out true. A model for a *set of* wffs is any (uniform) assignment of extensions that makes every wff in the set come out true. Some sets of wffs do not have models; sometimes the wffs in a given set *cannot* all be true, no matter what extensions are assigned to its terms.[1] Take the set containing just $\forall x(Fx \rightarrow Gx)$, Fa, and $-Ga$. (We can refer to that set using braces: $\{\forall x(Fx \rightarrow Gx), Fa, -Ga\}$.) It has no model, as you can easily verify for yourself by trying to construct one (do try it). When a set of wffs does have a model, it is called *satisfiable*. Intuitively, when a set is satisfiable, any of its models shows how things in the world could have been arranged in such a way that all the wffs in the set were simultaneously true. This is the **QL** analogue of a set of **PL** wffs' having at least one row in their common truth table at which each of the wffs takes the value T.

Now we may define *semantic validity* a little more formally. A sequent $A_1, A_2, \dots A_n \vdash B$ is semantically valid iff the set of wffs $\{A_1, A_2, \dots A_n, -B\}$ is not satisfiable (has no model); this is equivalent to saying that it's impossible to devise an interpretation of the sequent that has all true premises but a false conclusion. When a sequent is semantically valid, we say that its conclusion is a *semantic consequence* of its premises.[2] When a sequent is semantically *in*valid, we call any model that shows that a *countermodel* for the sequent. Whenever we show an argument or sequent to be invalid by the "method of counterexamples" recommended in Chapter Seven, we are providing such a countermodel.

Now, soundness and completeness for **QL** are analogous to soundness and completeness for **PL**. **QL** is sound iff every sequent provable in **QL** is semantically valid; **QL** is complete iff every semantically valid sequent is provable in **QL**.

Soundness

Since **QL** is based on **PL**, we can exploit the early structure of the soundness proof in *PLA*1. There we dealt with the problem of *infinitely many* sequents' being provable, by resorting to a technique called "mathematical induction;" we need not repeat all that here. We need only show that each of our three new rules, $\forall$O, $\exists$O and QE, is "safe." What we showed in *PLA*1 about each **PL** rule is that the rule cannot take us from a valid sequent to an invalid one. But since each of the three **QL** rules obeys the standard assumption-dependence principle, we need not worry about subproofs, and all we have to do is show, for each rule, that for any sequent proved using that rule, if all the rules used in the proof other than that rule are sound, the sequent's conclusion is a semantic consequence of its premises.

---

[1]It is a contentious philosophical question whether the set lacks a model because its wffs cannot all be true, or its wffs cannot all be true because it lacks a model.

[2]Semantic validity for **PL** sequents—truth-table validity—is also called "tautologousness," as in *PLA*1. But for reasons unknown to me, that term does not carry over to **QL** sequents.

It is quite easy to do that for ∀O and QE, by establishing simply that there is never any interpretation on which either of those rules takes us from a truth to a falsehood. ∀O applies to a universal quantification ∀$v$$Av$, resting on some (possibly empty) set of assumptions [α], and derives an instance of it, i.e., the result of replacing the variable v with some individual constant (or dummy name). According to the definition given above, ∀$v$$Av$ is true on an interpretation I iff on I, the open sentence Av is true of every individual in the domain. So any interpretation that made the derived instance false would also make the open sentence false of the individual in question and so would make ∀$v$$Av$ false as well. So there is no interpretation that makes ∀$v$$Av$ true but its instance false.

QE allows the derivation of ∃$v$$-Av$ from $-$∀$v$$Av$ and that of $-$∀$v$$Av$ from ∃$v$$-Av$. It is easy (and I leave it as an exercise) to show, using the foregoing definitions of the quantifiers and the truth-table definition of the dash, that on no interpretation can QE take us from a truth to a falsehood.

∃O cannot be checked so simply, because it involves a dummy name and restrictions. In fact, so far as I can tell, it is not possible to give a direct semantic argument for the soundness of ∃O. This is because ∃O is in effect an abbreviation of a somewhat different rule, EE as Lemmon calls it.[3] To show that ∃O is sound, we must demonstrate the soundness of EE and then exploit it by showing that all and only those sequents that can be proved using EE can also be proved using ∃O. Those tasks are too cumbersome to be fit in here, but they are performed on the CD that accompanies this book (see the file EO.pdf).

Completeness

For our completeness proof, we will need some elementary concepts from set theory. We have already introduced the notion of a *class*, or set, of things, and some notation: Braces are used to define a class by listing its members: {1,2,3,4}, {Bob, Carol, Ted, Alice}, {the Eiffel Tower, George W. Bush, my left elbow}. Additionally, a set can be *empty*; there is a unique "empty set" or "null class," the set with no members at all.

The *union* of two sets is the combined set that contains all the members of each. So the union of the first two sets mentioned above is {1,2,3,4, Bob, Carol, Ted, Alice}. The symbol for the union of X and Y is X ∪ Y; thus, {1,2,3,4} ∪ {Bob, Carol, Ted, Alice} = {1,2,3,4, Bob, Carol, Ted, Alice}. A set X *includes* a set Y iff X contains all of Y's members and perhaps more. So {1, 2, 3, 4, Bob, Carol, Ted, Alice} includes {1,3, Bob}, {Carol, Ted, Alice}, {4, Bob, Ted} and others, plus itself and the empty set. When X includes Y we also call it a *superset* of Y, and Y a *subset* of X.

---

[3]E.J. Lemmon, *Beginning Logic* (London: Thomas Nelson and Sons, 1965), on which Pospesel's *Propositional Logic* is based. For the present observation I am indebted to Keith Simmons. Thanks also to Simmons for his many other very helpful suggestions.

Now, to **QL**. The vocabulary of **QL** was specified in Section 13.4. I add only that we shall assume an infinite stock (each) of propositional constants, predicates, individual constants, and variables. In Chapter Two we used primes to number variables: w, x, y, z, w′, x′, y′, z′, w″, x″, y″, ..., and in Section 13.4 we did the same for constants and predicates.

The proof of completeness will come in four unequally sized stages. First, I shall motivate an Enumeration Theorem for **QL**. Second and third, I shall prove each of two preliminary metatheorems. Fourth, I shall deduce completeness from the two metatheorems.[4]

Stage 1

I shall not try to prove the Enumeration Theorem rigorously, but only show intuitively that it is true. What the theorem says is that all the wffs of **QL** can be arranged in a single list, with a first item, a second item, and so on (to infinity, of course, **QL** having infinitely many wffs). There are any number of ways in which this ordering or enumeration can be done. None is correct to the exclusion of the rest; the point is only to get the wffs ordered in some way or other.

Here is an easy one. We can order in part by *length* of wff. Every wff contains a particular number of symbols. ∃x(Fx & Gx), for example, contains nine symbols: the flipped-*E* and its variable, the left parenthesis, the predicate F and its variable, the ampersand, the predicate G and its variable, and the right parenthesis. So, for a start, the wffs of **QL** can be sorted into classes by number of symbols and then arranged in increasing order of length. Simple propositional wffs have the lowest number (one). Simple subject–predicate wffs have the second lowest (two)[5], and so on.

Now of course we also need to enumerate within each class. We can appeal to a kind of alphabetical order. Going back to the vocabulary list for **QL**, we can just stipulate an ordering of all the symbols it contains, perhaps starting with the individual constants in their pre-existing numerical order and then moving on to the predicates, and so on, and call that ordering **QL**'s "alphabet." Then we can rank the members of any like-numbered class alphabetically, just as in a telephone book. With each like-numbered class internally ordered and the like-numbered classes themselves rank ordered, all the wffs of **QL** will have been arranged in a single infinite list.

[4]The strategy for this proof is swiped from Leon Henkin, "The Completeness of the First-Order Functional Calculus," *Journal of Symbolic Logic* 14 (1949), 159–166. I am also heavily indebted to Benson Mates' *Elementary Logic* (Oxford: Oxford University Press, 1965), and to Keith Simmons' *Logic and Metalogic*, MS, University of North Carolina.

[5]Simple propositional negations also contain just two symbols.

Stage 2

For our two preliminary metatheorems, we shall need three important concepts:

A set of wffs is *D-consistent* iff no standard contradiction can be derived from that set. ("D" is for derivability.)

A set of wffs is *maximally D-consistent* iff (a) it is D-consistent and (b) if any further wff (at all) were to be added to it, the resulting set would not be D-consistent.

A set of wffs is *ω-complete* (the Greek letter ω is pronounced "omega") iff it does not contain an existential wff $\exists \nu A$ unless it also contains an instance of that wff (from which the existential wff could be derived by one step of $\exists$I). Let us use the notation "$A\nu/a_n$" for an instance of $\exists \nu A$, "a_n" meaning just some individual constant or other.

Now we aim to prove Metatheorem (*1*). It says: For any set Γ (pronounced "gamma") of **QL** wffs, if Γ is D–consistent, then there exists a set Δ ("delta") that includes Γ, is maximally D–consistent, and is ω-complete. We shall prove this first metatheorem by starting with an arbitrarily chosen set Γ, constructing a certain second set Δ that includes Γ, and then proving that Δ is both maximally D–consistent and ω-complete.

We begin by exploiting the Enumeration Theorem in a particular way. (Here again I will be intuitive rather than rigorous.) Given that all the wffs of **QL** have been arranged (on whatever basis) in a single list, that list can be rearranged into a revised list having the following property: Every existential wff on the new list is immediately followed by one of its instances, where the individual constant occurring in the instance has not appeared either in any of the previous wffs on the list or in any wff in Γ. To get a given existential wff immediately followed by one of its instances, we just insert a new instance after it, using a constant that has not been used before; no problem finding new constants, since there are always infinitely many.[6] (Then we delete the new instance from wherever it occurred in the original enumeration.) From now on we will work with the revised list, which shall now honorifically be called "The List."

As usual, we shall use script letters to stand for wffs, but now we shall also subscript them to indicate their place in The List. Thus, A_i would be the i-th wff on The List, B_j would be the j-th wff on The List, and so on.

Now we can get from any given set Γ of **QL** wffs to a more inclusive set Δ by constructing Δ out of Γ. Here is the construction, which from now on I'll call "the construction:"

---

[6]This presupposes that for any set Γ, **QL** still contains an infinite stock of individual constants that do not appear in any of the wffs in **QL**. That is easily seen to be true, so long as Γ is a finite set. But Γ may be infinite. To handle that case, there are tricks we must do to provide still more individual constants (e.g., Mates, *op. cit.*, p. 138), the details of which are not important here.

We shall define a series of sets whose first member is Γ. To obtain the immediate successor of Γ (call it Δ_1), add A_1 (first wff on The List) to Γ, *if* the resulting set ($\Gamma \cup \{A_1\}$) is D-consistent; otherwise we merely identify Δ_1 with Γ itself. To obtain the next member of the series, Δ_2, we add A_2 if $\Delta_1 \cup \{A_2\}$ is D-consistent, but otherwise we let Δ_2 be just Δ_1 itself. To obtain Δ_3, we add A_3 if $\Delta_2 \cup \{A_3\}$ is D-consistent, but otherwise we just identify Δ_3 with Δ_2; and so on until we have gone entirely through The List (an infinite task, of course).

To complete the construction, we let Δ be the union of Γ and all the Δ_i. That is, a wff A will be a member of Δ just in case A is a member of Γ or of at least one of $\Delta_1, \Delta_2, \ldots$. Obviously, Δ includes Γ, since it was constructed solely by adding wffs to Γ. What need to be shown are (Lemma 1) that Δ is maximally D-consistent and (Lemma 2) that Δ is ω-complete.

Lemma 1: Each of the Δ_i is D-consistent, because they were constructed that way. Now, suppose that Δ is not D-consistent. That means a standard contradiction can be derived from Δ. But whatever is derivable from an infinite set of wffs is derivable from some finite subset of that set (because every wff is finite in length, and no line of any derivation ever rests on more than finitely many assumptions[7]). So if a standard contradiction can be derived from Δ, there is also a finite subset Δ- from which the contradiction can be derived. It follows from a fact of set theory[8] that Δ- is also a subset of at least one of the Δ_i, say Δ_{27}. That would mean that Δ_{27} is *not* D-consistent, contrary to the construction. So our supposition is false; Δ is D-consistent after all.

We must further show that Δ is *maximally* D-consistent. Take any wff that is not a member of Δ. That wff is on The List, so for some number k, it is the k-th wff on The List; it is A_k. And since A_k is not a member of Δ at all, A_k is not a member of Δ_k in particular. But now, by the construction of Δ, if $\Delta_{k-1} \cup \{A_k\}$ were D-consistent, Δ_k would be identical to it, and so Δ_k would have A_k as a member. Therefore, $\Delta_{k-1} \cup \{A_k\}$ is not D-consistent. And so $\Delta \cup \{A_k\}$ is not either. ($\Delta_{k-1} \cup \{A_k\}$ is a subset of $\Delta \cup \{A_k\}$, and if a standard contradiction can be derived from a subset of $\Delta \cup \{A_k\}$, then obviously it can be derived from $\Delta \cup \{A_k\}$ itself.) But A_k was an arbitrarily chosen wff; the same argument would show for any wff whatever that that wff could not D-consistently be added to Δ. Thus, Δ is maximally D-consistent.

Lemma 2: Consider any existential wff that is a member of Δ, $\exists vA$. For some number j, $\exists vA$ is the j-th wff on The List; $\exists vA$ is A_j. By the construction of Δ (specifically the earliest part, where the revision made the original enumeration into The List), A_{j+1} is A/a_n, where a_n is a new individual constant. That is, a_n occurs neither anywhere in Γ nor in any wff that precedes A_{j+1} on The List.

---

[7] Actually, nothing in this book's presentation of the system **QL** guarantees that; for all that has been said here, a proof could begin with infinitely many assumptions and then go on to derive, for example, their infinite conjunction. But let us simply legislate against that.

[8] Namely, that any finite subset of a union of nested finite sets is a subset of at least one of the nested sets.

Again by the construction, $\exists v A$ is a member of Δ_j, because $\exists v A$ is A_j. (The only way $\exists v A$ could have got into Δ is by having been admitted to Δ_j.)

Now, suppose A_{j+1} is not a member of Δ_{j+1}. Then by the construction, $\Delta_j \cup \{A/a_n\}$ cannot have been D-consistent; a standard contradiction can be derived from it. Hence, $-A/a_n$ is derivable from Δ_j alone (by a single application of Dash Out). That means that $\forall v -A$ is also derivable from Δ_j.[9] And so $\forall v -A$ is also derivable from Δ as well. But since $\exists v A$ is a member of Δ, $-\forall v -A$ is also derivable from Δ (using QE and Dash In). Both $\forall v -A$ and $-\forall v -A$ being derivable from Δ, so is their conjunction, which is a standard contradiction; thus, Δ would not be D-consistent. But Δ is D-consistent, so our supposition has self-destructed. We reject it: A_{j+1} is after all a member of Δ_{j+1}.

A_j was an arbitrarily chosen wff. So if $\exists v A$ is a member of Δ, A/a_n is a member of Δ_{j+1} and hence a member of Δ also. Δ is ω. That concludes the proof of Metatheorem (1).

Stage 3

Metatheorem (2) says that every maximally D-consistent and ω-complete set of wffs is satisfiable (i.e., has a model).

So let Ξ ("xi") be any set that is both maximally D-consistent and ω-complete. We need to show that Ξ has a model. We shall accordingly offer an interpretation of the wffs in Ξ, and then show that on that interpretation, all of those wffs come out true.

The interpretation is somewhat degenerate, though entirely legal. Let the domain be the set of all of the *individual constants* in **QL**'s own vocabulary. (So far as set theory is concerned, symbols are just as much things that can be members of sets as are numbers or people or apples.) And let us begin the interpretation by assigning each constant to itself as its referent. (That is the degenerate part; it is unusual for a constant to name itself, but no worse than unusual. It sometimes happens in everyday English, as when we write "Hello, my name is Fred.") To each property predicate F, we assign as its extension the class of **QL** constants a_n such that the wff 'Fa_n' is a member of Ξ. (Let us here continue to ignore relational predicates, because that part of the interpretation would

---

[9]Though that is not obvious. If we were to avail ourselves of the rule $\forall$I provided at the beginning of Section 4.2, the derivation would be straightforward, since $\forall$I would allow us to infer $\forall v -A$ in a single step (subject to several restrictions, but the restrictions are met). But the system whose completeness we are proving does not contain $\forall$I. There is a way of deriving $\forall v -A$ without using $\forall$I, which I leave as a difficult exercise. Big hints: (1) Assume $-\forall v -A$ for Dash Out. (2) Use QE to get $\exists v --A$. (3) Apply $\exists$O to get A/a_m, for some new dummy name a_m. (4) Use a derivation parallel to the derivation (however it may go) of $-A/a_n$ from Δ_j, to get $-A/a_m$ from Δ_j, and then do your Dash Out. But the difficult part is: (5) Show that the derivation of $-A/a_m$ from Δ_j, no matter how it went, would not have violated any restrictions on the use of the dummy name a_m.

require fancier set theory.) Finally, for any propositional constant P, we shall say that P is true (is assigned the value T as in a truth table) iff P is a member of Ξ.

Call this slightly strange interpretation "I_s" ("s" for "slightly strange"). Now we shall show that for every **QL** wff A, A comes out true on I_s iff A is a member of Ξ. Call the latter claim "the Ξ Lemma."

In motivating the Enumeration Theorem, we spoke of the "length" of a given wff, which was the number of symbols occurring in that wff. Now we need a slight modification of that notion: Let us define the "operator length" of a wff as just the number of quantifiers and propositional connectives occurring in that wff, ignoring the groupers, variables, and constants. As we saw, the wff $\exists x(Fx \,\&\, Gx)$ is of length nine; but its operator length is only two, since it contains just one quantifier and one connective.

The Ξ Lemma is obviously true of simple statements. I_s assigns T to propositional constants iff they are members of Ξ, and the extensions of the property predicates are chosen in such a way as to make Fa_n true (for any individual constant a_n) when and only when Fa_n is a member of Ξ. All and only simple statements are of operator length zero.

Now, suppose there is some wff of operator length m, A_m, for which the Ξ Lemma is not true; i.e., it is false that A_m is true iff A_m is a member of Ξ. Suppose further that there is no wff of *lesser* operator length than A_m for which the Ξ Lemma fails (A_m is the operator-shortest wff of which the Ξ Lemma is not true). A_m must be of greater operator length than zero, because we have already shown that the Ξ Lemma holds for all wffs of operator length zero.

Since A_m is thus not a simple statement, there are just seven further possibilities as to what type of wff A_m might be: A_m might be a negation, a conjunction, a conditional, a biconditional, a disjunction, a universal quantification, or an existential quantification. We can run through those seven types one by one, and in each case we will be able to show that A_m is not a wff of that type. It follows that there is not in fact any such wff as A_m, since if there were, it would have to be either a simple statement or of one of the seven types.[10]

For brevity, though, I shall just give two illustrations.

Negation: If A_m is a negation, it is the negation of some wff B whose operator length is one unit less than A_m's. $-B$ ($=A_m$) is true on I_s iff B is not true on I_s. But B is true on I_s iff B is a member of Ξ, since by hypothesis the Ξ Lemma is true of any wff whose operator length is less than m. So B is true on I_s iff B is not a member of Ξ. But since Ξ is maximally D-consistent, either B or $-B$ must be a member of Ξ. (This follows immediately from the general fact, which we will use again, that for any maximally D-consistent set of wffs X (Greek "chi") and any wff C, either C or $-C$ must be a member of X; call that fact "C-fullness." Proof: If neither C nor $-C$ were a member of X, then neither

---

[10]If you followed the soundness and completeness proofs given in *PLA*1, you will recognize that the present strategy is again that of "mathematical induction," this time an induction on the operator length of wffs: the Ξ Lemma is true of wffs of operator length zero, and if the Lemma is true of a wff of operator length n, it is also true of a wff of operator length $n + 1$.

X $\cup$ {$\mathcal{C}$} nor X $\cup$ {$-\mathcal{C}$} would be D-consistent, because X is already maximally D-consistent. In that case, $-\mathcal{C}$ and $--\mathcal{C}$ would both be derivable from X, and so X itself would not be D-consistent.) Having established that either $\mathcal{B}$ or $-\mathcal{B}$ must be a member of Ξ, we have that $\mathcal{B}$ is not a member iff $-\mathcal{B}$ is a member. Therefore, $-\mathcal{B}$ $(=A_m)$ is true on I_s iff $-\mathcal{B}$ is a member of Ξ, which is to say, contrary to hypothesis, that the Ξ Lemma is true of A_m. So A_m cannot be a negation.

Universal quantification: If A_m is a universal quantification, it is a wff $\forall v \mathcal{B}$, where $\mathcal{B}$'s operator length is one unit less than A_m's.[11] $\forall v \mathcal{B}$ is true on I_s iff for every individual constant a_n, $\mathcal{B}/a_n$ is true on I_s. Since the Ξ Lemma holds for any wff of operator length less than m, this means that $\forall v \mathcal{B}$ is true on I_s iff for every constant a_n, $\mathcal{B}/a_n$ is a member of Ξ.

Now we show that for every constant a_n, $\mathcal{B}/a_n$ is a member of Ξ, iff $\forall v \mathcal{B}$ is a member of Ξ. First, right to left: Obviously any member of Ξ is derivable from Ξ (in one step). So $\forall v \mathcal{B}$ is derivable from Ξ. And therefore so will be each of its instances. Since each instance is derivable from Ξ, each instance is a member of Ξ. (Suppose an instance $\mathcal{B}/a_x$ were not a member of Ξ. Then by $\mathcal{C}$-fullness, $-\mathcal{B}/a_x$ would be a member of Ξ, hence derivable from Ξ. Since Ξ is D-consistent, $\mathcal{B}/a_x$ would not be derivable from Ξ.) Now, left to right: Suppose that for every constant a_n, $\mathcal{B}/a_n$ is a member of Ξ, but $\forall v \mathcal{B}$ is not a member of Ξ. Then by $\mathcal{C}$-fullness, the negation $-\forall v \mathcal{B}$ is a member of Ξ. Hence that negation is derivable from Ξ, and so, by an added step of QE, is $\exists v -\mathcal{B}$. By the reasoning given parenthetically five sentences back, then, $\exists v -\mathcal{B}$ is a member of Ξ. Since Ξ is ω-complete, there is also some constant a_0 such that $-\mathcal{B}/a_0$ is a member of Ξ. But by our supposition, $\mathcal{B}/a_0$ is also a member of Ξ; so, contrary to hypothesis, Ξ would not be D-consistent. So if it is true that for every constant a_n, $\mathcal{B}/a_n$ is a member of Ξ, then it must after all be true that $\forall v \mathcal{B}$ itself is a member of Ξ.

So we have two biconditionals: $\forall v \mathcal{B}$ is true on I_s iff for every constant a_n, $\mathcal{B}/a_n$ is a member of Ξ; and for every constant a_n, $\mathcal{B}/a_n$ is a member of Ξ, iff $\forall v \mathcal{B}$ is a member of Ξ. Chaining these, we obtain that $\forall v \mathcal{B}$ is true on I_s iff $\forall v \mathcal{B}$ is a member of Ξ, which is to say that the Ξ Lemma holds for the case of universal quantification. A_m cannot be a universal quantification.

The seventh, existential quantification case is excluded similarly.

By excluding all seven cases, we show that the putative A_m is neither a simple statement nor any other type of wff. So it does not exist; there is no such wff as A_m. That is, there is no wff that violates the Ξ Lemma and is the wff of shortest operator length to violate it. But if any wff at all violates the Ξ Lemma, there must be an operator-shortest wff that does. So there is no wff at all that does; the Ξ Lemma is true (of all wffs).

---

[11] $\mathcal{B}$ is not a wff, since it contains one or more free variables, but it still has an operator length as that notion has been defined.

And so our set Ξ has an interpretation, I_s, on which all its wffs come out true—which is to say that Ξ is satisfiable. Since Ξ was an arbitrarily chosen maximally D-consistent and ω-complete set, this establishes Metatheorem (2).

Stage 4

Putting Metatheorems (1) and (2) together: For every D-consistent set Γ of **QL** wffs, there is a maximally D-consistent and ω-complete set Δ that includes Γ. By (2), Δ is satisfiable. But any subset of a satisfiable set is itself satisfiable (by the same model, obviously). So Γ is satisfiable. Thus, any D-consistent set is satisfiable.

The step from this result to completeness is short. Let A be a wff and Θ ("theta") be a set of wffs of which A is a semantic consequence. Then, by definition, $\Theta \cup \{-A\}$ is not satisfiable. Hence, by the previous result, $\Theta \cup \{-A\}$ is not D-consistent; a standard contradiction can be derived from it. If so, then A can be derived from Θ alone, by a single application of Dash Out. Thus, since A and Θ were arbitrarily chosen, any semantic consequence of any set of wffs is derivable in **QL**.[12] **QL** is complete.

Undecidability

The completeness proof given for **PL** in *PLA*1 worked by means of a gigantic *algorithm*, a recipe for proof construction logically bound to succeed. That is, we came up with a set of instructions so general and so powerful that, when they're applied to any arbitrarily chosen tautologous sequent whatever, they reliably generate a correct **PL**-proof of that sequent. That is how we showed that every tautologous **PL** sequent is provable.

An algorithm is what logicians call an *effective method* for obtaining a result that one wants, a method of computing the result that is logically guaranteed to give the right answer (and no wrong answers) in a finite number of steps. Besides our completeness algorithm for **PL**, we have a second effective method for determining validity: The method of truth tables is one, and it is also an effective method for determining invalidity.

You may have noticed that our completeness proof for **QL** did not work by means of an overall algorithm, though several smaller algorithms were given within it. There is a good reason why not. In 1936, Alonzo Church[13] showed that despite the completeness of **QL**, there is no effective method for finding a proof of any given sequent of quantificational logic. In that sense, **QL** is *undecidable*. Church had previously proved the undecidability of a certain portion of

---

[12]That holds even if the set is empty. So the "tautologies" or logically valid wffs of **QL** are included.

[13]"A Note on the Entscheidungsproblem," *Journal of Symbolic Logic* 1 (1936), 40–41, 101–102.

number theory in mathematics; he then extended the result by showing that if quantificational logic were decidable, so would be the relevant portion of number theory.

It is a little eerie that we should know (by our completeness proof) that every semantically valid sequent is provable in **QL**, yet have no overall algorithm or other effective method for finding their proofs. But that is and will always remain the case.

APPENDIX 3

Using PredLogic

You can dive straight into *PredLogic* and learn how to use it as you go or, if you prefer, read about the program first in this appendix.

Getting Started

PredLogic is a tutorial program designed to help you master the material presented in *Predicate Logic*, 2nd ed. It will assist you as you learn to symbolize sentences and arguments, construct proofs of validity, devise counterexamples, and create truth trees. The program will assess your work, enabling you to catch errors as you make them, and it will offer hints for solving problems. System requirements are Windows 98 or later, a color monitor, and a mouse.

PredLogic can be run directly from the CD-ROM disk or from the hard drive of your computer. It is better to run the program from your hard drive for several reasons, including faster and smoother operation. You should run the program from the CD-ROM disk only if you are prevented from loading it on the hard drive. (This will likely be the case if you use a computer in a college computer lab.)

Installing *PredLogic* on Your Hard Drive

1. Click the *Start* button on the taskbar.
2. Click *Run*.
3. Type: D:Setup *(Here I assume that "D:" names the CD-ROM drive. If the CD-ROM drive is identified with a different letter, use that letter in place of "D.")*
4. Click *OK*.
5. Follow the instructions displayed on-screen.

Running *PredLogic* from Your Hard Drive (After Installation)

1. Click the *Start* button on the taskbar.
2. Highlight *Programs*.
3. Highlight *Logic*.
4. Click *PredLogic*.

Of course, if you place the *Shortcut to PredLogic* icon on the desktop, you can run the program by double-clicking that icon. (Instructions for placing the shortcut on the desktop are provided in the section on "Trouble Shooting.")

Running *PredLogic* from the CD-ROM Disk

1. Click the *Start* button on the taskbar.
2. Click *Run.*
3. Type: D:PredLogic *(Here I assume that "D:" names the CD-ROM drive. Make appropriate adjustments if necessary.)*
4. Click *OK.*

Using *PredLogic*

I'll start by explaining features that are found throughout the program and then provide explanations for each of the five sections of *PredLogic.*

Special logic symbols may be entered by pressing buttons at the bottom of the screen or by typing characters or pressing certain *F*-keys:

For this symbol	Type this character	Or press this F-key
∃	#	F5
∀	$	F6
↔	<	F7
→	>	F8
v	@	F9
&	&	F10
−	-	F11
⊢	+	F12

The symbol buttons at the bottom of the screen can be removed by invoking a command on the *View* drop-down menu (on the toolbar).

There are three main ways to navigate between the sections of *PredLogic:*

1. You can use the menu on the initial screen. Click on a section name to move to that section.
2. You can use the drop-down menu under *Sections.*
3. You can use the first five *F*-keys (with Shift). For example, pressing Shift-F1 takes you to the first section.

You can transfer sequents from one section of the program to another by moving to the new section by either the second or the third method described above. If you move via the first method, the sequent will be lost. (Note that invalid sequents cannot be transported to the PROOFS section and valid sequents cannot be moved to the COUNTEREXAMPLES section.)

Several buttons are common to most or all of the sections. Here is what they do:

NAME	*GRAPHIC*	*FUNCTION*
Help		Explains how the section operates.
Menu		Returns you to the main menu screen.
New		Erases the sequent *and* your work.
Clear		Erases your work but not the sequent.
Next		Sets the next practice problem.
Hint		Provides a hint.
Check		Checks your work.

I'll mention some miscellaneous matters next. (You might want to skip on to the instructions for using the program section you are most interested in and return to these points later.)

- Right-clicking often brings up a pop-up shortcut menu with common commands. Different sections have different shortcut menus.
- *PredLogic* installs some sample proof, CEX, and truth tree files. The files are located in *PredLogic*'s default working directory. Use the *Open* button (in the relevant section) to load one of these files.
- Sections three through five remember the four most recently used files. A list of these files may be found on the *File* drop-down menu.
- You may wish to print several problems on one sheet of paper. You can do this (in most sections) by saving the problems to be printed and then placing the file names on the printer manifest. You can use the *Move Up* and *Move Down* buttons on the printer manifest box to change the order in which problems will be printed. (Note that you can print multiple problems on one sheet only if the problems are of the same type, for example, all proofs. You cannot print more than one truth tree on a single sheet.)

- Correct answers are often identified with a green check mark, and incorrect answers are marked with a red *X*. In some sections, a non-wff is labeled with a purple slashed circle.
- All of the program's help messages can be accessed by means of the *Help* drop-down menu on the toolbar.
- You can turn off sounds via the *Options* drop-down menu.
- The program has several default settings and message reminders that can be turned off or overridden. To restore the default settings, use the command in the Options menu item on the Main Menu screen.

The Five Sections of *PredLogic*

Formulas Overview: In this section you learn to distinguish between formulas that are well formed (wffs) and those that are not well formed (non-wffs). The program explains why certain formulas are ill formed.
Instructions for using this section:

- Enter a formula in the white window. It will be checked automatically as you type. If your formula is well formed the *wff* box appears. If your formula is not well formed the *not a wff* box appears.
- Use the *Hint* button to get an explanation for why a formula is not well formed.
- Press the *About Wffs* button to study the definition of a well-formed formula.

Symbolizations Overview: In this section you symbolize textbook exercises while the program checks your work. This is particularly useful because mis-symbolizing an exercise will adversely affect the rest of your work on that exercise. The section also provides problems for further symbolization practice. The program catches your symbolization mistakes and offers hints designed to help you reach the correct symbolization.
Instructions for using this section:

- Select a chapter (2–13) from the white box in the upper left corner. Then select an exercise from either the *Book Exercises* or the *Practice Problems* box to the right of the *Chapter* box. (Note: Practice problems are available only for Chapters 2, 5, 10, and 13.)
- Enter your answer in the large white window. Each line is checked as you type. An evaluation symbol will appear to the left of each line to indicate whether it is correct (check mark), incorrect/incomplete (*X*), or not well formed (slashed circle).
- If a problem has you stumped, use the *Hint* button. The program will reveal the overall structure of the correct symbolization. Predicate letters, variables, individual constants, and sentence letters are represented by

P, *v*, *c*, and *S*, respectively. Propositional connectives appear in color in order to distinguish a wedge from any *v* that represents a variable. If the problem involves several sentences, you can tell the program which symbolization you want a hint for by using the arrow keys or mouse pointer to place the cursor on that line.

- If the program evaluates your symbolization as well formed but incorrect (by posting a red *X*), you may press the *Hint* button to obtain an explanation of the problem. Typically the program will inform you that your symbolization does not entail the sentence or that the sentence does not entail your symbolization (or both). It will often provide a brief proof to bolster its assessment. For example, to show that your symbolization does not entail the sentence, it may provide a wff that is entailed by the sentence but is not entailed by your symbolization.
- Note that to be correct a symbolization must have the same content as the sentence and must also "track" the sentence satisfactorily.
- A yellow smiley face will appear when the symbolization of a sequent is entirely correct. A correctly symbolized sequent may be saved, printed, and/or transported to other sections of the program.

Additional points:

- Exercises that are already symbolized in the book are included in the *Book Exercises* list as a convenience to the user. These sequents can be transported to other sections of the program without the user typing them in.
- Press the *Symbolization Guide* button for a list of English connective expressions and the symbols that translate them.

Proofs   Overview: In this section you construct formal proofs for valid sequents while the program checks your work and offers explanations of the mistakes you may make.

Instructions for using this section:

- Select a chapter (3, 4, 6, or 11) from the white box in the upper left corner. Then select an exercise from the white *Practice Problems* box. Or just create your own proof problem by typing premises and a conclusion in the proof box (one wff per proof line).
- Enter formulas and justifications in the appropriate columns. (The columns expand as you type.) To move between columns, use the tab or arrow keys or click on the columns or their headings. *PredLogic* creates line numbers for you and renumbers lines automatically as you insert or delete lines. It makes the necessary adjustments to the line numbers occurring in the justification and assumption-dependence columns. The assumption-dependence column appears when necessary.

- Use the *Check* button to check your proof.
- Use the *Hint* button for a more detailed explanation of an error in your justification column.

Additional points:

- To undo the most recent action, use the *Undo* button or the command on the *Edit* drop-down menu.
- If a quantification begins with two or more contiguous existential quantifiers or two or more contiguous universal quantifiers, the program permits the shortcut of instantiating all the quantifiers in one step. It supports a similar shortcut for steps of ∃I.
- To toggle between strict (default) and lenient line number checking, use the *Strict Checking* command on the *Options* drop-down menu. In strict checking, line numbers in justification entries are accepted in only one order, the order that corresponds to the statement of the rule.
- To toggle between wide and narrow columns, use the *Re-size Formula Column* button or the command on the *Edit* drop-down menu.
- Press the *Rules* button to see a list of the inference rules. Pressing on a rule name on this list will provide an example of the rule in use in a proof.
- Press the *Font Size* button to change font size. You can keep a long or wide proof from extending beyond the screen by reducing font size.
- The program includes eight sample proofs with file names like "example1.prf". Use the *Open* button to load a sample proof.

    Counterexamples   Overview: In this section you construct CEXes while the program checks your work.
    Instructions for using this section:

- Enter a sequent in the white edit box at the top. Place commas between premises and precede the conclusion with the turnstile ("+" or F12). Formulas that are not well formed will appear in red. Or you may import an invalid sequent from the Symbolization section or select an exercise from the white Practice Problems box.
- Select a domain by clicking on either the *Domains* drop-down menu or the *Domains* button. You may choose from among seven domains:

          Integers 0 to 100
          Integers −100 to 100
          Selected Integers
          People

Farmer Logik's Barn
Jay Leno's Garage
Dr. X's Aquarium

The first four are actual-world domains and the last three possible-world domains. Note that the *people* domain may not be used for relational sequents.

- Assign a meaning to each predicate and sentence letter in your sequent by making a selection from the drop-down list that appears next to the letter. Assign each individual constant in your sequent to some member of the domain.
- To check a CEX, press the *Check Counterexample* button. The truth value of each wff in the sequent will be shown (T = True, F = False, ? = Undetermined). A CEX is correct when and only when all predicate and sentence letters are defined, all individual constants are assigned to members of the domain, all premises are true (T), and the conclusion is false (F).
- Use the *Clear Counterexample* button (the eraser) to remove definitions and undo constant assignments.
- The program includes nine sample CEXes with file names like "example1.cex". Use the *Open* button to load a sample CEX.

Additional instructions for the three graphic domains:

- Assign members to the domain by left-clicking on any of the nine cells. Click repeatedly to change members. Note: your domain must have at least one member.
- Move the mouse pointer over a constant and it will become a lasso, a wheel, or a net. Hold down the left mouse button and drag the constant to the appropriate cell.
- Use the *Clear Counterexample* button to empty the domain (and erase definitions).

Truth Trees   Overview: In this section you construct truth trees while the program checks your work. The program will locate errors that you may make.

Instructions for using this section:

- Enter a sequent or a single wff in the white edit box at the top. Place commas between premises of a sequent and precede the conclusion with the turnstile. If every formula is well formed, the trunk of a truth tree will be constructed automatically. Or you can click on the down arrowhead and select a practice problem from the list that appears.
- Empty tree entries appear as red question marks. Left-click on the question mark (or subsequent red dot) until the correct rule has been applied

to the wff indicated by the yellow arrow. Wffs that have not been decomposed are red. Decomposed wffs marked with a plus are blue. Decomposed wffs marked with a check mark and wffs that cannot be further decomposed are black.

- When you decompose a quantification, an *Instantiation* box appears so that you can select the individual constant to be employed in the move. If the quantification begins with two or more contiguous existential quantifiers or two or more contiguous universal quantifers, the program permits the shortcut of instantiating all the quantifiers in one step.
- *PredLogic* positions the yellow arrow to help minimize tree length. You may use the tab or arrow keys to move the yellow arrow to another red (not yet decomposed) wff.
- If a completed branch contains no (blue) plus-marked wff or undispatched decomposable wff, you can mark it closed (*), open (o), or cycling (∞) by left-clicking the red question mark at the tip. If the branch contains a plus-marked wff or an undispatched decomposable wff, you can mark its tip by right-clicking the question mark and (if necessary) then left-clicking the tip.
- To check a truth tree, press the *Check Truth Tree* button. If the tree is correct, the program will ask what the tree demonstrates. If the tree is incorrect, the program will draw a red *X* at the spot (or one of the spots) where the tree goes wrong. If you move the mouse pointer to the *X*, the pointer will become an eraser. Left-click to remove the erroneous part of the tree, then make corrections in the usual fashion.

Additional points:

- To create a tree with a single wff on the right of the trunk, precede the wff by *R* and a period (.).
- When creating large truth trees, branches can overlap. Use the *Redraw Tree* button. To view more of a large tree, reduce font size with the *Change Font Size* button.
- Use the *Undo Move* button (repeatedly if necessary) to undo the most recent moves. To undo larger portions of a tree, move the mouse pointer over the region in question. When the pointer becomes a pair of pruning shears, left-click to undo the tree to that point.
- Press the *Rules* button to see a list of truth tree rules.
- You can stop the program from asking what a completed truth tree shows via a command on the *Options* drop-down menu.
- The program includes eight sample truth trees with file names like "example1.tre". Use the *Open* button to load a sample tree.

Trouble Shooting

Symptom: Logic symbols do not appear correctly on the monitor or printouts. For example, typing the "#" symbol produces "#" on the screen, rather than the flipped-*E*.

Cause: "Logic" font is not installed correctly.

Solution: Exit *PredLogic*. Use *Windows Explorer* to open the *Windows\ Fonts* folder on the hard drive. Look for font name *Logic* (file name: pl_fnt.ttf). If this font is not present, copy the file (pl_fnt.ttf) from the *PredLogic* CD-ROM disk into the *Windows\Fonts* folder. Restart *PredLogic*.

* * *

Symptom: The logic problem (proof or truth tree) does not entirely fit on the monitor screen.

Various Solutions:

(a) Reduce font size using the *Change Font Size* button.
(b) Increase screen resolution (choose *Settings* from the Start menu, click on *Control Panel*, double-click on *Display*, and then choose the *Settings* tab).
(c) Hide the Windows taskbar or other toolbars that occupy screen space. To hide the taskbar, click the *Start* button, highlight *Settings*, click *Taskbar*, check *Auto hide*, and click *OK*.
(d) Use the scrollbar that appears when the problem extends beyond the screen.

* * *

Symptom: The shortcut to *PredLogic* is not on the desktop.

Solution:

1. Run *Windows Explorer* (with part of the desktop exposed).
2. Locate the file *PredLogic.exe* in the folder *Program Files\PredLogic*.
3. Using the left mouse button drag the file name to the desktop.
4. Exit *Windows Explorer*.

Uninstalling *PredLogic*

1. Click the *Start* button on the taskbar.
2. Highlight *Settings.*
3. Click *Control Panel.*
4. Double-click *Add/Remove Programs.*
5. Click *PredLogic.*
6. Click *Add/Remove.*
7. Click *Yes* (to confirm file deletion).
8. Click *OK* (to exit uninstaller).
9. Click *Cancel* (to exit Add/Remove Programs).
10. Click *X* (to exit Control Panel).

Solutions to Starred Exercises

Chapter 2: Basic Symbolization

1. (b) $\exists x(Sx \, \& \, Nx)$ (Sx = x is a singular statement, Nx = x is negative)
   (f) $\exists x(Hx \, \& \, Ox)$ (Hx = x is a horse-drawn bus)
   (j) $\exists x(Mx \, \& \, Fx)$ *or* $\exists x(Fx \, \& \, Mx)$

2. (b) Janet Reno does not live in Ohio.
   (f) Some Ohioans are not politicians.

3. (b) $\forall x(Wx \rightarrow -Ex)$ (Wx = x is a wealthy person, Ex = x is executed)
   (f) $\forall x(Wx \rightarrow -Ax)$ (Wx = x is a woman who seeks to be equal to men)
   (j) $\exists x(Px \, \& \, Yx)$ (Px = x is a royal poinciana, Yx = x has yellow blossoms)
   (n) $\forall x(Rx \rightarrow Dx)$ (Rx = x dies rich, Dx = x dies disgraced)

4. (b) $\forall x(Ix \rightarrow Ax)$ (Ix = x is an insect, Ax = x has antennae)
   (f) $\forall x(Kx \rightarrow Lx)$
   (j) $\forall x(Bx \rightarrow Lx)$ (Lx = x is lonely, Bx = x is brave)
   (n) $\forall x(Hx \rightarrow Cx)$

5. (b) No salamanders are reptiles.

6. (b) I
   (f) A

Chapter 3: Proofs: ∀O and ∃O

1. (b)

2	(2)		
3	(3)		
4	(4)		
2	(5)		2 ∀O
4	(6)	Fe → Ge	4 ∀O
1,2	(7)		5,1 →O
1,2,4	(8)	Ge	6,7 →O
1,2,3,4	(9)		8,3 &I
	(10)		4-9 −I

2. (b) (1) ∀x(Ax → Fx)   A   *The one-line symboliza-*
        (2) −Fl   A   *tion of the argument is*
        (3) Al → Fl   1 ∀O   *omitted; the symboliza-*
        (4) −Al   3,2 MT   *tion can be read from the*
                                                      proof. Only one proof for
5.   (1) ∀x(Px → Ax)   A   *each problem will be*
        (2) ∀x(Ax → Mx)   A   *given, even though often*
        (3) −Ms   A   *there will be several cor-*
        (4) Ps → As   1 ∀O   *rect proofs.*
        (5) As → Ms   2 ∀O
        (6) Ps → Ms   4,5 CH
        (7) −Ps   6,3 MT

9. (b) 1   (1) ∀x(Bx → −Ax)   A
        2   (2) ∃x(Bx & Ax)   PA
        2   (3) Bc & Ac   2 ∃O
        1   (4) Bc → −Ac   1 ∀O
        2   (5) Bc   3 &O
        1,2 (6) −Ac   4,5 →O
        2   (7) Ac   3 &O
        1,2 (8) Ac & −Ac   7,6 &I
        1   (9) −∃x(Bx & Ax)   2-8 −I

13.   1   (1) ∀x(Ex → Cx)   A
        2   (2) ∀x(Mx → Ex)   A
        3   (3) ∀x(Cx → −Fx)   A
        4   (4) ∃x(Fx & Mx)   PA
        4   (5) Fa & Ma   4 ∃O
        1   (6) Ea → Ca   1 ∀O
        2   (7) Ma → Ea   2 ∀O
        3   (8) Ca → −Fa   3 ∀O
        1,2   (9) Ma → Ca   7,6 CH
        1,2,3   (10) Ma → −Fa   9,8 CH
        4   (11) Ma   5 &O
        1,2,3,4   (12) −Fa   10,11 →O
        4   (13) Fa   5 &O
        1,2,3,4   (14) Fa & −Fa   13,12 &I
        1,2,3   (15) −∃x(Fx & Mx)   4-14 −I

Chapter 4: Proofs: ∃I and QE

3.   (1) ∀x(Mx → Dx)   A   *I omit several wffs from this proof*
        (2) ∃x(Mx & −Sx)   A   *and from subsequent proofs. The*
        (3) Ma & −Sa   2 ∃O   *purpose is to encourage you to en-*
        (4)   1 ∀O   *gage in proof construction, rather*
        (5) Ma   3 &O   *than passively observing the results*
                                       of my work.

      (6)   4,5 →O
      (7)   3 &O
      (8) Da & −Sa   6,7 &I
      (9) ∃x(Dx & −Sx)   8 ∃I

7.   (1) ∀x(Bx → Mx)   A
         (2) ∃x(Ex & Bx)   A
         (3) Ea & Ba   2 ∃O
         (4)   1 ∀O
         (5) Ba   3 &O
         (6)   4,5 →O
         (7)   3 &O
         (8)   7,6 &I
         (9) ∃x(Ex & Mx)   8 ∃I

10. (b) 2   (2)
           1   (3)   1 QE
           2   (4)   2 QE
           2   (5)   4 ∃O
           1   (6)   3 ∀O
           1   (7)   6 DM
           1   (8)   7 AR
                (9)   8,5 &I
              (10)   2-9 −O

12. (a) 1   (1) ∀x(Px → Nx)   A
          2   (2) ∀x(Nx → Rx)   A
          3   (3) −∀x(Px → Rx)   PA
          3   (4) ∃x−(Px → Rx)   3 QE
          3   (5) −(Pa → Ra)   4 ∃O
          1   (6)   1 ∀O
          2   (7)   2 ∀O
         1,2 (8)   6,7 CH
        1,2,3 (9) (Pa → Ra) & −(Pa → Ra) 8,5 &I
         1,2 (10) ∀x(Px → Rx)   3-9 −O

13. (b) 1   (1) ∀x(Mx → Dx)   A
          2   (2) ∃x(Mx & −Sx)   A
          3   (3) −∃x(Dx & −Sx) PA
          3   (4)   3 QE
          2   (5) Ma & −Sa   2 ∃O
          1   (6)   1 ∀O
          3   (7)   4 ∀O
          2   (8) Ma   5 &O
        1,2 (9)   6,8 →O
       1,2,3 (10) −−Sa   7,9 CA

2	(11)		5 &O
1,2,3	(12)		11,10 &I
1,2	(13)	$\exists x(Dx \& -Sx)$	3-12 $-$O

15.	1	(1) $\forall x(Tx \rightarrow Dx)$	A
	2	(2) $\forall x(Dx \rightarrow Ux)$	A
	3	(3) $\forall x(Ux \rightarrow Nx)$	A
	4	(4) $-\forall x(Tx \rightarrow Nx)$	PA
	4	(5)	4 QE
	4	(6) $-(Ta \rightarrow Na)$	5 $\exists$O
	1	(7)	1 $\forall$O
	2	(8)	2 $\forall$O
	3	(9)	3 $\forall$O
	1,2	(10)	7,8 CH
	1,2,3	(11)	10,9 CH
	1,2,3,4	(12) $(Ta \rightarrow Na) \& -(Ta \rightarrow Na)$	11,6 &I
	1,2,3	(13) $\forall x(Tx \rightarrow Nx)$	4-12 $-$O

Chapter 5:   Intermediate Symbolization

1. (b) $\forall xSx$ (Sx = x sins)
   (f) $\forall x(-Gx \rightarrow -Mx)$
   (j) $\forall x(Ix \leftrightarrow Cx)$ *or* $\forall x(Cx \leftrightarrow Ix)$ (Cx = x has the capacity for suffering and enjoyment, Ix = x has interests)
   (n) $\forall x(Kx \leftrightarrow -Tx)$ (Tx = x is a transient)

2. (b) $-\forall x(Hx \text{ v } Bx)$ *or* $\exists x-(Hx \text{ v } Bx)$ (Hx = x is a hunk, Bx = x is a babe)
   (f) $\exists x[Fx \& (Cx \text{ v } Nx)]$ (Fx = x is a fish, Cx = x is a cardinal tetra, Nx = x is a neon tetra)
   (j) $-\forall x[Hx \rightarrow (Wx \text{ v } Gx)]$ *or* $\exists x[Hx \& -(Wx \text{ v } Gx)]$ (Hx = x is a comic book hero, Wx = x is white, Gx = x is green)
   (n) $\forall x[Jx \leftrightarrow (Mx \text{ v } Cx)]$ (Jx = x is a Jew, Mx = x's mother is Jewish, Cx = x has converted to Judaism)

3. (b) Not everyone is obese.
   (f) Some obese vegetarians do not diet.

4. (b) $\forall x[Sx \rightarrow (Lx \text{ v } Fx)]$ (Lx = x is a liar, Fx = x is a fool, Sx = x can call smoking safe)
   (f) $\forall x[Bx \rightarrow (Nx \text{ v } - Rx)]$ *or*
       $\forall x\{Bx \rightarrow [(Nx \text{ v } -Rx) \text{ v } (Nx \& -Rx)]\}$ (Nx = x is naive)

   The two symbolizations for 4(f) are equivalent.

   (j) $\forall x[(Wx \text{ v } Bx) \rightarrow (Cx \& -Ax)]$ (Bx = x is described as "black," Cx = x is a criminal suspect, Ax = x has been apprehended)

(n) ∀x[(Dx v Cx) → Tx] *or* ∀x[(Dx → Tx) & (Cx → Tx)] (Dx = x
is a drunkard, Cx = x is a child, Tx = x tells the truth)
The two symbolizations for 4(n) are equivalent.

8. (b) Pm v Po (m = the Michigan State team, o = the Wisconsin team,
Px = x will play for the national championship)
(f) P → (Lu v Lf) (Lx = x will lose)
(j) ∃x(T → Dx) (Dx = x dies)

9. (b) ∃xLx → Lf (f = the Florida Marlins)
(f) ∃xGx & −∀xGx
(j) ∀x(Bx → Lx) & −∀x(Lx → Bx) (Bx = x is a bobcat, Lx = x is a
lynx)

10. (b) ∀xEx → ∃xTx (Ex = x passes the exam, Tx = x will throw a
party)
(f) ∀x(Tx → Kx) (Tx = x touches the light pole, Kx = x will be
killed)
(j) ∀x[(Yx & −Wx) → Sx] & ∀x[(Ox & −Lx) → Fx] (Yx = x is
young, Wx = x has wept, Sx = x is a savage, Ox = x is old,
Lx = x will laugh, Fx = x is a fool)

11. (b) If someone is a Baptist, then someone is a Protestant.
(f) Everyone is either female or male.

Chapter 6: Intermediate Proofs

1. (b) 2   (3)   2 ∃O
1   (4)   1 ∀O
1,2   (5)   4,3 →O
1,2   (6)   5 ∃I
1   (7)   2 6 →I

3.   (1) ∀x[Ix ↔ (Gx v Sx)]   A
(2) −Gt & −St   A
(3)   1 ∀O
(4) It → (Gt v St)   3 ↔O
(5)   2 DM
(6) −It   4,5 MT

7.   (1) ∀xAx v ∀x−Ax   A   *The first premise may also be*
(2) −Ag   A   *symbolized: ∀xAx v −∃xAx*
(3)   2 ∃I
(4)   3 QE   *The conclusion may be*
(5) ∀x−Ax   1,4 DA *symbolized: −∃xAx*

10. (b) 1   (1) ∃x(Ax → Bx)   A
2   (2) ∀xAx   PA

1	(3)	Ac → Bc	1 ∃O
2	(4)		2 ∀O
1,2	(5)		3,4 →O
1,2	(6)		5 ∃I
1	(7)	∀xAx → ∃xBx	2-6 →I

13.

1	(1)	∀x(−Lx → −Ux)	A
2	(2)	∀x(Lx → −Mx)	A
3	(3)	−∀x(−Ux v −Mx)	PA
3	(4)		3 QE
3	(5)	−(−Ua v −Ma)	4 ∃O
1	(6)		1 ∀O
2	(7)		2 ∀O
1	(8)	Ua → La	6 CN
1,2	(9)	Ua → −Ma	8,7 CH
1,2	(10)		9 AR
1,2,3	(11)	(−Ua v −Ma) & −(−Ua v −Ma)	10,5 &I
1,2	(12)	∀x(−Ux v −Mx)	3-11 −O

15. (a)

1	(1)	∀x(Sx ↔ Cx)	A	*The second premise may*
2	(2)	∀x(Gx ↔ −Cx)	A	*be symbolized:*
3	(3)	−∀x(Sx v Gx)	PA	∀x(−Cx ↔ Gx)
3	(4)	∃x−(Sx v Gx)	3 QE	
3	(5)	−(Sa v Ga)	4 ∃O	
1	(6)	Sa ↔ Ca	1 ∀O	
2	(7)	Ga ↔ −Ca	2 ∀O	
3	(8)	−Sa & −Ga	5 DM	
3	(9)	−Sa	8 &O	
1	(10)	Ca → Sa	6 ↔O	
1,3	(11)	−Ca	10,9 MT	
3	(12)	−Ga	8 &O	
2	(13)	−Ca → Ga	7 ↔O	
2,3	(14)	−−Ca	13,12 MT	
1,2,3	(15)	−Ca & −−Ca	11,14 &I	
1,2	(16)	∀x(Sx v Gx)	3-15 −O	

18.

1	(1)	∀xLx	A
2	(2)	∀x(Lx → Ix)	PA
3	(3)	−∀xIx	PA
3	(4)	∃x−Ix	3 QE
3	(5)	−Ia	4 ∃O
1	(6)	La	1 ∀O
2	(7)	La → Ia	2 ∀O
1,2	(8)	Ia	7,6 →O
1,2,3	(9)	Ia & −Ia	8,5 &I
1,2	(10)	∀xIx	3-9 −O
1	(11)	∀x(Lx → Ix) → ∀xIx	2-10 →I

22.

1	(1)	$-\forall xJx \rightarrow -\exists xJx$	A	*The first premise may*
2	(2)	$\forall x(-Jx \rightarrow -Hx)$	A	*be symbolized:*
3	(3)	$-\forall xJx$	PA	$-\forall xJx \rightarrow \forall x-Jx$
4	(4)	$\exists xHx$	PA	
1,3	(5)	$-\exists xJx$	1,3 $\rightarrow$O	*The conclusion may be*
1,3	(6)	$\forall x-Jx$	5 QE	*symbolized:*
4	(7)	Ha	4 $\exists$O	$-\forall xJx \rightarrow \forall x-Hx$
2	(8)	$-Ja \rightarrow -Ha$	2 $\forall$O	
1,3	(9)	$-Ja$	6 $\forall$O	
1,2,3	(10)	$-Ha$	8,9 $\rightarrow$O	
1,2,3,4	(11)	Ha & $-Ha$	7,10 &I	
1,2,3	(12)	$-\exists xHx$	4-11 $-$I	
1,2	(13)	$-\forall xJx \rightarrow -\exists xHx$	3-12 $\rightarrow$I	

Chapter 7: Counterexamples

1. (b) **CEX dictionary:** domain: people; Fx = x is female,
a = Julia Roberts
CEX: Julia Roberts is female. (T)
So, everyone is female. (F)

3. **target dictionary:** Kx = x is a type of knowledge,
c = courage, Vx = x is a virtue
symbolization: Kc, Vc ⊦ $\forall x(Vx \rightarrow Kx)$
CEX dictionary: domain: integers; Kx = x is odd,
c = 3, Vx = x is less than 10
CEX: 3 is odd. (T)
3 is less than 10. (T)
So, all integers less than 10 are odd. (F)

Note: In the remaining solutions I omit the target dictionary.

6. (b) **symbolization:** $\forall x(Fx \rightarrow -Cx)$, $-\forall x(Hx \rightarrow Cx)$ ⊦ $\forall x(Hx \rightarrow Fx)$
CEX dictionary: domain: animals; Fx = x is a cat, Cx = x is a
dog, Hx = x is a mammal
CEX: No cats are dogs. (T)
Not all mammals are dogs. (T)
So, all mammals are cats. (F)

7. **symbolization:** $\forall x(Hx \rightarrow Px)$, $\forall x(Mx \rightarrow Px)$ ⊦ $\forall x(Hx \rightarrow Mx)$
CEX dictionary: domain: people; Hx = x is a dermatologist,
Px = x is a physician, Mx = x is a psychiatrist
CEX: All dermatologists are physicians. (T)
All psychiatrists are physicians. (T)
So, all dermatologists are psychiatrists. (F)

10. (b) **symbolization:** ∀x[(Lx v Hx) v Gx], −∀xLx, −∀xHx ⊢ ∃xGx
    CEX dictionary: domain: integers; Lx = x is even, Hx = x is odd, Gx = x is both even and odd
    CEX: Each integer is even or odd or both. (T)
    Not all integers are even. (T)
    Not all integers are odd. (T)
    So, some integers are both even and odd. (F)

The parentheses in the first premise wff of 10(b) may be positioned differently.

14. (b) Every animal (in the barn) is a chicken or a duck. (T)
    So, either every animal is a chicken or every animal is a duck. (F)

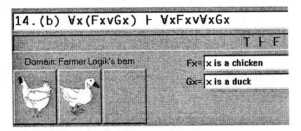

14.(b) ∀x(FxvGx) ⊢ ∀xFxv∀xGx
T ⊢ F
Domain: Farmer Logik's barn
Fx= x is a chicken
Gx= x is a duck

16. (a) Every duck (in the barn) is white. (T)
    No chicken is a duck. (T)
    So, no chicken is white. (F)

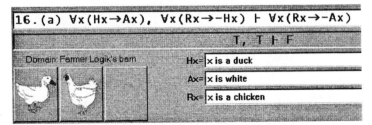

16.(a) ∀x(Hx→Ax), ∀x(Rx→−Hx) ⊢ ∀x(Rx→−Ax)
T, T ⊢ F
Domain: Farmer Logik's barn
Hx= x is a duck
Ax= x is white
Rx= x is a chicken

(e) All chickens are animals. (T)
    All chickens are birds. (T)
    So, all animals are birds. (F)

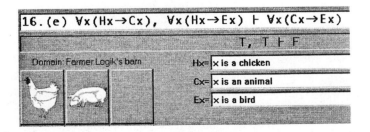

16.(e) ∀x(Hx→Cx), ∀x(Hx→Ex) ⊢ ∀x(Cx→Ex)
T, T ⊢ F
Domain: Farmer Logik's barn
Hx= x is a chicken
Cx= x is an animal
Ex= x is a bird

19. (b) If no chickens are on the third floor, then not all pigs are mammals. (T)
All pigs are mammals. (T)
So, either all animals on the third floor are chickens or all chickens
are on the third floor. (F)

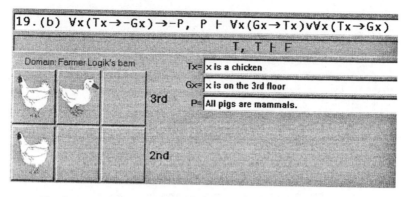

The first premise is true because its antecedent is false.

Chapter 8:   Truth Trees

1. (b) +∀xGx   The tree is closed.
            |
          ∃xGx+
       Ga ─┤
            |
           Ga
            ↓
            *

I omit the symbolization of the argument; it can be read from the tree.

2. (b) ✓∃x(Mx & −Sx)   valid
                      |
                    −∀xSx✓
           +∀xSx ─┤
          ✓Ma & −Sa
                Sa
                Ma
              ✓−Sa
                  |
                 Sa
                  ↓
                  *

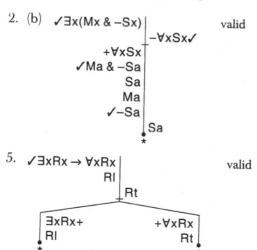

9.   valid

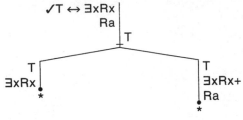

11. (b)   +∀x(Ix → Ux)   invalid
          +∀x(Mx → Ux)

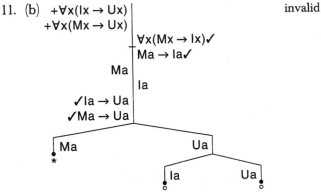

14.   valid

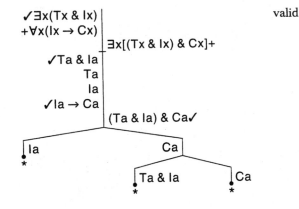

15. (d) +∀x(Gx → −Fx)   valid

18. (a)

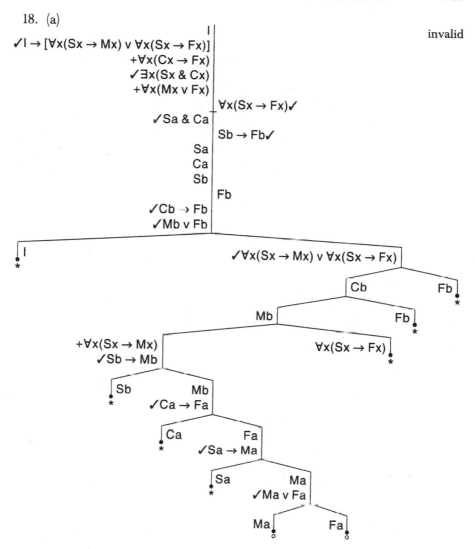

invalid

Chapter 9:   **Property-Logic Refinements**

1. (b) **symbolization:**   ∀xRx v ∀x−Rx
   status: contingent
   1st CEX dictionary: domain: people; Rx = x is a person

CEX: Either everyone is a person or no one is a person. (T)

2nd CEX dictionary: domain: people; Rx = x is female

CEX: Either everyone is female or no one is female. (F)

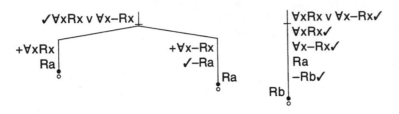

2. (c) **symbolization:** ∀xFx → ∃xFx

    status: logical truth

    1 (1) ∀xFx   PA

    1 (2) Fa   1 ∀O

    1 (3) ∃xFx   2 ∃I

    (4) ∀xFx → ∃xFx   1-3 →I

```
             ∀xFx → ∃xFx✓
      +∀xFx
                  ∃xFx+
        Fa
                  Fa
              *
```

4. (a) **symbolization:** −∀x(Sx → Sx)

    status: contradiction

    1 (1) −∀x(Sx → Sx)   A

    1 (2) ∃x−(Sx → Sx)   1 QE

    1 (3) −(Sa → Sa)   2 ∃I

    1 (4) Sa & −Sa   3 AR

```
       ✓−∀x(Sx → Sx)
                     ∀x(Sx → Sx)✓
                     Sa → Sa✓
             Sa
                     Sa
                 *
```

7. (b) **symbolization:** ∀x(Ax → −Lx) ⊢ ∃x(Ax & −Lx)

    CEX dictionary: domain: people; Ax = x is more than 12 feet tall, Lx = x is less than 10 feet tall

    CEX: Anyone over 12 feet tall is not less than 10 feet tall. (T)

    So, someone over 12 feet tall is not less than 10 feet tall (F)

```
        +∀x(Ax → −Lx)
                     ∃x(Ax & −Lx)+
          ✓Aa → −La
                     Aa & −La✓

           Aa              ✓−La
                                La
        Aa       −La✓
          °    La         Aa       −La
               °          °          *
```

supplementary premise: ∃xAx

(1) ∀x(Ax → −Lx)   A
(2) ∃xAx   A
(3) Ab   2 ∃O
(4) Ab → −Lb   1 ∀O
(5) −Lb   4,3 →O
(6) Ab & −Lb   3,5 &I
(7) ∃x(Ax & −Lx)   6 ∃I

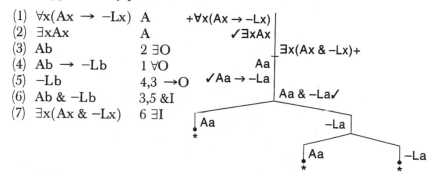

11. **symbolization:**   ∀x(Gx → Mx), ∀x(Mx → −Cx) ⊢ ∃x(Cx &−Gx)
    CEX dictionary: domain: integers; Gx = x is greater than 3, Mx = x
    is greater than 2, Cx = x is both even and odd

    CEX: All integers greater than 3 are greater than 2. (T)
    No integers greater than 2 are both even and odd. (T)
    So, some even-and-odd integers are not greater than
    3. (F)

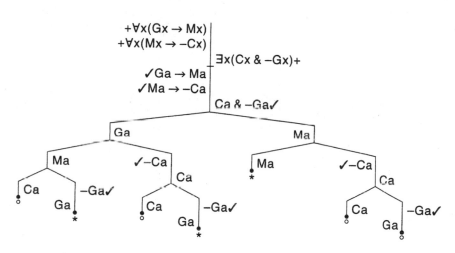

supplementary premise: ∃xCx
    (1) ∀x(Gx → Mx)   A
    (2) ∀x(Mx → −Cx)   A
    (3) ∃xCx   A
    (4) Ca   3 ∃O
    (5) Ga → Ma   1 ∀O
    (6) Ma → −Ca   2 ∀O
    (7) Ga → −Ca   5,6 CH
    (8) −−Ca   4 DN
    (9) −Ga   7,8 MT

(10) Ca & −Ga   4,9 &I
(11) ∃x (Cx & −Gx)   10 ∃I

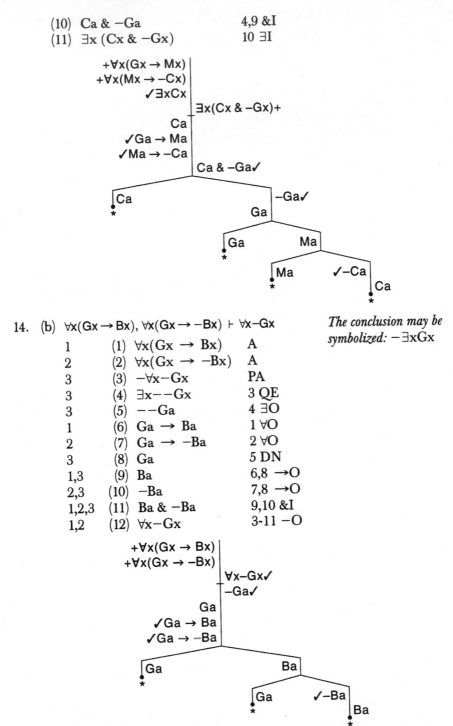

14. (b) ∀x(Gx → Bx), ∀x(Gx → −Bx) ⊢ ∀x−Gx   *The conclusion may be*
                                                       symbolized: −∃xGx

1	(1) ∀x(Gx → Bx)	A
2	(2) ∀x(Gx → −Bx)	A
3	(3) −∀x−Gx	PA
3	(4) ∃x−−Gx	3 QE
3	(5) −−Ga	4 ∃O
1	(6) Ga → Ba	1 ∀O
2	(7) Ga → −Ba	2 ∀O
3	(8) Ga	5 DN
1,3	(9) Ba	6,8 →O
2,3	(10) −Ba	7,8 →O
1,2,3	(11) Ba & −Ba	9,10 &I
1,2	(12) ∀x−Gx	3-11 −O

17. The entry for *L*

Chapter 10:   Relational Symbolization

1. (b) $\exists x L f x$
   (f) $\forall x \forall y L x y$
   (h) Someone loves himself or herself.
   (l) There is a person who does not love everyone.

2. (b) $\exists x[Px \ \& \ \forall y(Sy \rightarrow Kxy)]$
   (f) Every person knows no songs. *or* No one knows any songs.

3. (b) $\forall x \exists y L x y$
   (f) $\forall x \exists y(Kxy \ \& \ Py)$ (Kxy = x knows y, Px = x is a politician)
   (j) $\forall x \exists y(Kxy \ \& -Txy)$ (Kxy = x knows y)

4. (b) $\forall x \forall y(Cxy \rightarrow Dxy)$
   (f) $\forall x(-Dxx \rightarrow \forall y -Dyx)$ (Dxy = x deceives y)
   (j) $\forall x[Px \rightarrow \exists y(Py \ \& \ \exists z Lxyz)]$ *or* $\forall x[Px \rightarrow \exists y \exists z(Py \ \& \ Lxyz)]$

5. (b) $\forall x[(Ex \ \& \ Wx) \rightarrow \forall y(Uy \rightarrow -Axy)]$ *or*
   $\forall x[(Ex \ \& \ Wx) \rightarrow -\exists y(Uy \ \& \ Axy)]$ *or*
   $\forall x[(Ex \ \& \ Wx) \rightarrow -\exists y(Axy \ \& \ Uy)]$ (Ex = x is healthy, Wx = x is a wolf, Axy = x attacks y, Ux = x is a human)
   (f) $\forall x \forall y\{[(Dx \ \& \ Py) \ \& \ Syx] \rightarrow Gyx\}$ *or*
   $\forall x \forall y\{[(Px \ \& \ Dy) \ \& \ Sxy] \rightarrow Gyx\}$ (Dx = x is a day)
   (j) $\forall x \forall y[(Mx \ \& \ My) \rightarrow -(Wxy \ \& \ Wyx)]$ (Mx = x has McDonald's franchises)

6. (b) $\forall x[(Ox \ \& \ Px) \rightarrow -\forall y Gxy]$

7. (a) Two people each have chips (so S1 is false), and every chip belongs to someone or other (so F1X is true).
   (e) $\forall x[Px \rightarrow \forall y(My \rightarrow -Hxy)]$ *or* $\forall x[Px \rightarrow -\exists y(My \ \& \ Hxy)]$
   (i) No person has any chips.

Chapter 11:   Relational Proofs

1. (b)

2	(2)	
2	(3)	2 QE
1	(4)	1 $\exists$O
2	(5)	3 $\exists$O
2	(6)	5 DN
1	(7)	4 $\forall$O
2	(8)	6 $\forall$O
1,2	(9)	8,7 &I
1	(10)	2-9 -O

3. (a) (1) ∀x∀yLxy   A
         (2) Lcb   1 ∀O

    (e) (1) ∀x∀yLxy   A   *This proof can be done in four lines.*
         (2) Lba   1 ∀O
         (3) Lab   1 ∀O
         (4) Lba & Lab   2,3 &I
         (5) ∃x(Lbx & Lxb)   4 ∃I

6.   1   (1) ∀x(Rxi → −Rix)   A   *The premise may be*
     1   (2) Rii → −Rii   1 ∀O   *symbolized:*
     3   (3) Rii   PA   −∃x(Rxi & Rix)
     1,3 (4) −Rii   2,3 →O
     1,3 (5) Rii & −Rii   3,4 &I
     1   (6) −Rii   3-5 −I

10.   (1) ∀x∀y[Dxy → (Ax & Ay)]   A
          (2) −Am   A
          (3) Dsm → (As & Am)   1 ∀O
          (4) −As v −Am   2 vI
          (5) −(As & Am)   4 DM
          (6) −Dsm   3,5 MT

14. 1   (1) ∀xIxx   A
     2   (2) −∀xExx   A
     3   (3) ∀x∀y(Ixy → Exy)   PA
     2   (4) ∃x−Exx   2 QE
     2   (5) −Eaa   4 ∃O
     1   (6) Iaa   1 ∀O
     3   (7) Iaa → Eaa   3 ∀O
     1,3   (8) Eaa   7,6 →O
     1,2,3 (9) Eaa & −Eaa   8,5 &I
     1,2   (10) −∀x∀y(Ixy → Exy)   3-9 −I

18. 1   (1) ∀x∀y(Axy → −Exy)   A
     2   (2) ∀x[Dx → ∀y(Sy → Axy)]   A
     3   (3) −∀x[Dx → ∀y(Sy → −Exy)]   PA
     3   (4) ∃x−[Dx → ∀y(Sy → −Exy)]   3 QE
     3   (5) −[Db → ∀y(Sy → −Eby)]   4 ∃O
     3   (6) Db & −∀y(Sy → −Eby)   5 AR
     3   (7) Db   6 &O
     3   (8) −∀y(Sy → −Eby)   6 &O
     3   (9) ∃y−(Sy → −Eby)   8 QE
     3   (10) −(Sc → −Ebc)   9 ∃O
     3   (11) Sc & −−Ebc   10 AR
     3   (12) Sc   11 &O

3	(13)	$--Ebc$	11 &O
2	(14)	$Db \rightarrow \forall y(Sy \rightarrow Aby)$	2 $\forall$O
2,3	(15)	$\forall y(Sy \rightarrow Aby)$	14,7 $\rightarrow$O
2,3	(16)	$Sc \rightarrow Abc$	15 $\forall$O
1	(17)	$Abc \rightarrow -Ebc$	1 $\forall$O
1,2,3	(18)	$Sc \rightarrow -Ebc$	16,17 CH
1,2,3	(19)	$-Ebc$	18,12 $\rightarrow$O
1,2,3	(20)	$-Ebc \ \& \ --Ebc$	19,13 &I
1,2	(21)	$\forall x[Dx \rightarrow \forall y(Sy \rightarrow -Exy)]$	3-20 $-$O

The second premise may be symbolized: $\forall x \forall y[(Dx \ \& \ Sy) \rightarrow Axy]$
The conclusion may be symbolized: $\forall x \forall y[(Dx \ \& \ Sy) \rightarrow -Exy]$

Chapter 12:   Relational CEXes and Trees

1. (b) **symbolization:** $\exists x \exists y Lxy \vdash Lcc$
   CEX dictionary: domain: integers; Lxy = x is greater than y, $c = 1$
   CEX: Some integer is greater than some integer. (T) So, 1 is greater than 1. (F)

   (f) **symbolization:** $\exists x \exists y Lxy \vdash \forall x \forall y Lxy$
   CEX dictionary: domain: integers; Lxy = x is greater than y
   CEX: Some integer is greater than some integer. (T) So, every integer is greater than every integer. (F)

2. (d) **symbolization:** $Kdh \ \& \ Kdr \vdash Khr$
   CEX dictionary: domain: people; Lxy = x is taller than y, d = Michael Jordan, h = Queen Elizabeth, r = Tom Cruise
   CEX: Michael Jordan is taller than Queen Elizabeth and Tom Cruise. (T) So, Queen Elizabeth is taller than Tom Cruise. (F)

6. (a) **CEX dictionary:** domain: people; Bxy = x is mother of y, a = Hillary Clinton, Cxy = x is father of y
   CEX: Hillary Clinton is mother or father of someone. (T) So, Hillary Clinton is mother and father of someone. (F)

   (e) **CEX dictionary:** domain: people; Jxy = x is sibling of y
   CEX: If one person is sibling of another, the other is sibling of the one. (T) So, each person is his or her own sibling. (F)

10. **symbolization:** ∃x∃y(Pxy & −Cxy) ⊢ −∀x∀y(Cxy → Pxy)

   CEX dictionary: domain: people; Pxy = x is a parent of y,
   Cxy = x is mother of y

   CEX: Someone is parent of someone but is not
   mother of that person. (T)
   So, it is false that a mother of a person is a parent of that person. (F)

13. (c)
```
    +∀x∃yRxy
              ⌐−∀x∃y−Ryx✓
  +∀x∃y−Ryx
     ✓∃yRay
       Rab
  ✓∃y−Ryb
    ✓−Rcb
            Rcb
     ✓∃yRcy
       Rcd
  ✓∃y−Ryd
    ✓−Red
              Red
              ∞
```

14. (b)
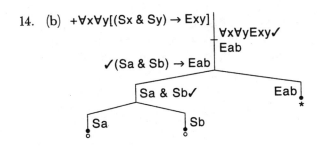
```
   +∀x∀y[(Sx & Sy) → Exy]
                          ⌐∀x∀yExy✓
                           Eab
      ✓(Sa & Sb) → Eab
              ┌──────────────┴──────────────┐
           Sa & Sb✓                        Eab
         ┌────┴────┐                         *
        Sa        Sb
        ∘          ∘
```

16. (b)
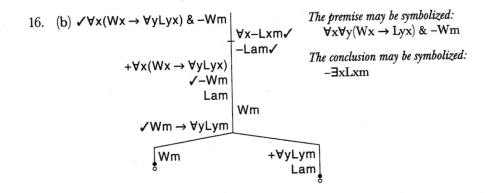
```
   ✓∀x(Wx → ∀yLyx) & −Wm
                          ⌐∀x−Lxm✓
                           −Lam✓
      +∀x(Wx → ∀yLyx)
          ✓−Wm
           Lam
                           Wm
      ✓Wm → ∀yLym
         ┌──────────┴──────────┐
        Wm                  +∀yLym
        ∘                     Lam
                               ∘
```

The premise may be symbolized:
∀x∀y(Wx → Lyx) & −Wm

The conclusion may be symbolized:
−∃xLxm

17. (d)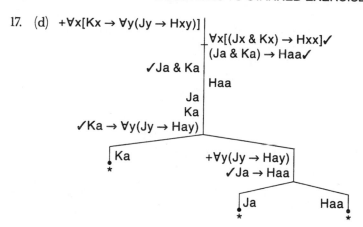

The premise of 17(d) may be symbolized:
∀x∀y[(Kx & Jy) → Hxy]

The conclusion may be symbolized:
∀x[(Kx & Jx) → Hxx]

18. (c)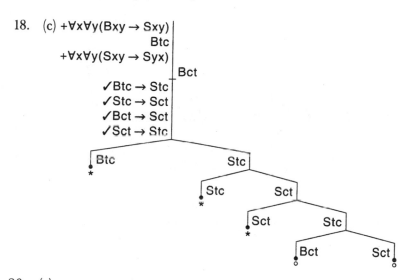

20. (a) ✓∃x∀y−Hyx
              ∀x−∀yHxy✓
     +∀y−Hya
              −∀yHby✓
     +∀yHby
     ✓−Hba
              Hba
        Hba
           •
           *

The premise may be symbolized:
∃x−∃yHyx

The conclusion may be symbolized:
−∃x∀yHxy

22.

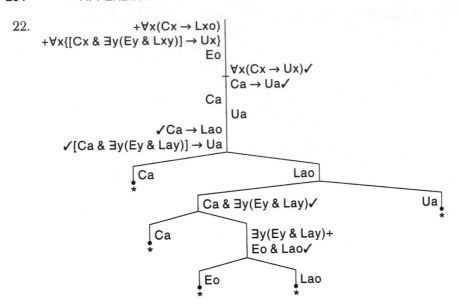

The second premise may be symbolized:
∀x{[Cx & ∃y(Lxy & Ey)] → Ux}

Chapter 13:   Relational-Logic Refinements

1. (b) ∃x(Ex & Rx) → −P, ∀x[(Ex & Rx) → −P]
   (f) ∀x[∃y∃z(Sxy & Syz) → Hx], ∀x∀y∀z[(Sxy & Syz) → Hx]

2. (b)

1	(1)	∃x(Fx → P)	A
2	(2)	∀xFx	PA
1	(3)	Fa → P	1 ∃O
2	(4)	Fa	2 ∀O
1,2	(5)	P	3,4 →O
1	(6)	∀xFx → P	2-5 →I

(f)

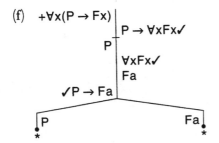

3. (b)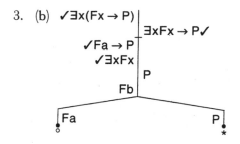

4. (b) ∀x∃y(Fy → Gx)

8. (b) ∀x∃yGyx

9. (b) There is a person who is loved by each person at some time or other.
   (f) For each person and each moment someone loves that person at that moment.

10. (b)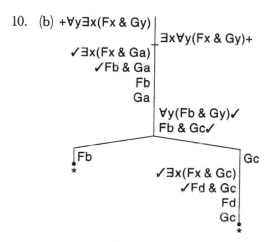

12. (b)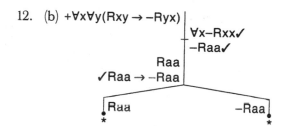

   (f) 1   (1) ∀x∀y∀z[(Rxy & Ryz) → Rxz]   A
        2   (2) ∀xRxx   A
        3   (3) ∀x∀y(Rxy → −Ryx)   PA

2	(4)	Raa	2 ∀O
3	(5)	Raa → −Raa	3 ∀O
2,3	(6)	−Raa	5,4 →O
2,3	(7)	Raa & −Raa	4,6 &I
2	(8)	−∀x∀y(Rxy → −Ryx)	3-7 −I

The assumption-dependence entry on line 8 shows that the conclusion follows from the second premise alone.

13. (b) **symbolization:** ∀x∀y(Rxy → Ryx) ⊢ ∀x∀y∀z[(Rxy & Ryz) → Rxz]
CEX dictionary: domain: people; Rxy = x is of a different sex than y
CEX: If one person is of a different sex than a second, then the second is of a different sex than the first. (T)
So, if one person is of a different sex than a second and the second is of a different sex than a third, then the first is of a different sex than the third. (F)

(f) **symbolization:** ∀x−Rxx ⊢ ∀x∀y(Rxy → −Ryx)
CEX dictionary: domain: people; Rxy = x is spouse of y
CEX: No person is his or her own spouse. (T)
So, if one person is spouse of a second, then the second is not spouse of the first. (F)

16. Missing premise: Nothing is better than itself (*or* "Being better than" is irreflexive).

1	(1)	∀x−Bxx	A
2	(2)	∀xBhx	PA
1	(3)	−Bhh	1 ∀O
2	(4)	Bhh	2 ∀O
1,2	(5)	Bhh & −Bhh	4,3 &I
1	(6)	−∀xBhx	2-5 −I

20.
```
     ✓−Sab
            −(Sca & Scb)✓
            Sab
  ✓Sca & Scb
     Sca
     Scb
            o
```

Missing premises:
Synonymy is transitive. Synonymy is symmetrical.

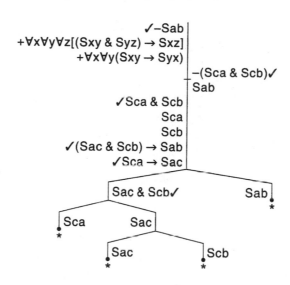

Chapter 14:   Natural Arguments

*Often there is more than one acceptable formalization of a natural argument. In the
solutions below I omit demonstrations of validity and invalidity.*

1. formalization: Brian crawled before he walked, and he is not a
   good reader.
   So, it is false that children who don't crawl before
   walking will not be good readers.
   dictionary: domain: children; b = Brian, Cx = x crawls before x walks, Gx = x is a good reader
   symbolization: Cb & −Gb ⊢ −∀x(−Cx → −Gx)
   form: invalid

2. formalization: Fed gators become aggressive.
   Gators that become aggressive are destroyed.
   So, fed gators are destroyed.
   dictionary: domain: alligators; Fx = x is fed, Ax = x becomes aggressive, Dx = x is destroyed
   symbolization: ∀x(Fx → Ax), ∀x(Ax → Dx) ⊢ ∀x(Fx → Dx)
   form: valid

3. formalization: Capital punishment is morally acceptable only if the system is perfect.
                      No system is perfect.
                      So, capital punishment is not morally acceptable.

   dictionary: domain: systems; A = Capital punishment is morally acceptable, c = the system of capital punishment, Px = x is perfect

   symbolization: A → Pc, ∀x−Px ⊢ −A
   form: valid

5. formalization: Substances that can exist apart from each other are distinct.
                      The mind and the body are substances that can exist apart from each other.
                      So, the mind and the body are distinct.

   dictionary: domain: substances; Axy = x and y can exist apart from each other, Dxy = x and y are distinct, m = the mind, b = the body

   symbolization: ∀x∀y(Axy → Dxy), Amb ⊢ Dmb
   form: valid

Alternate treatment for 5:

   formalization: Substances that can exist apart from each other are distinct.
                      Minds and bodies are substances that can exist apart from each other.
                      So, minds and bodies are distinct.

   dictionary: domain: substances; Axy = x and y can exist apart from each other, Dxy = x and y are distinct, Mx = x is a mind, Bx = x is a body

   symbolization: ∀x∀y(Axy → Dxy), ∀x∀y[(Mx & By) → Axy]
                      ⊢ ∀x∀y[(Mx & By) → Dxy]
   form: valid

9. formalization: If we don't have water, then we cannot raise pigs.
                      If we raise pigs, we have income.
                      So, if we don't have water, we don't have income. (unstated)

   dictionary: W = We have water, P = We raise pigs, I = We have income

   symbolization: −W → −P, P → I ⊢ −W → −I
   form: invalid

13. formalization: No cause follows its effects.
                    If all causes are contemporary with their effects,
                    then all events are simultaneous.
                    It is false that all events are simultaneous.
                    So, each cause occurs before its effects.

    dictionary: domain: events; Cxy = x causes y, Bxy = x oc-
                    curs before y, S = All events are simultaneous

    symbolization: ∀x∀y(Cxy → −Byx),
                    ∀x∀y[Cxy → (−Bxy & −Byx)] → S,
                    −S ⊢ ∀x∀y(Cxy → Bxy)

    form: invalid

Index

A

A-statement, 8, 12–14
Adequate symbolization, 113
Algorithm, 233
All, 12
All ... are not, 15–16
Ampersand (&), 216
Amphiboly, 16 n., 134–35
Any, anyone, 12, 65–66
Argument, natural, 197–206
Aristotelian logic, 43
Arrow (→), 216
Assumption, 217
    dependence, 23, 217–18
Asymmetry, 185
At least one, 10

C

Capital, 191
Categorical:
    proposition, 5, 8
    syllogism, 42–43
CEX (*see* Counterexamples, method of)
Charts (*see* Tables)
Circular (*see* Circularity)
Circularity (*see* Circular)
Comics and cartoons, 38, 75, 76, 81, 89, 93, 104, 105, 106, 152, 162, 169, 182, 183, 190, 208, 211
Completeness of QL, 226–33
Connective, 192, 216
Constant, individual, 6, 191
Contingent statement, 110, 112
Contradiction, 110–12
    standard, 23 n.
Contradictories, 13, 32, 44–45
Converse, 36, 40
Copula, 6 n.

D

Counterexamples, method of, 83–87, 90–93, 156–61
    actual CEXes, 83–87
    compared with truth trees, 103
    domain, 85
    mixed wff, 86
    possible-world CEXes, 90–93
    relational, 156–61
    requirements, 85, 92
    target argument, 83
    tests:
        contingency, 112
        invalidity, 83–84
    tips, 85

Dash (−), 216
Definitions, 191–96
Diagrams, method of (*see* diagrams.pdf *on CD-ROM disk*)
Dispatch mark, 96–97, 167
Domain, 54–55, 67 n.
    in counterexamples, 85
Double arrow (↔), 216
Dummy name, 28, 31
Dyadic connective, 192
Dyadic relational predicate, 129–30

E

E-statement, 8, 14–16
Each, 12
Effective method, 92–93, 168, 233
Entailment, 36 n.
Enthymeme, 165
Equivalence, logical, 14 n.
Evaluation of form and content, 198

Proof Rules

and

Truth Tree Rules

Propositional Proof Rules

<table>
<tr><th colspan="3">Primitive Inference Rules</th></tr>
<tr><th></th><th>In</th><th>Out</th></tr>
<tr>
<td>→</td>
<td>From the derivation of B from assumption A (and perhaps other assumptions) derive $A \rightarrow B$.</td>
<td>From $A \rightarrow B$ and A derive B.</td>
</tr>
<tr>
<td>&</td>
<td>From A and B derive A & B.</td>
<td>From A & B derive either A or B.</td>
</tr>
<tr>
<td>v</td>
<td>From A derive either A v B or B v A.</td>
<td>From A v B, $A \rightarrow C$, and $B \rightarrow C$ derive C.</td>
</tr>
<tr>
<td>↔</td>
<td>From $A \rightarrow B$ and $B \rightarrow A$ derive $A \leftrightarrow B$.</td>
<td>From $A \leftrightarrow B$ derive either $A \rightarrow B$ or $B \rightarrow A$.</td>
</tr>
<tr>
<td>−</td>
<td>From the derivation of B & $-B$ from assumption A (and perhaps other assumptions) derive $-A$.</td>
<td>From the derivation of B & $-B$ from assumption $-A$ (and perhaps other assumptions) derive A.</td>
</tr>
</table>

<table>
<tr><th colspan="2">Derived Inference Rules</th></tr>
<tr>
<td>Modus Tollens (MT)</td>
<td>From $A \rightarrow B$ and $-B$ derive $-A$.</td>
</tr>
<tr>
<td>Disjunctive Argument (DA)</td>
<td>From A v B and $-A$ derive B.
From A v B and $-B$ derive A.</td>
</tr>
<tr>
<td>Conjunctive Argument (CA)</td>
<td>From $-(A$ & $B)$ and A derive $-B$.
From $-(A$ & $B)$ and B derive $-A$.</td>
</tr>
<tr>
<td>Chain Argument (CH)</td>
<td>From $A \rightarrow B$ and $B \rightarrow C$ derive $A \rightarrow C$.</td>
</tr>
<tr>
<td>Double Negation (DN)</td>
<td>From A derive $--A$ and vice versa.</td>
</tr>
<tr>
<td>De Morgan's Law (DM)</td>
<td>From $-(A$ & $B)$ derive $-A$ v $-B$ and vice versa.
From $-(A$ v $B)$ derive $-A$ & $-B$ and vice versa.
From $-(-A$ & $-B)$ derive A v B and vice versa.
From $-(-A$ v $-B)$ derive A & B and vice versa.</td>
</tr>
<tr>
<td>Arrow (AR)</td>
<td>From $A \rightarrow B$ derive $-A$ v B and vice versa.
From $-A \rightarrow B$ derive A v B and vice versa.
From $A \rightarrow B$ derive $-(A$ & $-B)$ and vice versa.
From $-(A \rightarrow B)$ derive A & $-B$ and vice versa.</td>
</tr>
<tr>
<td>Contraposition (CN)</td>
<td>From $A \rightarrow B$ derive $-B \rightarrow -A$ and vice versa.
From $A \rightarrow -B$ derive $B \rightarrow -A$.
From $-A \rightarrow B$ derive $-B \rightarrow A$.</td>
</tr>
</table>

Predicate Proof Rules

Universal Quantifier Out (∀O)	From a universal quantification derive any instance of it.
Existential Quantifier Out (∃O)	From an existential quantification derive any instance of it, *provided that* the individual constant being introduced is a dummy name that is new to the proof.
Existential Quantifier In (∃I)	Derive an existential quantification from any instance of it.
Quantifier Exchange (QE)	From $-\forall x A x$ derive $\exists x - A x$ and vice versa. From $-\exists x A x$ derive $\forall x - A x$ and vice versa.

Propositional Truth-Tree Rules

LEFT	RIGHT
✓ −A | |A	|−A✓ A|

✓ A & B |
   A
   B |
	|A & B✓
	 A B

✓ A ∨ B | A B	|A ∨ B✓ A B
✓ A → B | A B	A |A → B✓ |B
✓ A ↔ B | A A B B	|A ↔ B✓ A A B B

Predicate Truth-Tree Rules

LEFT	RIGHT
+ ∀xAx | Ac |	|∀xAx ✓ |Ac *c* is new to the branch
✓ ∃xAx | Ac | *c* is new to the branch	|∃xAx + |Ac

SINGLE PC LICENSE AGREEMENT AND LIMITED WARRANTY

READ THIS LICENSE CAREFULLY BEFORE OPENING THIS PACKAGE. BY OPENING THIS PACKAGE, YOU ARE AGREEING TO THE TERMS AND CONDITIONS OF THIS LICENSE. IF YOU DO NOT AGREE, DO NOT OPEN THE PACKAGE. PROMPTLY RETURN THE UNOPENED PACKAGE AND ALL ACCOMPANYING ITEMS TO THE PLACE YOU OBTAINED THEM.

1. GRANT OF LICENSE and OWNERSHIP: The enclosed computer programs ("Software") are licensed, not sold, to you by Prentice-Hall, Inc. ("We" or the "Company") and in consideration of your purchase or adoption of the accompanying Company textbooks and/or other materials, and your agreement to these terms. We reserve any rights not granted to you. You own only the disk(s) but we and/or our licensors own the Software itself. This license allows you to use and display your copy of the Software on a single computer (i.e., with a single CPU) at a single location for academic use only, so long as you comply with the terms of this Agreement. You may make one copy for back up, or transfer your copy to another CPU, provided that the Software is usable on only one computer.

2. RESTRICTIONS: You may not transfer or distribute the Software or documentation to anyone else. Except for backup, you may not copy the documentation or the Software. You may not network the Software or otherwise use it on more than one computer or computer terminal at the same time. You may not reverse engineer, disassemble, decompile, modify, adapt, translate, or create derivative works based on the Software or the Documentation. You may be held legally responsible for any copying or copyright infringement which is caused by your failure to abide by the terms of these restrictions.

3. TERMINATION: This license is effective until terminated. This license will terminate automatically without notice from the Company if you fail to comply with any provisions or limitations of this license. Upon termination, you shall destroy the Documentation and all copies of the Software. All provisions of this Agreement as to limitation and disclaimer of warranties, limitation of liability, remedies or damages, and our ownership rights shall survive termination.

4. LIMITED WARRANTY AND DISCLAIMER OF WARRANTY: Company warrants that for a period of 60 days from the date you purchase this SOFT-WARE (or purchase or adopt the accompanying textbook), the Software, when properly installed and used in accordance with the Documentation, will operate in substantial conformity with the description of the Software set forth in the Documentation, and that for a period of 30 days the disk(s) on which the Software is delivered shall be free from defects in materials and workmanship under normal use. The Company does not warrant that the Software will meet your requirements or that the operation of the Software will be uninterrupted or error-free. Your only remedy and the Company's only obligation under these limited warranties is, at the Company's option, return of the disk for a refund of any amounts paid for it by you or replacement of the disk. THIS LIMITED WARRANTY IS THE ONLY WARRANTY PROVIDED BY THE COMPANY AND ITS LICENSORS, AND THE COMPANY AND ITS LICEN-SORS DISCLAIM ALL OTHER WARRANTIES, EXPRESS OR IMPLIED, IN-CLUDING WITHOUT LIMITATION, THE IMPLIED WARRANTIES OF MERCHANTABILITY AND FITNESS FOR A PARTICULAR PURPOSE. THE COMPANY DOES NOT WARRANT, GUARANTEE OR MAKE ANY REPRE-SENTATION REGARDING THE ACCURACY, RELIABILITY, CURRENT-NESS, USE, OR RESULTS OF USE, OF THE SOFTWARE.

5. LIMITATION OF REMEDIES AND DAMAGES: IN NO EVENT, SHALL THE COMPANY OR ITS EMPLOYEES, AGENTS, LICENSORS, OR CONTRACTORS BE LIABLE FOR ANY INCIDENTAL, INDIRECT, SPECIAL, OR CONSEQUENTIAL DAMAGES ARISING OUT OF OR IN CONNECTION WITH THIS LICENSE OR THE SOFTWARE, INCLUDING FOR LOSS OF USE, LOSS OF DATA, LOSS OF INCOME OR PROFIT, OR OTHER LOSSES, SUSTAINED AS A RESULT OF INJURY TO ANY PERSON, OR LOSS OF OR DAMAGE TO PROPERTY, OR CLAIMS OF THIRD PARTIES, EVEN IF THE COMPANY OR AN AUTHORIZED REPRESENTATIVE OF THE COMPANY HAS BEEN ADVISED OF THE POSSIBILITY OF SUCH DAMAGES. IN NO EVENT SHALL THE LIABILITY OF THE COMPANY FOR DAMAGES WITH RESPECT TO THE SOFTWARE EXCEED THE AMOUNTS ACTUALLY PAID BY YOU, IF ANY, FOR THE SOFTWARE OR THE ACCOMPANYING TEXTBOOK. BECAUSE SOME JURISDICTIONS DO NOT ALLOW THE LIMITATION OF LIABILITY IN CERTAIN CIRCUMSTANCES, THE ABOVE LIMITATIONS MAY NOT ALWAYS APPLY TO YOU.

6. GENERAL: THIS AGREEMENT SHALL BE CONSTRUED IN ACCORDANCE WITH THE LAWS OF THE UNITED STATES OF AMERICA AND THE STATE OF NEW YORK, APPLICABLE TO CONTRACTS MADE IN NEW YORK, AND SHALL BENEFIT THE COMPANY, ITS AFFILIATES AND ASSIGNEES. THIS AGREEMENT IS THE COMPLETE AND EXCLUSIVE STATEMENT OF THE AGREEMENT BETWEEN YOU AND THE COMPANY AND SUPERSEDES ALL PROPOSALS OR PRIOR AGREEMENTS, ORAL, OR WRITTEN, AND ANY OTHER COMMUNICATIONS BETWEEN YOU AND THE COMPANY OR ANY REPRESENTATIVE OF THE COMPANY RELATING TO THE SUBJECT MATTER OF THIS AGREEMENT. If you are a U.S. Government user, this Software is licensed with "restricted rights" as set forth in subparagraphs (a)-(d) of the Commercial Computer-Restricted Rights clause at FAR 52.227-19 or in subparagraphs (c)(1)(ii) of the Rights in Technical Data and Computer Software clause at DFARS 252.227-7013, and similar clauses, as applicable.

Should you have any questions concerning this agreement please contact in writing: Legal Department, Prentice Hall, One Lake Street, Upper Saddle River, NJ 07458. If you need assistance with technical difficulties, call: 1-800-677-6337. If you wish to contact the Company for any reason, please contact in writing: Deborah O'Connell, Media Editor for Humanities, Prentice Hall, One Lake Street, Upper Saddle River, NJ 07458.